John Mooney and Michael O'Toole

Black Operations

The Secret War Against the Real IRA

MAVERICK HOUSE PUBLISHERS
Published by Maverick House,
Unit 115 Ashbourne Industrial Estate,
Ashbourne, Co. Meath
info@maverickhouse.com
http://www.maverickhouse.com

Copyright © 2003 John Mooney and Michael O'Toole

First published in 2003

ISBN 0-9542945-5-6

Printed by Mackays of Chatham Ltd
Typeset by Jean Harrington

'Only the dead have seen the end of the war.'

PLATO

BLACK OPERATIONS

John Mooney dedicates BLACK OPERATIONS
to Jean and Aoileann.

Michael O'Toole dedicates this book
to the memory of his father, Gerry O'Toole, RIP.
Thanks for the sunshine, pops.

CONTENTS

CONTENTS

ACKNOWLEDGMENTS

John Mooney

BLACK OPERATIONS IS primarily about the secret war waged by the Irish security services against the republican Michael McKevitt and the Real IRA. However, the book is as much about the 29 people and unborn twin girls who were murdered by the Real IRA when it bombed Omagh, a market town in County Tyrone, on 15 August 1998. The bombing was the single greatest loss of life in the history of the Northern Ireland conflict.

My only frustration in writing *Black Operations* is knowing that the families of those massacred will find on paper no more than a written account of the terrible grief and trauma they endured. I was humbled to meet the Omagh families and hear their stories.

In this regard, I offer my eternal thanks to Donna Maria and Victor Barker, whose son James died in the Omagh massacre. Their willingness to recount the nightmare of losing their son was a truly heart-rending and unforgettable experience.

But I am indebted to all the families—particularly the Gallaghers, Lawrence Rush, Kevin Skelton and Mark Breslin—who gave their time freely and spoke openly about their losses. I would also like to thank Pat McElhatton, who filmed the Omagh bombing, and Joan Kernan.

On a personal note I would like to thank my friends and family, particularly my parents, and my friends Fr. Joe Whelan, Alan Faherty and Susie Harrington. It is only fitting to posthumously thank my friend Robert Harrington, who died earlier this year, for all his help and good advice. I also wish to thank my wife Jean for her help and solid support. This book would not have been written without her loyalty, good advice and friendship.

A number of colleagues helped with the research. I would like to thank Seán McMahon of *The Anglo Celt*, Liam Clarke and John Lee of *The Sunday Times*, and Vincent Kearney and Brendan McCourt of the BBC. Gerard Colleran, editor of *The Star*, was also generous in affording me time off to write the book. Fiona Barry and Michael Kealey of William Fry Solicitors were more than accommodating in preparing the manuscript for publication.

A number of republicans also spoke freely about the Real IRA and Continuity IRA. Many spent long hours explaining the intricacies of the republican movement and why they opposed the Provisional IRA's journey into constitutional politics. They made an important contribution to *Black Operations*.

My final thanks go to sections of An Garda Síochána. The task of combating the Real IRA fell largely on their shoulders and it is no exaggeration to say the secret work of certain garda departments saved countless lives and helped constitutional politics flourish in Northern Ireland. If the Real IRA had not been infiltrated and spied on, there is no doubt that many more innocent people would have died.

The garda departments worthy of sincere praise are Crime and Security, the National Surveillance Unit and Special Branch. The detective units at Monaghan and Dundalk Garda Stations, which investigated the Omagh atrocity, also curtailed the Real IRA and secured justice for the Omagh families. Their task was not an easy one.

I believe that future historians will properly acknowledge the role of these garda units and individual detectives, who fought the Real IRA and helped stop the gruesome violence that perpetuated the Northern Ireland conflict for so long.

ACKNOWLEDGMENTS

Michael O'Toole

I WISH TO thank those sources, both republican and from the security agencies, who spoke on condition of anonymity. They are many; each of the sources provided information vital to our research. Without their help, this book could not have been written. Many other people spoke on the record and I also thank them, including Joe Dillon, Rory Dougan and Francie Mackey. Thanks also go to Donal. I also wish to thank the Garda Press Office for its help. I want to reserve a special thanks for Mavis McFaul, who welcomed me into her house and spoke so candidly about the loss of her partner, David Caldwell, in the most trying of circumstances. I wish also to thank all my colleagues in *The Star*, particularly editor Gerard Colleran, Gary Ashe, Shane Doran, Catherine Halloran, and Jason O'Brien. I also thank Robert, Michael, Brian, and Humphrey. My eternal thanks go to the inestimable Diarmaid Mac Dermott of Ireland International News Agency. I want to thank him for his advice, help and, above all, friendship over the last six years. Thanks also go to Robert Kennedy-Cochrane, Eamon Dillon, Liz Trainor, Séamus McKinney and Tony Bailie. I also thank my wonderful family: my parents Gerry and May, for everything, and my siblings Jim, Gerry, Kev, Kathy, Brendan, and my best friend of 33 years, Conor. I want to thank the Larkin family for their encouragement and support. But, above all, I wish to thank my beloved wife, Olga, who has given me a unique gift: happiness.

INTRODUCTION

by Victor Barker

THERE IS NO DOUBT that my British Ancestors were responsible for acts of unforgivable cruelty and repression on the island of Ireland. The force of British imperialism was, at times, uncompromising and callous.

Following the 1916 Easter Rising and the birth of the Irish Free State, the bitterness, which was left in the hearts of so many Irish people, still runs in the blood of many who call themselves Irish republicans. The separation of the six counties left a physical and religious divide which remained a breeding ground for that bitterness and hatred.

But times change and with understanding and compromise on both sides the Good Friday Agreement was reached in 1998, an agreement which was acceptable to the vast majority of all people on the island of Ireland, as a means of solving their differences. The cornerstone of that agreement was mutual respect and understanding—but above all a respect for the dignity of human life.

I remember that afternoon vividly—a journey back from Belfast airport with my wife and three children in the car, passing through the Glenshane Pass on our way to our home in Buncrana County Donegal. We heard the news of the Good Friday Agreement and I was relieved to think that any danger that my children once faced when visiting the North was diminished.

Yet still in this atmosphere there were those on both sides who would not accept the democratic will of the people and who took it upon themselves to continue the fight for Irish Sovereignty or blind loyalty to Her Majesty.

Little did we even suspect that on the 15 August 1998 whilst on a school trip to Omagh, County Tyrone, our own 12-year-old son James would be amongst the many innocent victims of an atrocity perpetrated by the Real IRA. 29 people lost their lives along with two unborn children and many hundreds were left physically and mentally scarred. The Real IRA claimed responsibility—to their eternal shame.

The past five years have been as difficult for me as they have been for all those effected by the Omagh Bomb. But as I have visited Ireland in the weeks and months since James' death I have begun to appreciate the enormity of the suffering endured by so many during the years of the conflict, and also witnessed the inner strength of so many of their families. Ordinary people who have pursued the quest for truth with grim determination.

I have had the privilege of meeting so many good Irish people, some of whom have even told me that after Omagh they felt ashamed to be Irish. One of those good people is the co-author of this book, John Mooney. Through my friendship with him I have learnt much about the history of Ireland and I have tried to understand the republican psyche.

Those within the Real IRA have convinced themselves that the quest for Irish Sovereignty has greater value than human life - and that those who lose their lives as a result of their campaign of violence are simply casualties of war. Can you describe the murder of innocent women and children in a busy shopping centre on a Saturday afternoon as part of a war?

IT IS NOT until the people of violence on both sides realise that human life has far more importance than nationalism—that there will be true peace in Ireland. It is the many victims of violence—

whether Catholic or Protestant—that have endured the suffering of terrorism who are the Real Irish Freedom Fighters. Their fight is not for the freedom of a nation or loyalty to a queen—but the fight to live in peace and freedom—freedom from the shackles of terror and violence.

But above all we must not turn away from those who feel compelled to continue a campaign of terrorism—they must be brought to face the human consequences of what they do and to examine their own consciences. If my son's death leads one of them to turn away from violence and continue their struggle by peaceful democratic means—then it would not have been in vain. This book looks at the Real IRA—and tries to understand them as I have done. I only hope that one day I will also find the strength to forgive them.

October 2003

1

THE QUARTERMASTER GENERAL

HE GLANCED OVER his shoulder to reassure himself that no one was watching. It was minutes after 5 p.m. on the evening of 16 October 1997. The roads around the sea swept village of Blackrock in County Louth were poorly lit. Although the darkness limited his vision to a few hundred feet, his senses reassured him there was no danger lurking in the shadows. Paranoia was a healthy state of mind for Michael McKevitt; he was the Quartermaster General of the Provisional IRA, the man who provided the underground army with arms to fight its bloody war against the British.

McKevitt's senses were more alert than usual that night because he was travelling to an Extraordinary General Army Convention of the IRA. This was a secret gathering of delegates drawn from across the 32 counties of Ireland.

The meeting was due to take place in a hall near the remote village of Falcarragh in County Donegal. As he did every time he attended an IRA gathering of such magnitude, the Quartermaster General made sure no one was tracking his movements. He travelled in a van with blacked out windows. His driver was instructed to follow a carefully chosen route of back roads to avoid encountering checkpoints mounted by the security forces.

In accordance with IRA internal security procedures, McKevitt switched vehicles twice during the journey. During the first vehicle transfer, an IRA security team searched his companions for anything that might contain a transmitter. Once the security team assured themselves that none of his delegation were compromised, McKevitt and his companions were waved onwards.

As he travelled to Falcarragh that October night, McKevitt feared for the future of the IRA. He felt drained and alone; his fundamental beliefs in militant republicanism were now under serious threat.

The IRA Army Council had announced a second ceasefire without consulting him. He now viewed the IRA leadership with suspicion, particularly Gerry Adams and Martin McGuinness, the two Sinn Féin leaders.

As far as McKevitt was concerned, these men could not be trusted. They were once revolutionary IRA volunteers but now appeared ready to condemn violence as an illegitimate form of struggle. McKevitt saw them as threatening the very cause to which he had dedicated his life.

The Quartermaster General arrived in Falcarragh around 10 p.m. McKevitt felt unease the moment he walked into the Convention.* Those assembled glared coldly at him. He noticed Adams staring intently at him. McKevitt was an expert at reading body language, and he knew by the way the delegates threw mistrusting glances in his direction that trouble lay ahead. His analysis was correct.

TWELVE MONTHS EARLIER in October 1996, McKevitt had mounted a successful coup within the Provisional IRA when he launched a full-scale assault on the policies advocated by the Army Council at an Extraordinary General Army Convention of the IRA. This Convention was held on the Cooley Peninsula in County Louth and was called to debate the IRA's embracing of constitutional politics.

A republican to the bone, McKevitt had vehemently opposed Adams' talk of constitutional politics and used the occasion to

---

* Interview with member of Real IRA Army Council

spread dissent through opportune timing and advocating traditional republican ideals.

IRA conventions are by their very nature formal affairs. Regional leaders and commanders vote on motions, discuss strategies, engage in robust debates and elect new leaderships. The Chief of Staff usually delivers a report on the IRA's activities and outlines his future plans.

At the time, the IRA had just broken its first ceasefire (known as *sos* in republican circles). This ceasefire, declared in August 1994, had allowed Adams and the IRA leadership to enter into political dialogue with the Irish and British governments. Although the Irish public supported the IRA's tentative steps into democracy, the move had the effect of demoralising rank and file IRA members whose dedication to armed insurgency against the British in Northern Ireland was proverbial.

McKevitt possessed many talents but one of his most important skills was the natural born ability to gauge the feelings of IRA volunteers. He knew there was a prevailing sense of unease in the IRA and used this to his own advantage. He made sure politics was the main subject of debate at the Cooley Convention. Of the 130 motions presented to the Convention that night, most concerned decisions made by the Army Council in the fledgling Peace Process.

McKevitt was more direct in his approach. He chastised the Army Council, and accused them of betraying the IRA by proffering the idea that Sinn Féin politics should take precedence over IRA operations. He believed politics, or even the acceptance of political debate on the status of Northern Ireland, weakened the IRA. For this reason, he and others like him had come to be known as 'the dissidents'.

THOUGH HE WAS first a confirmed militarist, he had some political acumen. He realised he could not defeat his internal enemies and secure a change of republican strategy from outside the IRA, or even by issuing warnings about the organisation's future demise from the sidelines. He was much too clever for that.

Instead he chose to remain inside the IRA and introduce new rules through his leadership of the IRA Executive, the 12-person committee of guardians that govern the future direction and policies of the secret army. At the Cooley Convention, McKevitt and his supporters on the Executive proposed amendments to the IRA's constitution which guaranteed there could be no acceptance of anything less than a 32-county socialist republic before the IRA could disband or destroy its own weapons. His motions were carried, but at a cost.

In the months that followed, relations between the IRA Executive and the Army Council deteriorated, with both sides eyeing the other suspiciously. The Executive supported McKevitt; the Army Council saw the Quartermaster General as a threat. The tension came to a head on 16 July 1997 when Martin McGuinness, who was chairman of the Army Council, told McKevitt that a second IRA ceasefire would be announced four days later. McKevitt and the other Executive members responded angrily at the news; there had been no consultation or discussion. According to one member of the Executive, McGuinness flatly refused to enter into a debate about the merits of the planned ceasefire.

'He simply said there was going to be another ceasefire in a matter of days. When we kicked up a stink, he just replied, "If you don't like it, elect a new fucking Army Council."'

The ceasefire was called on 20 July as the dissidents tried to canvas opposition. Tensions were further exacerbated when Sinn Féin later accepted the 'Mitchell Principles of Consent and Non Violence' on 9 September 1997. The guidelines were drafted by the American Senator George Mitchell, who had been appointed by the US Administration. The principles committed all political parties involved in the Northern Ireland Peace Process to adhere to the principle of consent. McKevitt saw the guidelines as the end of the IRA. A showdown loomed.

BY THE TIME he walked into the Falcarragh Convention some months later he had developed a pathological fear of Sinn Féin. Although the Falcarragh Convention had ostensibly been called to debate the Mitchell Principles, he believed the Army Council wanted to pass a motion that allowed them to ignore the IRA Constitution. The Quartermaster General didn't need a fortune-teller to tell him that he would be removed from power if this happened. Moments before the Convention got formally underway, McKevitt was made aware of the Army Council's strategy. They wanted 'dispensation' to ignore the IRA constitution if they felt it necessary. The dissidents knew this could mean only one thing: permission to decommission IRA weapons. The Constitution strictly forbade the destruction of IRA arms short of a United Ireland. McKevitt knew his hand was being forced.

THE FALCARRAGH CONVENTION began with an address by the chairman of the IRA Executive. The chairman was the IRA's Director of Finance and an ally of McKevitt's. He had been alerted to the dispensation motion. When he heard about this, he decided to meet the Army Council head on. In his speech he pleaded with delegates to prohibit any IRA volunteer from endorsing the Mitchell Principles, or to even consider decommissioning.

The Mitchell Principles were based on constitutional politics and consent; principally that the people of Northern Ireland should decide their own future. The IRA, the chairman insisted, could never agree to achieve a 32-county republic through solely peaceful means. He rounded on the Army Council, accusing them of misleading IRA volunteers.

His words fell on deaf ears. The Army Council had planned their strategy well. For many delegates, Falcarragh was their first IRA Convention. To them, republicans like McGuinness and Adams *were* the Provisional IRA. The two Army Council members were almost mythical figures—hardened republicans, who in the eyes of most IRA staff, would never do anything to damage the republican movement. The chairman's criticisms made no sense to these people.

However, the chairman's carefully chosen words ignited a fierce debate. He continued to deliver his speech to the amazement of the delegates who listened to him accuse the Army Council of deliberate lies and sacrileges. McGuinness, he said, had withheld documents that clearly showed the Army Council had told the Executive in May 1997 there would be no ceasefire but 'we had only to wait a few weeks to see this commitment flounder.'

McGuinness stood to his feet to deny the allegation, prompting McKevitt to stand and raise his own voice. The Quartermaster General called McGuinness a liar—much to the disbelief of those gathered. McKevitt later told friends he felt ready to snap. In an attempt to reach a compromise, he suggested that only Sinn Féin, and not the IRA, should be party to what would later constitute the Good Friday Agreement. The vote, however, went against the rebel.

The dissidents were in the process of losing the battle when the Army Council made its move. One carefully chosen delegate loyal to Adams rose to his feet and began debating the issue of decommissioning and whether the leadership should be granted a dispensation from the Constitution. The general message conveyed during that debate was that decommissioning would never happen. The dissidents on the Executive, however, not alone saw it as a possibility but a probability.

McKevitt and his dissidents opposed the motion, though he and his followers knew they had no chance of winning. The Quartermaster General refused to yield and a fierce argument erupted over the sanctity of the IRA's Constitution. McKevitt's supporters launched fragmentary arguments but they failed to marshal significant support.

Certain that the leadership was about to win revenge for the earlier embarrassment it had suffered at the Cooley Convention, McKevitt finally realised that his appeal for support had fallen on deaf ears. When the matter was put to a vote, only 30 percent supported the dissidents. The Army Council won the motion; it now had the power to decide if there should be decommissioning. The dissidents were defeated but waited for the elections to the Executive and Army Council to take place. Then something happened that no one expected.

The delegates re-elected the same Executive that opposed the Army Council. Defeated at the vote, the dissidents had expected to lose all power. Then the same Army Council was elected but this time it contained one new face. A republican who McKevitt sincerely trusted, had switched sides in return for a guaranteed promotion to the Army Council; the Executive though remained full of militant republicans.

THE TRUTH WAS that by this stage it didn't matter; McKevitt knew he was finished. He knew he would soon be replaced as Quartermaster General because he was no longer trusted by the Army Council and Sinn Féin leadership. The position of Quartermaster General would be another man's destiny. He found this intolerable.

McKevitt's opposition to the Peace Process was not simply born out of revulsion at the prospect of decommissioning. He was steadfastly opposed to any change in the republican view of the six counties that made up Northern Ireland as proposed by the Peace Process. In his opinion, if Northern Ireland was regarded within republican circles as anything other than territory occupied by Britain, the Provisional IRA had no right to exist.

If there was a difference between McKevitt's version of republicanism and that held by the Army Council, it was his belief in the absolute authority of the IRA. He saw the IRA as an underground organisation steeped in history, which should always exist and maintain the military challenge to Britain. He viewed Adams and McGuinness not as true republicans, but as men who joined the IRA to fight against civil rights abuses in Northern Ireland.

His IRA was different; his IRA was the defender of the Republic, a defender of Irish sovereignty.

WHEN THE FALCARRAGH Convention ended that night, McKevitt took a deep breath and regained his composure. Some of his supporters were so agitated they could not hide their feelings; they openly attacked the people who had betrayed their cause. McKevitt knew his life would never be the same again. The drive home that night took hours. Those who knew him knew he did not intend letting the matter rest. Even though he was a member of the Provisional IRA, and carried out orders for its leadership, his department was always a circle within a circle. Factors other than republicanism drove the dissidents together and a common heritage also sustained their obsession with being part of an underground movement that upheld fundamental republicanism.

When McKevitt and his supporters were defeated at Falcarragh, Adams and McGuinness wrote them off, believing they were headed for oblivion. That confidence would soon dissipate.

Two weeks later on 26 October, McKevitt and his supporters resigned from the Executive en masse.* McKevitt was the first person to walk and called on the IRA not to accept the Mitchell Principles. Five members of the Executive followed—four of them were senior IRA officers. The Provisional IRA was now headed for oblivion as far as they were concerned but the dissidents strand of republicanism was far from dead.

When they left, the IRA Chief of Staff tried to placate the defectors.

'"Lads," he said. "Will you not think about how bad this will look in the newspapers when they get their hands on it?" That's all he was interested in. How it would appear to outsiders—they didn't give a shit that they were witnessing a split,' recalled one of the Executive.

Within hours the dissidents set about building a new organisation, which they called Óglaigh na hÉireann, or simply the IRA. As far as they were concerned, they had remained faithful to the IRA's Constitution; they were the Real IRA.

* Interview with member of Real IRA Army Council

2

THE NEW ARMY

IF THE ARMY Council hoped McKevitt's defeat at Falcarragh would bring about his ultimate demise, they were sorely mistaken. Even though all sides in the republican movement had anticipated a bitter split, none had foreseen the way it happened, nor how fast. If anything, McKevitt's resignation from the Executive placed him in a position where he was forced to act. He seemed to have foreseen what would eventually happen as far back as 1994. At the time he assembled a group of confidantes who would meet in secret to discuss IRA policy and the future direction of the underground army. This select group talked a good deal among themselves; the common denominator was that none trusted the Army Council. All watched Adams' pronunciations with frightening attention, analysing his comments and public statements with microscopic interest.

They all believed in McKevitt's every word, and when he finally resigned from the Executive, it was almost as if all his prophecies had come true. No longer members of the IRA, they did not know what to do, or to what extent the Quartermaster General's resignation would affect their own lives.

McKevitt was equally anxious. He found resigning traumatic; the IRA had shaped and consumed his adult life. The feeling of betrayal was inevitable; although he reflected deeply on the events, he quickly regained his composure. He realised the situation was more complex and hazardous than he had first thought. For a start, he had anticipated more support from long serving IRA volunteers. He had wrongly predicted the IRA's former Chief of Staff would join the rebellion. But in spite of everything, there was hope.

Within a week of his resignation, IRA representatives from across Ireland contacted him seeking clarification on what had happened. His message was simple and direct; the IRA was headed for military oblivion. He said the IRA Army Council was now operating outside the Constitution and would eventually destroy the IRA. He advised the membership to wait for further instruction and urged them not to lose heart.

The truth was that by this time McKevitt had already made plans for the future. He knew the constant whirlwind of speculation, claim and counterclaim about the Falcarragh Convention was not only putting him under serious strain—but his adversaries on the rival Army Council were also feeling the heat. He knew that, by continuing to preach his message, he would sow serious dissension in the IRA—which could only be of benefit to him. His message would generate solidarity—and hopefully—revolutionary indignation.

Matters had now reached a stage where action was demanded. If the Army Council was managing to stave off resignations, then it was McKevitt's job to eliminate the ambiguities that were holding the republican movement together. He would restart the war against the British.

FUELLED BY HIS indomitable beliefs in the IRA, McKevitt began creating a new military organisation within weeks. His strategy was to assemble a small organisation, bomb targets in Northern Ireland and Britain at strategic times, and eventually seize control of the IRA. An absolute self-belief in his personal capability and strengths fuelled his plan. The knowledge that a significant portion of the IRA, among them hardened bombers and gunmen, had said they would follow his command, led him to conclude that in spite of the obstacles, he could take control of the Provisionals. His failing was that, unlike Adams, he could not see the bigger picture.

In recent years, as peace negotiations commenced, a more pragmatic climate had swept through Ireland and indeed the IRA. McKevitt chose to ignore that reality. He would not accept the indisputable fact that the Provisionals' reputation was not at the high level of its terrorist successes but rather at the abysmal level of its failures. Operations had been compromised and volunteers were behind bars.

Crime and Security, the spying department of the Garda, and MI5, the British Security Service, had recruited high-ranking agents that gave them the upper hand. The IRA was also financially ready to implode; it was cash starved and weakened, though it still enjoyed support in many parts of Ireland.

McKevitt's myopic analysis of the Peace Process had already allowed him to be out-manoeuvred by the Army Council but his most serious error was to believe there was still an appetite for militant republicanism; there wasn't.

A combination of pride and determination urged him to establish a new IRA. But in spite of how undesirable and dangerous this decision could prove; the military route was still open and that was all that mattered. McKevitt was undeterred; if he did have any reservations, he didn't reveal any clues or the slightest doubt to anyone who knew him. As Sinn Féin prepared to enter into end-game political talks, he made plans to destroy the fledgling political process.

THE REAL IRA was born at a meeting that took place in the farming town of Oldcastle in County Meath that November. The town was the birthplace of Oliver Plunkett, the Catholic Archbishop of Armagh who was hanged, drawn, and quartered in England in 1681 on false charges. The symbolism was un-intentional; McKevitt chose the location because he could guarantee a secure meeting place. He was granted access to a remote farmhouse where there would be no interruptions. There were less than ten people in attendance.

The underlying problem the small group faced was how to proceed. For some weeks, McKevitt had been thinking that he should do something that would shake the IRA and the entire republican movement.

Sitting at the table, McKevitt spoke with energy and precision to his comrades. The events of Falcarragh were discussed; they all shared the same analysis of that night—they were right, the IRA was wrong. McKevitt suggested two things: the election of a caretaker Army Council and the resumption of the IRA campaign. The group would claim all operations using the name Óglaigh na hÉireann, or the IRA. Though in time they would become known as the Real IRA: RIRA.

'The philosophy was simple,' said one of the dissidents who attended the meeting.* 'The view was taken that we were not breaking away from the IRA, it was the Provos who were doing the splitting. They were discarding the Constitution—we were protecting it. They were now an illegal organisation, a militia; we were the real IRA.'

The rebels elected their caretaker Army Council that same night. The new Army Council was made up of seven people; the most important was the Chief of Staff. McKevitt was nominated for the position but refused. It was not because he was afraid. McKevitt knew his rebel history, his personal life with its tragedies and republican credentials, would enter the public domain if he became Chief of Staff.

He had experienced a hard life. Henry Michael McKevitt was born on 4 September 1949 at 11 McSweeney Street in Dundalk in County Louth. Everyone called him Mickey after his father who worked as a labourer. He had known grief and tragedy all his life. His first wife Majella and their unborn child were killed in a motorcycle accident near Dundalk shortly after they married. Some time later he married another woman and the couple had two children but the relationship broke down. He began courting Bernadette Sands—whose brother Bobby had died in 1981 on a hunger strike—after she moved to Dundalk. The relationship produced three children.

* Interview with Real IRA Army Council member

McKevitt had joined the IRA in his teens and risen through the ranks. He was a dangerous republican who commanded IRA units that engaged in notorious killings, assassinations, and bombings. His speciality was arms procurement and he excelled when appointed Quartermaster General.

He argued that his appointment as Chief of Staff to the RIRA Army Council would be counterproductive. Instead he proposed a bomb maker called 'Frank McGuinness'.

The nomination was approved by all present except one; 'McGuinness' voted against himself. In a half-joking, half-serious way, he asked them what they wanted him to do. He knew before they answered.

'Frank McGuinness' was the most skilled bomb-maker and improvised weapons expert ever trained by the IRA. He lived in Dublin.

His father was a republican and introduced him to the IRA when he was a teenager. The youth graduated through the ranks of the IRA but never got involved in Sinn Féin or local politics. He liked to live in the shadows, building and designing new types of mortars and bombs; that was his speciality.

His other expertise lay in security and counter-surveillance. Few outside the hierarchy of the IRA knew of his existence. He used the name Frank McGuinness as a cover; he was paranoid about informants.

'He would turn up at Executive or GHQ meetings and he would be known as Frank McGuinness. He mustn't have trusted any of us, at any time. We were all shocked to find out that wasn't his name at all,' said one dissident.[*]

Security was paramount. The bomb-maker never travelled the same route twice; he proved an elusive quarry for any garda ordered to log his movements. He would weave through traffic to lose unmarked patrol cars. When such methods didn't work, he would drive up a cul-de-sac, park his motorbike, and jump over a wall where another motorbike would be waiting.

McKevitt first met him when 'McGuinness' joined the Engineering Department. The section supplied the Quartermaster

* Interview with Real IRA Army Council member

General with a steady stream of weapons, hence the two men had to work together. When 'McGuinness' was made Director of Engineering and was elected to the IRA's Executive, they became close associates, whilst maintaining a tempestuous relationship. McKevitt recognised the Dubliner's engineering talent but found his temperament difficult to handle; 'McGuinness' was cocky and too sure of himself. He was prone to bouts of his own self-importance; he had a habit of overstepping his authority and challenging anyone who issued an instruction he didn't approve of.

He was brought down to size on several occasions by McKevitt, who once famously told him that he would do whatever he wanted, for as long as he wanted, or he would kill him. On that occasion, 'McGuinness' backed down.

'McGuinness' was no fool. While he may have been Chief of Staff he knew McKevitt was boss. In plain language, the Dubliner could do anything once he had McKevitt's permission; he had the throne but no real power.

McKevitt himself was proposed and elected to the position of Quartermaster.

The role of Director of Training was given to Séamus McGrane, a volunteer who had resigned from the Executive in solidarity with McKevitt. An unassuming and slightly overweight man, he lived with his family in the townland of Dromiskin near Dundalk. He had been convicted of IRA membership and jailed for a year in 1976 but had managed to evade the gardaí ever since.

The group also ratified the appointment of a Director of Operations for Northern Ireland. This job went to Liam Campbell, a mastermind smuggler who lived at Upper Faughart in County Louth with his wife and their two children.

Campbell had nerves of steel and a good tactical eye for operations. He earned a living through smuggling diesel, contraband, cattle, and alcohol, but this had brought him into conflict with the IRA Army Council, who dismissed him after announcing the 1997 ceasefire because he would not stop smuggling. He had always been close to McKevitt.

Campbell came from a staunch republican family. His brother Seán died on active service in December 1975 when he and a fellow IRA volunteer were blown up when a landmine they were preparing exploded. His brother Peter was also a convicted IRA volunteer having served 14 years for terrorist offences in Northern Ireland.

Campbell followed in his brothers' footsteps, only he was more ruthless. He came to the attention of the security services on both sides of the border in the 1980s. The campaign of violence he organised reached such a crescendo in the summer months of 1983 that he forced the British government to bestow upon him the highest honour granted to an IRA volunteer. That July, he became the subject of an exclusion order issued by the Northern Ireland Secretary who banned him from crossing the border. He looked an archetypal traditional republican. He stood six feet tall, was of athletic build, and spoke with a soft County Louth accent. Campbell would organise and command all bomb attacks in the North.

A Dubliner was appointed Director of Finance to oversee robberies and other fund-raising activities. This man was Pascal Burke, a 34-year-old from Ballyfermot in Dublin's south inner city. He had been an important member of the IRA's Dublin Brigade. He gave the fledgling organisation credibility in the city through his work with the anti-drugs movement and community groups.

Two Cork men were given non-operational positions on the new Army Council. An IRA volunteer from the village of Fermoy in County Cork was made commander of the Southern Brigade. The second appointee was made Adjutant General and charged with recruiting new members. This man had previously been the IRA Quartermaster for the Munster region.

The group also elected a Director of Publicity. This man was a militant republican from north County Dublin. During his youth, he had robbed banks and organised heists for Saor Éire, an ultra left republican group. He was trustworthy. And so began the RIRA.

THE TALK FOR the rest of the night concerned the type of warfare that would strike fear into the heart of Britain. There was deep division about how best to proceed. 'McGuinness' wanted to adopt a new approach and was very clear sighted about the situation. As the republicans listened with placid attention, he said a murderous campaign against British soldiers and police would be the best approach.

Convinced that time was against them and the political climate was shrouded in uncertainties, he urged the Army Council to engage the British military. If the new army began assassinating soldiers in broad daylight, it would spread fear and panic.

In particular, he was keen for the new army to strike militarily at the British Army, whom he argued that IRA volunteers viewed as an army of occupation. 'He felt the whole thrust of any operations should have been Óglaigh na hÉireann mounting attacks on the British Army,' recalled one member of the new Army Council.

'McGuinness' argued against using car bombs to destroy towns and commercial targets. Such attacks were useless and didn't advance the cause. Firstly they were inherently dangerous: innocent people and passers-by were sometimes murdered, they had the potential to destroy homes located near target sites and regularly failed to explode, thus providing the security services with forensic evidence.

Campbell thought otherwise. Large bombs made an impact and sent a clear message to the British government; bombings made Northern Ireland ungovernable. He also argued that there was a greater chance of success with a car bomb than trying to shoot a British soldier, or shoot down a helicopter. Car bombs were relatively simple to construct, easy to deliver and detonate. They were also cheap to manufacture.

The new Army Council felt there was merit in 'McGuinness'' argument but considered it essentially flawed. Among the many atrocities carried out by the IRA, assassinations stood out as among the most cold-blooded and cruel. Such killings made the war personal. The British government made heroes of victims; this would be counter-productive.

Campbell was permitted to run whatever military campaign he felt was necessary. 'McGuinness' was satisfied once there was a relentless onslaught against the British; he was content to let the matter rest. Another reason why he didn't oppose the strategy was that he needed more operators. He had kidnappers, expert bomb-makers, smugglers, and logistical experts but few men and women capable of carrying out the day to day work of the paramilitary group: shootings and bombing. He ordered an immediate recruitment drive.

One army council member recalled experiencing a feeling of exhilaration that night. 'There was a real sense of watching history in the making. We were all overwhelmed with solidarity and a pure determination to make Adams and Martin McGuinness accountable for their abandonment of Irish sovereignty. We were so confident. We could see that things were going to go our way, that we were going to win the argument and that people were going to join us. We were on the crest of a wave, there was no doubt about that. We felt great.'

THE DRAMATIC RESIGNATIONS of McKevitt, 'McGuinness', and McGrane from the IRA Executive were seen as a momentous occurrence within the republican movement. Bitter feuding was not a new element in Irish history and none of the previous incarnations of the IRA had escaped the destabilising process that inevitably followed. This time things were different because the stakes were higher. With no political agenda other than to collapse the ongoing peace negotiations, there was no doubting the threat the RIRA represented.

McKevitt's brand of republicanism soon became a focal point for sceptical IRA men uneasy with constitutional politics. The rebellion began. The bulk of the resignations took place in republican strongholds in Counties Louth, Monaghan, Dublin, Tyrone, and Armagh.

The Provisional Army Council knew they had a problem immediately. This was exacerbated because entire Active Service Units resigned together, with the intention of pledging allegiance to the RIRA. The calibre of volunteer that defected also terrified the IRA and Sinn Féin. For example, there were mass resignations from the Engineering Department, which accounted for 20 percent of the IRA's manpower.*

This worried the IRA Army Council more than anything else; McKevitt and 'McGuinness' were respected within IRA circles for their respective skills. The Quartermaster General's operations down through the years, with their exemplary style and perfect execution, began to look so easy that the Army Council had fooled themselves into believing they were easily organised; only those who worked alongside McKevitt knew the sacrifices he had made and the risks he took.

'McGuinness' was held in similar standing. When he created a new mortar, he personally loaded the prototype into a car he drove around the country lanes of Scotstown in County Monaghan to prove to nervous volunteers that the device was safe to transport.

The Dublin Brigade was next to divide. Burke wanted to supplant the IRA's control of the capital city. Many IRA volunteers living south of the border rejected out of hand the Army Council's handling of the Peace Process. They hoped the IRA would soon be condemned to the realms of history; that the RIRA would emerge as the true challengers to the British presence in the North.

Then suddenly the revolt stopped when the Provos moved to curb McKevitt's influence. It took the IRA Army Council a month to realise they had made a disastrous mistake by ignoring the dissidents.

Sinn Féin and the IRA Army Council had chosen to ignore the rebels because McKevitt's words had more than a ring of truth. To curtail the recruitment drive, the IRA were forced to act. Martin Ferris, a Sinn Féin candidate from County Kerry, was instructed to stop McKevitt's recruitment drive. It proved to be a decisive move.

Ferris had an equally hard reputation. Although he was a convicted gunrunner and IRA operator, having turned to politics he articulated what many IRA members knew but didn't want to accept. 'The truth,' he said without fear of contradiction, 'was that Northern Ireland was trapped in a vicious circle. On one hand, the

* Information collated by Garda Intelligence

IRA could continue with the war and get nowhere. On the other hand, the British were relentless in their pursuit of IRA volunteers.' He spoke honestly and his words had the desired impact on the volunteers. His intervention made sure the RIRA found it impossible to make its presence felt outside Leinster.

The task of organising meetings across the country to generate support also proved too much for McKevitt. The RIRA simply didn't have the manpower to send delegates to every county; Sinn Féin and the IRA did. When they realised their mistake, the mainstream republican movement also moved quickly to take control of Northern Ireland, although McKevitt did manage to generate a significant support base in Belfast.

Despite the IRA's counter-offensive, McKevitt had conducted a relatively successful recruitment drive. He amassed a formidable force of volunteers. The recruits were hard-line republicans; they saw the IRA not as a political organisation but as a religion.

Some were fundamentalist republicans. Their ideology was greatly different from those of the Provisionals. They studied Irish history and would often refer to men like Padraig Pearse, the leader of the 1916 rebellion who sacrificed his own blood for his dream of a United Ireland.

Amongst themselves, they would debate how the old IRA was defeated in 1923 by former comrades during the Irish Civil War. The IRA, they said, were more interested in fighting for Catholics than a United Ireland; there was a distinct difference. However, the RIRA also recruited criminal types. Some recruits had no knowledge of the IRA, and were considered to be undesirables in their own communities. Their allegiance to the movement would prove to have serious consequences.

PERHAPS THE FIRST people to learn of the resignations from the IRA Executive were the Garda and MI5, the British Security Service. The intelligence agencies had watched the seismic row unfold through the eyes of several informants who were paid handsomely for their information. Garda Headquarters had predicted a split but did not believe that McKevitt would harm the

IRA to any great degree. This was based on analysis of intercepted telephone traffic and information supplied by informants. It was Garda policy to spy on the IRA through two separate departments. The first was Special Branch, which collected a lot of good material, often in the area of internal IRA business and command structures.

The second department that monitored the IRA was Crime and Security. This section worked in conjunction with MI5, the Special Branch wing of the Royal Ulster Constabulary, and Scotland Yard in London. Although bureaucratic sounding in name, Crime and Security was tasked with mounting the most sensitive and secretive of all garda activities: black operations.

Crime and Security existed in the netherworld and operated from the shadows. Their operations provided the sort of intelligence sought by governments. The department operated out of offices in the Phoenix Park and was divided into different sections, which were sub-divided into smaller units. The first section was intelligence analysis; this division collated and analysed information gleaned from informants, the transcripts of intercepted telephone calls and other eavesdropping devices. The second section handled all operational matters and was called the National Surveillance Unit, or NSU for short. The NSU in turn was sub-divided into crime and subversive.

Suspects were tailed 24 hours a day. The NSU would shadow a targets every move. Such black operations were never officially recognised or even sanctioned by the Government but gave the State the upper hand in its dealings with the IRA. Command of the department fell on Dermot Jennings, a garda officer of Chief Superintendent rank. He was a native of County Sligo and had joined the Garda Síochána in 1973. Jennings spent his entire career in Special Branch and intelligence, and spoke with a mild accent, which belied a sharper tongue. His personality traits were caution and mistrust; he trusted few and acted as his own counsel.

When it came to the IRA, Special Branch and Crime and Security were expert at distinguishing between the line of truth and fantasy, particularly when assessing information from informants. Jennings had watched McKevitt spread dissension from the sidelines but was reliably informed that few at the upper echelons of the IRA supported him. This analysis was confirmed by dozens of intelligence reports that landed on his desk on a daily basis.

Crime and Security was the designated intelligence agency appointed to work with MI5. In security parlance, MI5 was code-named Snuff-Box, or Box, while Crime and Security was referred to as Bridgewater.

Box's prime concern since its founding in 1909 had been to counter the penetration of UK organisations by foreign intelligence services. However, the focus shifted in the 1980s when the IRA began its bombing campaign in Britain.

MI5 assumed full responsibility for countering the IRA in October 1992 when the Metropolitan Police were unburdened of the job. This proved to be a mistake on the part of the British government. Between 1992 and 1999, MI5 operations accounted for a mere 21 convictions for terrorist-related offences although it claimed to have averted many large city-centre bombings.

MI5 operated out of lavish buildings in central London, not far from the Palace of Westminster, where it maintained a staff of 1,850. A fraction of these worked on the Irish desk, a department referred to internally as T-branch. At the time, Stephen Lander was the Director General of the service having assumed the role in April 1996, but direct responsibility for countering the IRA rested with a quintessential Englishman, whose only connection to Ireland was through his grandmother, who was Irish. This man was called 'Webster.' He stood six feet tall, had unusual looking curly hair and always dressed formally.

MI5 had no real grasp of the RIRA. It had successfully penetrated the IRA in Northern Ireland to a far greater extent than anyone realised but knew little about the workings of the IRA south of the border, never mind the fundamental politics of the newly born RIRA. Therefore it relied on Crime and Security for help. But there were complications. Although the Garda and MI5 had a good working relationship, neither side trusted the other.

The security service specialised in running clandestine operations against the republican movement. MI5 also often drew scorn by trying to recruit informants from within the republican movement when they left Ireland to go on holiday. Crime and Security would inevitably learn of the failed operations. The golden rule was that they shared intelligence but not sources of information.

Rather than admit they knew little about McKevitt, Box forecast that half of the IRA would side with McKevitt. MI5 were convinced that two members of the IRA Army Council were toying with McKevitt, exploiting the situation, waiting to see if he could generate support.

Box attempted to enter into secret talks with the dissidents at this point in a last ditch effort to prevent the inception of another IRA faction. MI5 agents secretly approached one member of the new Army Council in Cork but the approach came to nothing. The security service also approached some of McKevitt's associates living near the border. These efforts were also wasted.

The British government had no wish to fight the RIRA for another 30 years or so but they were now left with no choice.

The Garda was of the opinion that the IRA would not split if the RIRA were contained. MI5 reluctantly agreed. If Crime and Security was saying there would be no serious defections, since that was Jennings' opinion, then their job was to brief the British government to eliminate the ambiguities and accept assurances given by Sinn Féin. All that was left to do was manage the RIRA, thus allowing the Provisionals and Sinn Féin to continue to negotiate with the Irish and British governments. This became the security agencies' main objective, though in reality, responsibility for containing the threat fell on Jennings' shoulders.

3

SOVEREIGNTY

THE INCEPTION OF the Real IRA was part of a well-defined policy to protect and conserve traditional republicanism. The RIRA—which everyone knew was a trade name for McKevitt—rejected any peace negotiations with the British out of hand, while at the same time saying they were fighting for Irish reunification.

McKevitt and his supporters called themselves the true IRA. Though in reality, the creation of the RIRA mirrored an historic tradition unique to the republican movement. First came the bitter division in the IRA over policy, next the appointment of a new Army Council, and finally the establishment of a new political party to represent the army.

The same thing had happened in the early 1920s when the IRA split into pro and anti-treaty forces. Similar events took place in 1969 when the Provos broke away from the Official IRA. More recently in 1986, Republican Sinn Féin and the Continuity IRA were created over Sinn Féin's decision to recognise Leinster House and the Dáil.

The same sequence of events happened in the autumn of 1997. While most Sinn Féin members supported the hard decisions taken by Adams and the IRA, a percentage opposed what they interpreted as a sell out.

These political dissenters were fundamentalist republicans who had been central to Sinn Féin's successes, though unlike the IRA volunteers who resigned, few were high profile figures. But they were important behind-the-scenes negotiators and activists.

Rory Dougan was one of the political dissenters. He first joined Sinn Féin in 1975. For him Sinn Féin was much more than politics; it was a way of life; his life. He held virtually every position in the Dundalk branch of the party before his resignation in late 1997.

Like many who resigned, his fears dated back to 1994 when the IRA declared the first *sos*. He didn't believe there was any reason for the IRA to declare a ceasefire as the British government had made no promise to withdraw from Northern Ireland.

'I had real doubts about the ceasefire. The British had given no commitment to leave. While people were saying it, and genuinely believed that a deal had been done, I did not believe it. I fervently believed that to enter into a ceasefire without a position from the British—other than nothing had been agreed—was the road to nowhere.'

Dougan was a stalwart Sinn Féin and IRA supporter. When the IRA blew up the Harrod's Store in London, he made a point of selling *An Phoblacht*, the official Sinn Féin newspaper, in Dundalk town centre that same afternoon. He was not afraid to be a republican; he socialised with IRA volunteers and invited them to his home. He wore his republicanism and political beliefs on his sleeve.

Dougan was one of the few people in Sinn Féin who truly understood the internal mechanisms that shaped the party. He became cautious of the party in 1996. His enthusiasm for the republican movement was further eroded when he saw Sinn Féin promoting people who had not been active in politics for decades. He interpreted the elevations as a prelude to something more sinister; he slowly came to believe that the IRA was headed towards oblivion.

'On the eve of the first ceasefire, there was a meeting in Dublin that I attended. Pat Doherty was there. We were sitting and we were talking away. At the end of it I said, "Look, a lot of people aren't happy," and Pat said, "What are they unhappy at?" I said, "They're afraid of you selling out." He jumped ten feet in the air and said, "How dare you say this to me? I'm in the republican movement," and all this.

'I said, "So what? It doesn't matter what your position is. It doesn't matter if you are selling papers for 40 years or you are sitting on the Ard Comhairle—we're still part of the same movement." It was a bit heated.'

Privately Dougan believed the IRA would surrender weapons. No matter what way he examined the situation, he could not support Sinn Féin. Two years later in 1997, when Sinn Féin applied for office space in the House of Commons, he resigned. 'That was the final straw for me.'

The temperament Dougan kept under control rebelled at this point, and his manner and political views underwent a transformation. He berated Sinn Féin for its indifference and coldness in not fulfiling what he felt was its constitutional obligation to achieve a 32 county republic.

Dougan was one of many Sinn Féin activists who knew McKevitt. Not knowing what future lay ahead, or how the situation could be retrieved, and unable to remain within Sinn Féin, he and others converged around McKevitt's partner Bernadette Sands.

Working in tandem with McKevitt, she was in the process of building a new political pressure group to defend core republican issues, the most important being sovereignty. The issue of who has a right to run the country was the only question the dissidents were interested in. They felt the mainstream republican leadership, especially Sinn Féin, was targeting a political settlement short of a United Ireland. For the dissidents, this was the only issue worth fighting for.

Sands had impeccable republican credentials. She moved south of the border to County Louth in the late 1970s and met McKevitt not long after and they began a relationship.

Sands commanded respect. She set about establishing an alternative to Sinn Féin. This was part of a dual strategy devised by McKevitt.

Matters had reached the stage where political and paramilitary dissidents felt it was time to act. To begin with, Sinn Féin's dialogue with the Irish and British governments left the possibility wide open for the disbandment of the IRA. Sands saw this as Sinn Féin's greatest weakness—and her best argument. She envisaged that her organisation wouldn't be interested in electoral politics but more intent on applying pressure on Sinn Féin from within. The grouping would welcome members from any party who wanted a United Ireland; it would be the only membership criterion.

The point of the exercise was to make Sinn Féin's support base question the decisions the party made. Until now she had criticised Adams from the sidelines. Now she was openly hostile. First she wanted to know how far Sinn Féin was authorised to negotiate on behalf of the IRA, and second, how and when the IRA had decided to abandon the physical force tradition. Sinn Féin and the IRA remained silent.

She articulated her argument well using a panel of republican analysts who advised her on the best way to achieve her aims. These key figures were Dougan, a republican from north Dublin called Joe Dillon and Marion Price. Dillon had been a hardline republican all his life. He vehemently opposed the policies advocated by Adams and the Sinn Féin leadership. Price was another dissident. She had been an IRA volunteer and was convicted for bombing Britain with her sister Dolours. Their political credentials were impeccable.

THE NEW POLITICAL pressure group emerged from a republican meeting held in the seaside village of Rush in north County Dublin on 7 December 1997. Dillon arranged the venue. In preparation for the gathering, he drafted a series of discussion documents on Sinn Féin and the party's decision to embrace the Mitchell Principles, which he argued made the IRA an illegal militia. These documents mirrored the views of the RIRA Army Council. From McKevitt's point of view it was imperative that these views were circulated to as wide an audience as possible.

The meeting itself was arranged by word of mouth. Over 100 people attended to discuss the bitter split that had engulfed the

IRA. Dillon asked Mick Ahern, a veteran republican to chair the debate, which ended up being a highly charged discussion, according to Dougan.

'The concept and idea of sovereignty evolved. It appealed to me that we weren't going to be a political party. It was a purely republican position we were taking. And from there it just evolved.'

Dillon was the driving force behind the new movement and made his presence felt that night. His contributions to the debate concerned key issues. In his opinion, Adams and Sinn Féin could not win any debate on the issue of sovereignty because they were planning to accept a deal well short of unity. He repeatedly emphasised the absolute importance of protecting the issue, which he described as vital to the very existence of the new movement.

Dillon had by this stage been suspended from Sinn Féin for raising similar issues. In his opinion, the most serious problem they faced was Adams.

'The reality was that he negotiated the republican movement into a position where the IRA were unlawfully under arms. So the IRA went from being the lawful armed forces of the Irish nation in occupied Ireland to being an unlawful army,' Dillon told the meeting.

This was the crux of the debate as far as many were concerned. Those assembled had no aspirations to run for election, nor did they want to nominate themselves as an alternative political party to Sinn Féin. Instead, they wanted to exert pressure on Sinn Féin to return to fundamental republican politics.

One of the most vocal critics of Sinn Féin's path to constitutional politics had been Francie Mackey, a Sinn Féin councillor for Omagh in County Tyrone since 1985. Ignoring Dillon's advice, he had resigned from Sinn Féin.

Many of those in attendance looked in his direction for leadership. He had protested at Sinn Féin conferences in a charged and outspoken manner. Most IRA and Sinn Féin members held him in high esteem although he was never involved in any IRA operations. But he had built up a formidable Sinn Féin branch in Omagh town in County Tyrone, which campaigned on a whole range of issues. Many republicans had secretly contacted him in the weeks prior to the Falcarragh Convention, urging him to publicly take a stand.

'There were people from all over the country. The leadership knew there was uneasiness across the support base. Nobody used the word sell out, but people weren't very happy. It was only when the rumblings led to a split within the IRA that people like myself saw that others right across the republican spectrum were unhappy about the direction that things were going.

'I have to admit, the leadership, in their handling of it and how it was choreographed, were exceptional. The leadership were going one direction, the base were following, and it was choreographed in such a way that things were a *fait accompli*,' he recalled.

He also attended the meeting in Rush. All those assembled agreed that immediate action was required. To constrain Sinn Féin, the republicans formed a pressure group that Dillon named the 32 County Sovereignty Committee. Mackey was elected President; Sands Chairman while Dillon became its press officer.*

The Sovereignty Committee found itself caught up in a whirlwind of political activity from the moment of its inception. To exert as much pressure as possible, the republicans decided to move without delay. If there was one area of republican thinking that Sands wanted to influence more than anything else, it was America.

To construct any credible organisation, it was imperative the dissidents' views were considered on the far side of the Atlantic. This was crucial. American money had enriched the Provisionals' coffers enabling the IRA to mount bombing campaigns. Sinn Féin had also benefited greatly. More important was the influence of Irish Americans. The only way the Sovereignty Committee could influence the Peace Process was through American policy and opinion. If the 32 County Sovereignty Committee could obtain just a tiny percentage of the financial support that Sinn Féin received from Irish strongholds in New York and Boston, their fortunes could be greatly improved. Hence they concentrated on building a support base there.

* Interview with member of the 32 County Sovereignty Committee

When the leadership of Sovereignty Committee first met, the organisation drafted a blueprint plan to send Sands to the United States with this sole aim. A number of unrelated factors assisted them in this regard. At the time, the largest group to support the aims of Sinn Féin was NORAID, the American organisation. At the time, NORAID was in the throes of bitter internal disputes and rivalries. Sinn Féin no longer sought the help of leading NORAID activists in New York and other cities after Adams helped set up a new group called 'Friends of Sinn Féin'. This raised funds for political activities through lavish dinner parties rather than small collections in Irish bars, which was the forte of NORAID. Naturally this move sparked off a bitter resentment in NORAID. Its supporters desperately wanted to strike back at the republican movement for what they perceived as treachery. This ill will towards Adams and Sinn Féin worked to the advantage of Sands. The Sovereignty Committee was far more flexible on the issue of cash than Sinn Féin.

IN THE FIRST few weeks after the Rush meeting, Sands had barely time to talk to anyone, she was exhausted by the job of organising meetings and convening debates that urged attacks on Sinn Féin.

However, she remained focused and endeavoured to develop a support base in America. Martin Galvin assisted in this mammoth task. He was a New York based lawyer, who had resigned from NORAID a year earlier. Not alone did Galvin pledge his support for the new pressure group and set about raising funds, he also agreed to bring Sands to America to canvass support. As one observer recalled, 'He became a driving force in the whole thing. They spoke on the phone morning, noon, and night.'

Like Sands, Galvin had an intense passion for republicanism. All observers agree that his support was instrumental in the creation of the Sovereignty Committee. This had special significance.

There was one other republican organisation actively attacking the British presence in Northern Ireland. By the time the IRA declared its second ceasefire in the summer of 1997, a new republican group had already revealed itself when it bombed the

Killyhevlin Hotel in the town of Enniskillen in County Fermanagh in July 1996. Responsibility for the attack was claimed by a then unknown group called the Continuity Army Council of the IRA: CIRA. Two months before the inception of the RIRA, the same group bombed the RUC station in Markethill in the centre of County Armagh. CIRA was the military wing of RSF, the political party that had left Sinn Féin in 1986 when the latter decided to recognise Leinster House—the Irish parliment.

That split bore uncanny resemblance to the events of Falcarragh. RSF had built up a noteworthy support base in America, which had raised considerable amounts of cash for republican prisoners. For the RIRA to succeed, it needed to do the same.

CIRA was intent on keeping up the war. When its leadership learned about McKevitt's resignation, they flirted with the notion of an amalgamation.

Ruairí Ó Brádaigh, the IRA commander and the president of RSF, spearheaded the effort. He had watched the events unfold, albeit from a distance, with more than a degree of interest.

'This was just a repeat of what happened. For me, it was a typical example of how the revolutionary went down the constitution path. We forecast in 1986 that this would happen. Martin McGuinness said the war would never end short of Irish freedom because they accepted Leinster House, but it did. All that really changes are the personalities.'

When McKevitt departed from the IRA, Ó Brádaigh sent a secret message requesting a meeting. He wanted to find out what had happened.

A meeting was arranged between the two sides immediately after the Sovereignty Committee was set up. Ó Brádaigh attended the meeting with a republican friend. Representing the Sovereignty Committee was Phil Donoghue, an IRA veteran from County Kilkenny, who had been appointed to the central executive of the Sovereignty Committee.

The dialogue wasn't very productive. The Sovereignty Committee saw their republican counterparts as being trapped in history.

'They were unable to let their difficulty with the Irish government rest. They wanted us to renounce the Dáil and attack the political institutions in the Republic. We had no interest in doing that,' according to one of the Sovereignty negotiators.

Ó Brádaigh, on the other hand, saw the CIRA and RSF as being the only legitimate republican group.

'The talks weren't very progressive. They weren't prepared to object to Leinster House. As we saw it, in 1986 the Provisionals broke the constitution and we brought it with us. There was no recrimination. They were totally wrapped up in their own situation, where they were heading. You could call it a friendly gesture. Each party, if you like, knew the others situation,' Ó Brádaigh has said.

Friendly gesture or not, that meeting was a meeting of minds. If the two political pressure groups could converse, there was no reason why their military wings couldn't co-operate. In time, the two sides would do a lot more than talking.

THE RIRA WAS formally baptised on 7 January 1998. Following his appointment as Director of Operations for Northern Ireland, Campbell chose to begin his bombing campaign at once. The new Army Council considered it imperative that the RIRA send out a clear message. They decided to bomb the town of Banbridge in County Down.

Situated to the north west of the county, Banbridge covers a total of 175 square miles of countryside. Campbell was personally familiar with the thriving town, which is surrounded by the Slieve Croob Mountains to the east and the meandering River Bann valley to the west; the town made an ideal target.

An attack there would come as a complete surprise. It would also show the IRA, the security services and the British and Irish governments that the RIRA was a formidable force. More importantly, it would embarrass Sinn Féin. Adams would no longer speak for the entire republican movement. Another factor was the town's location; Banbridge was situated on the main A1 route between Belfast and Dublin. The RIRA had no interest in disrupting traffic but knew an attack would infuriate Unionist politicians.

Campbell selected a bomb team drawn from County Louth. 'McGuinness' oversaw the construction of the bomb. The device itself consisted of 500lbs of home-made explosive with a booster containing Semtex explosive. The bomb was assembled at a secret location in Dundalk and inserted into a Ford Sierra bought in the town months earlier.

It was a typical IRA operation. Minutes before the device was due to explode, the RUC received an urgent call from LMFM Radio, a provincial station that broadcasts in County Louth.

The station had been warned by a group which called itself Óglaigh na hÉireann. Minutes later the Samaritans in County Down called to say a similar warning had been made to their offices in Newry. The RUC moved fast to locate the car, which was parked on Newry Street. The bomb was made safe after an ordinance disposal unit from the British Army carried out several controlled explosions. This was certainly not the start McKevitt and Campbell had hoped for. It was a disaster.

EXACTLY 12 HOURS after the Banbridge bomb was defused Joe Dillon heard a bang on the door of his semi-detached home in the fishing village of Skerries. He knew that someone at his door just after 7 a.m. meant only one thing: a garda raid.

He awoke from his slumber and made his way slowly downstairs. He could see several men standing outside. He unbolted the door slowly but it was pushed in before he had a chance to stand aside. Armed detectives from the Emergency Response Unit pushed him to the ground.

'There was a fella poking a gun at my stomach at the door,' he recalled. 'I didn't know he was a Harrier.* It could have been anyone. So I tried to grab the gun. I nearly got it too. I was trying to get the pistol off him, wrestling on the floor of the kitchen with him. He's lucky I didn't get it too.'

In the end, three officers overpowered him. He was arrested under Section 30 of the Offences Against the State Act and taken from his

---

* A republican term of abuse for a garda officer

home into a squad car which transported him to Whitehall Garda Station in central Dublin.

At the same time, three other men were being arrested in Howth, a seaside village in north Dublin. Special Branch had found one and a half tonnes of fertilizer—the main ingredient of HME—at a disused fishmongers on Howth Pier.

The discovery was the result of a surveillance operation overseen by Jennings. The NSU had spent weeks watching the fishmonger's shop before they decided to move. Dillon had been seen entering another disused house in Bettystown in County Meath where a bag of fertilizer was found.

Dillon was later charged along with three others who all fought and won their cases. The republican had not been aware of his own profile in the media until his arrest. The national press seized the opportunity the arrest afforded. This was a disaster for the new committee, which had only been formed a month earlier. Dillon, though, found the episode amusing and correctly stated that no charges would stick.

The RIRA Army Council got over the failure of Banbridge. No one suspected that anything untoward had happened.

As a precaution McKevitt and Campbell decided to transfer the bombing operations deeper into the republic. McKevitt turned to a proven and trusted ally in County Kildare seeking help. In time, he would learn that this decision was the greatest mistake he ever made.

4

THE INFORMANT

PADDY DIXON WAS a quintessential criminal from Blanchards-town, a thriving community in west Dublin. He enjoyed a chaotic life. He didn't eat at regular hours, hardly got any sleep, listened to loud music, and never kept the same girlfriend for too long. He was a wild teenager who stole cars for enjoyment as well as serious financial gain. He left school without any formal education, though the education he learned on the streets compensated for his successive failures at school. He had few distinguishing features; he was slightly overweight, stocky, and didn't possess a good posture. He spoke in a flat accent and looked every part the rough cut Dubliner he was.

Auto theft was his specialty. If it was possible to have a natural ability to steal cars, Dixon possessed that special gift. He could disable car alarms without much thought in just a few seconds. By the time he was 20, he was an expert thief who provided much sought after services to criminal gangs across Dublin city. Friends of his say he knew far more about cars than most mechanics. Car ringers* and corrupt garage owners would pay him to provide stolen vehicles to order. As his reputation grew, so did his notoriety. He became a wanted man. Gardaí would stop and search him on sight. They were eager to put him behind bars.

* Car ringers fit stolen cars with registration plates from crashed cars in order to launder them into the legitimate motor trade

It was not in Dixon's nature to be security conscious despite the obvious Garda interest in him. Even he accepted that he would eventually end up in jail given his nocturnal acts of crime. It came as a surprise to no one when, in the summer of 1985, a young detective from Blanchardstown caught him in possession of a stolen car. The detective's name was John White.

Just as Dixon was a typical criminal, White was a classic example of someone who becomes a garda. Born in County Tipperary, he spoke with a soft rural voice, was thickset, stood under six feet tall and could easily have passed himself off as a farmer or minor civil servant. Appearances though, can be deceptive—White was sharp. He was a savvy, experienced detective who could tell when someone was lying. He honed his police skills on the streets of Dublin and in the Murder Squad. He knew how the underworld worked and how gardaí interfaced with criminals.

When he caught Dixon, he made sure the thief knew it was the end of the road. Dixon realised he was going to jail. The young man had a pathological fear of prison. He simply could not contemplate spending a period of his youth behind bars in Mountjoy Prison.

When Dixon was arrested, he was brought to Blanchardstown Garda Station for processing. When Dixon had completed the necessary custodial procedures, he was brought into an interrogation room for the purpose of taking a statement. But Dixon interjected and said he wanted to exchange some information for his freedom. White agreed to listen, after thinking about the proposal for a time. He told the prisoner that he was taking a great risk even listening to his story. White knew Dixon was a car thief but sensed there was something else worrying the prisoner.

Dixon began to talk slowly. He spoke as if trying to convince his captor that the weight of the world lay on his shoulders. He trembled as he spoke. White could see the dread of jail was to the forefront of his mind, but guessed there was something else gnawing at Dixon. White waited in anticipation. In an instant, Dixon named the criminal to whom he supplied stolen cars. The man he named was called 'Jones' and he ran a lucrative business in County Kildare.

Dixon waited for White to recognise 'Jones'' name but there was no reaction. When the car thief mentioned 'Jones' again he lowered his voice; it was clear that he was terrified of this man. Dixon chose his words carefully and spoke with absolute gravity. The two men never lost eye contact, with White giving the impression that he knew exactly who and what Dixon was referring to—but the truth was that White had no idea what Dixon was even talking about.

Dixon did not notice the deception. As the minutes ticked by in the interrogation room, Dixon began to tell his story. He said he supplied special order cars to 'Jones'. His words were lost on White who still didn't understand what he was talking about until Dixon explained in plain language that the stolen cars were for the IRA.

It is noteworthy that Dixon claimed he was paid nothing for his services. Any cars he supplied for the cause were free. The only thing he was asked to do was wear latex gloves when taking the vehicles, to avoid leaving fingerprints. White did not work with Special Branch, the force's anti-terrorist unit, and therefore had no way of ascertaining if the information was true or not.

White's reaction quickly led Dixon to conclude that the detective was out of his league. Once he realised his error by opening up to the officer, he started issuing ultimatums, insisting he would never give evidence against the IRA. But it was too late. White had other ideas. He might not have known who 'Jones' was, but he knew a valuable asset had just dropped into his lap. The detective made sure Dixon walked away a free man—but at a cost.

IN THE YEARS that followed, Dixon became White's eyes and ears in the underworld. Between 1991 and 1994, he provided information on the Dublin crime scene. White even befriended Dixon and treated him like a brother. The informant and his handler would organise secret meetings where Dixon would provide information on murders, drug dealing, and the IRA.

Dixon became White's vehicle to success. Information from the informant gave White the means to ingratiate himself with his superior officers, who rewarded the detective for his sterling work.

The situation in which Dixon found himself was very different, however. He was trapped in a vicious circle. On one hand, he had White offering a degree of immunity from prosecution if he was ever arrested. On the other hand, he was a dead man walking. Should he make one false move, he was dead.

The IRA and criminals denounced informants as traitors. No mercy was shown if one was identified. Informants were shot dead; no questions asked. No one cared. The only friend he felt he could confide in about his difficulties was White. But the detective was no friend; he was his handler.

Sometimes Dixon and White would talk several times a day. At other times, weeks would go by without any contact. Dixon made the best of his predicament and embraced his role as best he could. The two men almost became friends. The reality of the situation was not lost on Dixon; he knew he was only as good as the information he provided. He was expendable.

'JONES' LIVED IN the shadows of the underworld. He shied away from republican politics, but was firmly committed to the IRA. He was a millionaire who commanded fear in his local community. He stood six feet tall, was broadset and spoke with a coarse Kildare accent. The twin foundations of his fortune were fear and intimidation. He was hated by his neighbours and despised in his local community where he was regarded as a bully and a thug. He intimidated anyone who crossed him.

He was a republican supporter who was trusted and admired by the Quartermaster's Department. His function was to manufacture HME. For his services, he became a wealthy man. He traded on the IRA's name and reputation. If you made a deal with 'Jones', you made a deal with the IRA. Few business associates crossed him. Car ringing, smuggling alcohol, and criminality earned him a fortune. His adversaries assumed all the profits went to the IRA, the truth was that 'Jones' and his family were the chief beneficiaries. His wife and children wanted for nothing. They lived on the proceeds of crime and were despised for it.

'Jones', for some inexplicable reason, confided in Dixon. He had a senseless trust in the car thief. He departed sensitive information on the IRA without giving it a second thought. Looking back on the events, many observers today believe 'Jones' was simply trying to embellish his own standing in the IRA.

As the years passed, Dixon gained a valuable insight into 'Jones'' criminal empire, though he gave up stealing special orders in 1994 when the IRA announced their first ceasefire.

White, though, never used the informant to his full potential. Dixon was a career criminal; he cared nothing for the gardaí, or the IRA for that matter. His life revolved around money and power. He got involved in every form of crime.

At one point, he came under death threat from the IRA and anti-drugs campaigners for drug trafficking. On that occasion, 'Jones' intervened to make sure nothing happened. His actions betrayed other republicans who fought against the scourge of drugs sweeping through Dublin. In the end, the Provos who targeted Dixon turned a blind eye to his profiteering in narcotics. It was all the same to Dixon; his criminal career flourished. He became a professional; he didn't compromise himself. He operated a 'hands off' policy and hired miscreant teenagers to do his bidding.

DIXON WAS TOLD his special skills were no longer needed when the IRA went on ceasefire in 1994. Three years later, he received an unexpected telephone call from his old friend 'Jones'. He wanted two vans—special orders.* Dixon wondered why the IRA wanted stolen cars if it was on ceasefire. Dixon relayed the news to White. He did not know what to make of the request. The vans were not provided for an assortment of reasons, but a week later 'Jones' called again. The two men had a brief conversation and arranged to meet later that day. The meaning of the conversation was so vague that it took the informant a few minutes to register its true meaning, which he later relayed to White when they met. Dixon, in his hardened Dublin accent, whispered, 'The boys are back in business.'

White was so struck by the information that he immediately began compiling an intelligence report. He sent this to officials at

* Information provide by Detective Sergeant John White to Northern Ireland Police Ombudsman

Crime and Security, who ensured the file landed on Dermot Jennings' desk.

The Chief, as Jennings was known, was already monitoring McKevitt's activities but was unaware of any change in the RIRA's modus operandi. He read White's report with interest and instructed the detective to monitor the situation. The Chief knew McKevitt was in the process of moving his operational base out of County Louth. If White's information was accurate, having an informant inside a RIRA base was a monumental intelligence coup.

Jennings, who was a man known to work every hour, passed his mobile telephone number to White. If he was unavailable, he instructed the detective to call his deputy, Superintendent Phil Kelly, the head of the NSU. Neither garda thought anything would come of White's informant. McKevitt was far too clever to make a mistake, never mind trust a petty criminal. However, Jennings suspected that circumstances might force McKevitt's hand, that he might make a mistake. And he was right.

ON THE MORNING of 13 February 1998, White received an urgent telephone call from Dixon. 'Jones' wanted a special order again. When the informant relayed news of the request to White, the garda noticed that he sounded flustered. Dixon was scared, but that morning White demonstrated his agent handling skills by calming the informant down. White coaxed Dixon into promising that he would tell him everything about 'Jones'' request—even though the car thief was terrified of being exposed as an informant. It was an important telephone call and Dixon would later regret opening his mouth at all; but it was now too late. White knew something was happening.

The hours passed without any contact and at 8 p.m. White decided to call. The informant didn't want to talk but White persisted. Dixon confirmed he had sourced a Mazda for 'Jones'. The car was parked outside a residential address in Dublin. It had not yet been stolen, though Dixon said his gang was ready to move. They planned to steal the car at 2 a.m.

The information gave rise to the inevitable question: what to do next? Every chance to intercept a stolen car destined for the IRA was an opportunity not to be missed. White called Jennings on his mobile phone, however, it was switched off. As instructed, he proceeded to call Kelly with the news.

Dixon's gang in the meantime stole the Mazda. White believed the car would be delivered to a yard in Clane, a small town near Kilcock. The owner of the yard had been pressurised into helping 'Jones' and the Real IRA.

Kelly was asleep when he was woken by White's call. He told White that he would deal with the matter in the morning. White was unaware that an NSU officer was already monitoring the yard which had been identified weeks earlier. In any case, the Mazda was not driven to Clane but moved elsewhere.

MCKEVITT MAY HAVE been in the process of relocating his bombing team to County Kildare, but he was still forging ahead with his plans to wreak havoc across Northern Ireland. The RIRA was now fully operational. Jennings' spies had built up a detailed picture of the new Army Council from well placed informants. Crime and Security knew everything. They knew who was involved and who gave the orders. Campbell was of particular concern, as was 'McGuinness'. A number of Continuity IRA members living along the border had also switched sides and joined the RIRA; this created further problems for the security services.

'It was a meeting of minds. It wasn't a case of what politics someone believed in. It was a case of who could build the biggest bombs,' later recalled a member of the RIRA.

For the first time since its inception, the RIRA was on the move. McKevitt now wanted to demonstrate just how effective his new army was. To bomb Northern Ireland, McKevitt needed an endless stream of cars to carry the bombs. He had turned to 'Jones' for practical support. McKevitt knew nothing about 'Jones'' relationship with Dixon, nor how his trusted lieutenant spoke loosely to common criminals. He also wanted 'Jones' to manufacture consignments of HME, which 'McGuinness' and his engineering team could turn into car bombs. For the cars, 'Jones' in turn relied on Dixon and his gang.

THE TWO MEN met on 16 February at 2 p.m. 'Jones' came straight to the point.

'There will be mayhem, Paddy,' said 'Jones'.

'Absolute mayhem.'

The purpose of the meeting was to extract a commitment from Dixon that he would supply vehicles to the new army. In the misguided belief that Dixon was reliable, he asked him to start stealing Mitsubishi Pajeros and Isuzu Troopers as soon as possible. Dixon readily agreed. After the meeting, he called White to inform him of the development.

White had been told to continue gathering intelligence and instruct Dixon to operate within the RIRA as a participating garda informant. The hope was that Dixon would provide valuable information on what the RIRA was up to, and perhaps save lives in Northern Ireland. Dixon agreed to the proposal but he was nervous; he didn't wish to die young. His greatest fear was that he would be forced to meet other gardaí. He trusted White implicitly but the detective's superiors were another matter.

And so the black operation against the RIRA began, with Dixon playing the central role of the spy. The operation was largely a waiting game. It took two days for anything to happen. Then at 3.20 p.m. on 18 February, Dixon called White to say he had stolen a jeep from outside a house on the South Circular Road in Dublin city. The car was en route to Clane in County Kildare where it would be left in the yard.

'Jones' was so heavily involved in car theft and criminality that the intelligence specialists figured the vehicle was simply being stolen for resale. White was adamant, however, that this was terrorist related. He also told Jennings that a criminal called Damo, who came from Blanchardstown, had taken possession of another Pajero jeep, which would be used in a bombing north of the border. Dixon had warned him about the possible attack.

Jennings was cautious of White but he knew 'Jones' was fast becoming a force within the RIRA. The information he possessed from other sources suggested that Campbell was planning a series of attacks from areas near the border.

Meanwhile the business of crime and terrorism continued as normal. 'Jones' traded in stolen cars and anything else for that matter. The RIRA was his hobby. On 19 February, he asked Dixon to steal another jeep.

Jennings indicated that he wanted Dixon to hand over the next stolen vehicle. If indeed 'Jones' was taking possession of stolen cars, Crime and Security were interested. 'Jones' had escaped arrest many times before. Intelligence gleaned from informants had linked him to arms finds but there was never enough evidence to press charges.

Jennings believed the secret services of the NSU should now be deployed against 'Jones'. One system used by the NSU enabled its officers to monitor the movement of stolen cars through the attachment of a transmitter to the vehicles. The devices were called beacons and there were two kinds. The first was battery operated and was attached to the underside of a car by two magnets. These transmitted signals to a receiver.

The second device was more sophisticated. These beacons were inserted into a target car's electrical system and operated from the vehicle's own battery. They enabled the NSU to track a car from a spotter plane. These beacons were intelligent; they automatically turned off when anti-bugging sweeps were carried out. If a beacon was inserted, Jennings argued that 'Jones'' entire operation could be compromised.

As the days passed, it became clear to Jennings that White's informant was indeed an insider in the RIRA. The situation changed drastically. White now felt under pressure to deliver. It was imperative that the NSU gained access to one of the stolen cars.

White remonstrated with Jennings saying Dixon wouldn't agree to the beacon plan. If the RIRA checked the stolen car and found a transmitter, Dixon was sure to be blamed. And if the car was later intercepted by gardaí, he would also be blamed. It was a no-win situation from Dixon's point of view. The truth was that White and Dixon were out of their league. They didn't know what to do. After hours of debate, White was told in no uncertain terms how to proceed.

The detective sergeant was told to instruct Dixon to take sole possession of the next car the RIRA wanted stolen. The stolen vehicle would be delivered to the Phoenix Park. White would follow the stolen car in his own car. Once the car was delivered to the Phoenix Park, Dixon would join White while the NSU inserted the beacon. When the NSU had completed their work, White would escort Dixon to the drop off point and drive him home.

Jennings was a master handler. He suggested offering Dixon cash from the Government's Secret Service Fund. Dixon had never taken money but Jennings told White to keep the pressure on. The money would give White a psychological advantage over his informant.

When Dixon was told of the plan, he refused to do anything and said he would be signing his own death warrant if he co-operated. Handing control of a stolen car to the gardaí was inconceivable. His secret work had given him a unique insight into the RIRA. By this stage he had familiarised himself with their modus operandi, which he quoted verbatim to White. If any car he provided was intercepted, it would result in an internal inquiry. As far as he was concerned, he would be blamed, possibly abducted, likely tortured, and certainly murdered.

Jennings insisted. Crime and Security had obtained information that corroborated White's information. McKevitt's boys were indeed back in business.

ANY EARLIER SETBACKS inflicted on McKevitt by Crime and Security were quickly overcome. The RIRA set about organising a bombing campaign with the intention of collapsing the Peace Process. Working in absolute secrecy, the RIRA assembled three bombing teams and various ASUs. 'McGuinness' headed one bombing team that operated out of Dublin. His team conducted their work alone.

'McGuinness' would personally design and build TPUs—time-and-power units—while other members of his engineering unit would hollow out steel tubes and fill them with Semtex. He trained engineers in the art of bomb-making. He worked in conjunction with Campbell, who was tasked with organising a steady stream of attacks in Northern Ireland. 'Jones' provided logistical support. He was tasked with preparing the stolen cars for bombing missions. 'Jones' made sure the cars were already fitted with industrial shock absorbers to carry the weight of HME. 'Jones'' team also manufactured HME using fertilizer and sugar. When the vehicle with the explosive mixture was ready and waiting at a safe location, 'McGuinness' would arrive and construct the bomb. This usually meant that he fitted the TPU. As a security precaution, he inserted TPUs at workshops north of the border—where the Garda had no authority to operate.

THE FIRST SUCCESSFUL bomb produced by the RIRA was delivered to the town of Moira in County Antrim on 20 February 1998. The bomb was hidden in a Pajero, which carried 500lbs of explosives armed with a Semtex booster. 'Jones'' unit played no role in the attack. The vehicles used in the attack were purchased in Northern Ireland.

A 15-minute warning was given but there was no code word. The warnings were telephoned to the Maze Prison and Maghaberry Prison. As RUC officers rushed to evacuate the town, the bomb exploded, injuring 11 people. Three days later on 23 February, another car bomb exploded, this time in the loyalist town of Portadown in County Armagh. The bomb was hidden in a grey BMW parked on Edward Street. The location was close to the junction with High Street and 300 yards from the town's RUC station. The RIRA delivered a warning 40 minutes before the explosion.

Two clothes shops took the brunt of the explosion; a burned-out gaping hole with smoke billowing towards the sky was all that remained of them. Buildings on the opposite side of the street were also badly damaged. Roofs sat at dangerous angles to facades on adjoining buildings and large cracks showed through the brickwork. Windows were blown out in premises throughout the centre of the town. Portadown was a strategic target.

The town lay in the heartland of fundamental loyalism. It was also the biggest town in the Ulster Unionist leader David Trimble's Upper Bann constituency. Although no one was injured, the attack had the desired effect. Billy Hutchinson of the Progressive Unionist Party, which is linked to the loyalist terrorist group the Ulster Volunteer Force warned the loyalist ceasefire was close to breaking point. The attacks continued.

DIXON WAS NO liar and had provided accurate information on the RIRA from the start. White was now somewhat out of his depth and asked the Chief to meet the informant personally. For this meeting White asked a colleague if he could use his house in Porterstown in County Dublin as a safe place to meet. Everything was arranged. A few days later, White took Dixon to the meeting where Jennings was already waiting.

Jennings introduced himself as Dennis. He didn't give his rank, nor reveal his position, but shook Dixon's hand, congratulating him on his work. The purpose of the meeting was to advise Dixon on personal security. White had no specialist training in this field but Jennings had. What Jennings realised was that Dixon was like everyone else; he wanted money. He wasn't helping the Garda for ideological reasons but for personal incentives. Yet, in his own mind, Dixon couldn't see himself as an informant. He viewed his relationship as an arrangement between two parties.

At the time, his minibus company was sub-contracted to a firm in west Dublin. He rambled on about his work before telling Jennings that gardaí had seized his vehicle.

Jennings saw his opportunity and made a proposition. He would help Dixon financially conditional on the criminal handing over to Garda all special order cars he stole. Dixon was reluctant. He said he would appreciate the return of the minibus but thought handing over the stolen vehicles would be too dangerous. Jennings reiterated his offer; this time offering £1,000 cash as an incentive.

Dixon agreed, but stipulated one condition; he did not wish to take any money, but he would accept a loan. 'It's only for a few weeks, things are a bit hard,' he said.*

When Dixon agreed, Jennings handed him £1,000 saying he didn't want it back. Dixon took the money and left. Afterwards the Chief walked out into the evening air having accomplished a difficult task. Dixon now belonged to Crime and Security; there was no turning back.

Although Dixon had been recruited as an informant, the gardaí still had little or nothing to work on until 'Jones' sought another special order. Dealing with the RIRA was a game of nerves.

Every scrap of intelligence on the secret army suggested that McKevitt planned weekly attacks. In the meantime, surveillance on McKevitt was stepped up. This was straightforward enough. He lived in Blackrock and rarely took anti-surveillance measures.

'McGuinness', however, proved an elusive quarry. He drove everywhere with one eye on the road while the other watched for following cars. Even when the NSU deployed dozens of cars to tail him, it proved a futile exercise. In an instant he would spot unmarked police vehicles pulling out of garages and small lay-bys waiting for him to appear.

'We would get intelligence from mobile telephone calls where he would have arranged to collect a bomb component. We could have 20 men on surveillance waiting at the collection point. The operation would have taken months to arrange, then someone else would show. He was a nightmare to follow. He trusted no one and never took the same route twice,' a garda said later. Such was his success at spotting surveillance that some detectives came to suspect that he knew exactly when he was being followed but were not sure how.

While waiting for 'Jones' to move, the NSU maintained a watchful eye on those identified as joining the RIRA. At other times, sheer luck was on their side.

On 24 February, detectives located a 250lbs bomb outside the village of Redhills, a townland situated between County Cavan town and Newtownbutler in County Fermanagh. The device was

* Information provide by Detective Sergeant John White to Northern Ireland Police Ombudsman

hidden in a ditch. Although a detonating cord had been attached there was no detonator, making it relatively harmless.

Almost two weeks later, on 2 March, surveillance on RIRA suspects resulted in the capture of a car bomb in Hackballscross in County Louth. This time, the bomb was being assembled in a disused hay barn on the Concession Road, about a mile from the County Louth border with County Armagh. There was 400lbs of HME concealed in a Renault 21, which was fitted with false registration plates.

Bales of hay had been placed around the car to hide it from passers-by. Local gardaí had conducted surveillance on the barn for weeks but no one approached the car. 'It became too expensive to watch it for any longer,' said an officer on the operation.

A week later, the RIRA struck again. On 10 March, five mortars were fired at the RUC station in Armagh city just after midnight. The missiles were fired by remote control from a metal-framed firing base set up on waste ground behind the barracks on Friary Road, near Armagh Rugby Club.

One missile landed in the middle of the road, another fell among neighbouring houses on Newry Road, and two others fell on waste ground. The last one failed to fire and was found in its tube. Although none of the missiles struck the station; the attack did serve its purpose. It embarrassed Sinn Féin.

WHITE CONTINUED TO exert psychological pressure on the informant. He told Dixon in no uncertain terms that many lives depended on him; that he would be responsible for murder and mayhem if he did not help Crime and Security. Dixon found the pressure unbearable. He felt the weight of the world resting on his shoulders. He felt trapped, that he was no longer in control of his own destiny.

On one hand, Crime and Security were watching his every move; he had accepted cash for information and couldn't renege on the deal. He was also the central player in the black operation being run by Jennings against the RIRA.

On the other hand, 'Jones' was exerting pressure on him to steal more cars and if he refused, he knew it would look suspicious. He was running out of options fast. If he continued to deliver the special orders, sooner or later he would fall under investigation by the RIRA when the cars were later intercepted. Furthermore, if his role was compromised, he was a dead man; there was no way out. No matter how hard he tried to think up a plan to escape, he could not see any way out.

He was willing to play a little rough and dirty with White by threatening to quit, but events quickly overtook him. In reality he had only one choice and that was to continue working for the Garda strictly on the condition that he would be protected if his secret role were ever compromised. The assurance was given.

'JONES" DECISION TO involve Dixon in the RIRA was a stroke of good fortune for Jennings. It was an unexpected bonus that enabled Crime and Security to gain an insight into the structure of the new IRA. The intelligence services already knew a good deal about McKevitt. But Dixon opened up new avenues of investigation, which meant new targets to spy on.

'Jones' answered directly to McKevitt, Campbell, and 'McGuinness'. A strong friendship already existed between McKevitt and 'Jones'; the two men trusted each other like brothers. 'McGuinness' had also known the criminal for years. McKevitt had come to genuinely admire 'Jones' but there is no doubt that he would have severed all links with him if he had known how he spoke about sensitive IRA matters with people the Quartermaster would probably have regarded as petty thieves. McKevitt also hated drug dealers and would not tolerate them.

'It was almost unbelievable,' said a Crime and Security officer afterwards. 'McKevitt would never utter as much as a word to someone who hadn't proven themselves but here was his immediate subordinate talking about bombing campaigns to a petty thief.'

If Dixon gave away any signs of his clandestine relationship with the Garda, 'Jones' didn't possess the skills to notice. He continued to request more special order cars from Dixon. These were delivered by Dixon's gang, which consisted of two young car thieves from Blanchardstown. The first was Vinny, a master thief who had the outward appearance of a small and thin youth who seemed to fidget incessantly. Vinny had mastered the craft of stealing cars but was also a self trained cat burglar. If Dixon required a stolen car with its own set of keys, Vinny was the man for the job. He could easily break into any home and steal personal belongings from inside.

The second gang member was Chang. Like Vinny, he was small and thin; his dark complexion gave him an oriental appearance, hence the nickname Chang. He was another expert car thief.

The two youths dabbled in drugs, lived for house music, fast women and adored cars. In the company of Dixon, they were loud and obnoxious; when out stealing cars and plundering houses in the suburbs, they worked with the skill of a specialist military unit.

Dixon was careful to distance himself from crimes committed by the thieves and so monitored everything from afar. When the thieves were sourcing special orders, he provided them with latex gloves. He never travelled with the gang but collected the cars at pre-arranged drop off points. This suited everyone. The only people exposed to the risk of arrest were the thieves. Dixon remained one step removed from the actual thefts while 'Jones' remained two steps away. This was most important from 'Jones'' point of view. All he needed to know was that Dixon's gang were reliable. There were only two rules for Dixon's gang: don't get caught and if you do get caught, say nothing.

5

CAT AND MOUSE

THE SEARCH FOR suitable vehicles for the Real IRA would often extend beyond the suburbs of Dublin city. On 25 February 1998, the thieves travelled to the town of Navan in County Meath to steal a jeep. It was another special order for 'Jones'. The jeep was required to deliver a bomb into the North. Vinny found a Mitsubishi Pajero and took it at 1.45 a.m. that same night. The jeep was driven into Blanchardstown where Dixon had earlier arranged to take possession of the car in the Coolmine Industrial Estate in west Dublin. When Vinny arrived there at 2.25 a.m. the industrial estate was deserted.

When Dixon took the car, he ordered Vinny to go home. Almost as soon as he vanished a second car pulled up. It was White. The informant had earlier alerted his handler to the theft; Jennings in turn had put the NSU on full alert. White had convinced the informant to hand over the jeep for an hour.

Dixon drove the car out of the industrial estate taking a left, which took him through the villages of Blanchardstown and Castleknock. White followed behind. The two cars reached the Phoenix Park in the space of 15 minutes because there was no traffic on the roads. As instructed, Dixon drove to the park's gate entrance situated across from the Phoenix Park Racecourse. He parked the jeep beside a clump of trees, stepped out of the car, took a deep breath and walked over to White's car. Once the informant sat into his car, White called the NSU to say the vehicle was in position. He spoke on the phone to a man he knew only as Dave. The call lasted no more than ten seconds.

As the detective and his informant drove away, they could scarcely make out the images of faceless men emerging from the undergrowth. It was pitch black.

The two men expected the operation to take an hour but it actually took longer. To insert the beacon, it was necessary for the jeep's dashboard to be removed. This took time and given the circumstances and lack of facilities, the operation proved a difficult task for the NSU.

In the meantime, Dixon began to panic. He accused White of putting his life in danger. 'Time is everything. How am I going to explain being late?' the informant asked. White had no answers but told the spy to relax.

The jeep was destined for delivery to Clane later that same night. After an hour had passed, Dixon lost control of his senses. He asked White how he would explain the time delay. Worse again, how would he explain his movements if the jeep was later intercepted with explosives and the RIRA ordered an inquiry? Again White had no answers. It took a further two hours before Dave called to say the jeep was ready for collection. By this time, Dixon was in the throes of panic.

The four-wheel-drive had been fitted with a tracking device no larger than a Walkman, which permitted the surveillance unit to follow the moving vehicle from a low flying plane to within 100 feet of ground level.

When he received confirmation that the jeep was ready for collection, White drove Dixon back to the vehicle. The NSU had long since vanished into the night. Dixon and White saw nothing. Dixon sat back into the car and turned the engine. He drove straight to Clane, taking a circuitous route on winding back roads and country lanes. White followed behind.

The roads were dark and poorly lit but this didn't stop the spy driving at speed. This was a matter of life and death from Dixon's perspective. Every second counted. He had to get to Clane, and fast.

The two car convoy arrived at 'Jones'' yard around 5.20 a.m. It was dark and freezing cold. Once the jeep was parked up, Dixon called 'Jones' on his mobile to say the car was in place—ready for collection. He left a message on 'Jones'' answering machine because his phone was powered off.

THE NSU SATURATED the area with undercover detectives. The jeep was first left in the yard at Clane where 'Jones' assumed it was safe from prying eyes. But it took the NSU just minutes to insert surveillance teams into the surrounding countryside. Detectives dressed in combat fatigues hid in the undergrowth watching everything. Unmarked cars driven by plainclothes officers occasionally drove past to reconnoitre the location as part of the same covert operation. The identities and car registrations of anyone who entered the yard were logged; their identities were also checked against all files held by Crime and Security.

Two days after the jeep's theft, 'Jones' sent his men to prepare the vehicle for terrorism. Johnny McNamara was a hard-line republican from Kilcock who had joined 'Jones' and the RIRA. Dixon had met him several times but did not know him by name. He knew him only as the Big Fella—a name that baffled the gardaí.

McNamara took personal care of 'Jones'' special orders. He was a giant of a man: he stood six feet five inches, was of muscular build and looked every part the IRA hardliner.

'Bull' was the second trusted member of 'Jones'' unit. He arrived to collect the jeep with McNamara at Clane. On the day in question, the two walked into the yard but didn't engage in any unnecessary conversation. According to McNamara, they were instructed to prepare the vehicle for transport to Dundalk in County Louth.

'There were no number plates on the jeep when we got there. We met at the garage and we hadn't much conversation. We knew the job we had to do and we set about doing it,' McNamara would later tell gardaí.*

McNamara and 'Bull' removed a set of chrome bull-bars from the vehicle and affixed false registration plates. They also disabled the locking mechanism on the rear door because Vinny had not stolen the keys for the jeep. This took an hour. When they were finished, they used a screwdriver to turn the engine.

At this stage, the vehicle was empty and contained no explosives. 'Jones' had instructed the two men to deliver the jeep to the long-term car park at Dublin Airport. 'Bull' drove the stolen Pajero while McNamara followed behind. When he arrived at the Airport Car Park, 'Bull' collected a ticket for the car. This was later passed to 'Jones'.

The NSU watched the conspiracy unfold. For the detectives assigned to tail the jeep it was a game of waiting. And this is the way Jennings ran the black operation. After three weeks of watching and waiting, the jeep was collected. The beacon in the dashboard told the NSU it was headed towards the border.

Back in Garda Headquarters, Crime and Security scrambled a spotter plane to tail the vehicle. Several unmarked cars drove ahead of the vehicle while others tailed behind. From the skies, the spotter plane monitored the jeep travel along the Dublin to Belfast Road and turn towards Dundalk. The vehicle travelled into the town centre and made its way to a shed in Legion Avenue, a row of terraced houses in the town centre. All the time, the NSU followed their target, but from a safe distance. Jennings knew Campbell's modus operandi. It was probable that he would be conducting a counter-intelligence exercise to see if the gardaí were present.

Now it was time to watch. On 22 March, two men approached the site and were arrested by Special Branch when they entered the shed.

A more thorough examination of the vehicle revealed that a RIRA engineering team had fitted the vehicle with 1,200lbs of home-made explosive. To give the bomb extra blast power, the engineering team had inserted tubes packed with explosives; this

* Taken from statement made by John McNamara to gardaí

would help explode the ammonium nitrate-sugar mixture, which made up the bulk of the bomb.

The construction of this type of bomb was similar to the giant devices planted in the city of London in 1993. It also resembled the device that destroyed Canary Wharf in London in February 1996, and the bomb that exploded four months later in a Manchester shopping centre. The RIRA Army Council planned to detonate the bomb on St. Patrick's Day when Gerry Adams was due to visit the White House. The interception was a huge success for the Garda and an equally huge blow to McKevitt's Army Council.

While the object of the black operation was to prevent bombings and counter the RIRA, the ongoing surveillance also allowed Crime and Security to target specific dissidents. Jennings wanted to make it virtually impossible for McKevitt to distinguish between the line of truth and the contagious suspicions in the RIRA's internal security department. This served a number of useful purposes. The principle aims were to terrorise the republican group, create divisions and draw suspicion away from Dixon.

News of the bomb capture and arrests made the national headlines within an hour. 'Jones' was dumb-founded. Most surprising was his absolute belief that the security breach had not emanated from his unit. Although he didn't suspect Dixon, nor any of his own men, he issued a few threats. McNamara was one of the first people he threatened when they met in a pub in Kilcock that same night. McNamara later recounted what happened.

'He said, "Did you see the news?" and I said, "No."

'He said, "The jeep you left at the airport had been found in a shed in Dundalk." He warned me that I wasn't to talk to anyone or I would be going into a hole.'*

IN SPITE OF the traumatic circumstances in which he found himself, Dixon continued to work as a minibus driver. He was also earning money from Jennings who paid him in cash. He also earned money from crime. The gardaí were happy to turn a blind eye. If anything, his involvement in crime and car ringing added to his credibility within 'Jones'' gang. As the weeks passed, Dixon

* Taken from statement made by John McNamara to gardaí

continued with his criminal operation and supplied stolen cars to various gangs. It was inconceivable to suggest that he could be working for the Garda.

On Wednesday 18 March, Dixon called White; 'Jones' had just requested another car. This time he was looking for a BMW. White travelled from his home in County Donegal the next day, arriving in Dublin at 9.30 a.m. He wanted to discuss the request with the informant face to face.

After the meeting, White briefed Jennings on the current state of play. Jennings told White to instruct Dixon to relay any information on stolen cars that 'Jones' ordered.

White said Dixon was terrified. If another car was intercepted, he would be blamed. The fact that two men had already been arrested was almost certain to spark off an internal inquiry by the RIRA. This time he might not be so lucky. However, Jennings felt that White was the nervous party.

Jennings urged White to reassure the agent. The security of the state and the future of the fledgling Peace Process were at risk and these took precedence over everything else.

For the purpose of maintaining security, he also handed White two pay-as-you-go mobile telephones. He told the detective to give one to Dixon and keep one for himself; they were for secure communications.

Jennings was specific in his instructions. He ordered White to only contact the informant using a clean phone. If the RIRA began searching through Dixon's telephone bills, he would be compromised. Jennings then handed White a telephone number for the NSU. He should call this when Dixon had possession of the car.

That Friday, at 2.15 a.m. on 20 March, White received an urgent telephone call, which lasted five minutes. It was Dixon to say his gang had stolen a red BMW 318 and he was en route to collect the car at Coolmine Industrial Estate. White hung up and called the NSU a minute later at 2.21 a.m. Everything was running according to plan—officers were already ready and waiting.

Dixon arrived in Coolmine at 3 a.m. Vinny was already there to meet him. The two engaged in some discussion before Dixon ordered the thief to go about his business.

THE TRUTH WAS that Dixon was terrified. He wanted out; he did not want to get killed. He was afraid that 'Jones' would sense his fear. The informant was panic-stricken. He called White who was parked in Blanchardstown village in anticipation.

He said he was pulling out. White remained calm and instructed the spy to deliver the car to the rendezvous point, but Dixon was having none of it. He remonstrated with his handler. He said he was on the verge of fainting. White ignored Dixon's melodramatics. But when he realised he was not joking, he drove straight to the industrial estate and pulled up behind the car thief, who was still sitting in the BMW. White never said a word but signalled Dixon to follow him. The informant did as he was instructed. The two cars left the industrial estate and took a right turn, which brought them into the village of Clonsilla. They drove through the village and took the next left onto a winding lane that runs behind the Garda Golf Club in Westmanstown.

There was no street lighting and the two men drove with extreme caution as they made their way along the deserted road. It was the dead of night. White drove for about a mile and suddenly stopped in the lane; Dixon did likewise. He turned the car engine off and left the keys in the ignition. He then joined White, who called the NSU once Dixon sat into the passenger seat.

Dixon's uncertainty had intensified. He looked scared; petrified even. The risk of being uncovered grated his already frayed nerves. He pleaded with White to think of his position, he said he could not cope and couldn't live with himself. The NSU had promised they would not stall and would return the car within an hour but they took nearly three. The informant cursed the ground they walked on and swore he would never help again.

The BMW was eventually delivered to Clane at 5.10 a.m. that same morning. White drove behind the stolen car in a red Toyota Corolla. Neither Dixon or White saw anyone, nor did they observe any suspicious activity. The BMW was parked at the yard in Clane at 5.40 a.m. as dawn broke.

In what was now standard practice, Dixon called 'Jones' to say the car was in position. White made the same call only to the NSU. Another black operation was in progress.

THE ARRESTS AT Dundalk were still a mystery to the RIRA. The fear of incarceration caused 'Jones' to introduce some security measures to protect himself. The vehicle he ordered Dixon to steal would be fitted with a bomb but they would put counter-surveillance measures in place to deter the gardaí; this was more for peace of mind than anything else. McNamara and 'Bull' were charged with overseeing the operation from beginning to the end.

McNamara would later tell gardaí of his arrival at Clane to collect the BMW. He did not need to fit false registration plates, someone else had already changed the registration. All he had to do was drive the car to an apartment block in the university town of Maynooth in County Kildare.

The apartment complex was a redeveloped convent located at the top of the town. McNamara later said, 'We parked the car in the spaces that belong to the apartments. 'Bull' drove the BMW to Maynooth and I took him back in his own car.'*

The BMW contained no explosives, however, McNamara did notice a blanket, which he threw in the boot and a pair of Wellington boots.

Days later, 'Jones' asked him to drive the car to a man called 'Padraic'. He worked alongside 'Jones' but he also ran a small workshop in County Meath.

After hearing 'Jones'' new instructions, Jennings suspected that 'Jones' had someone watching the car from one of the apartments in Maynooth to see if the car was interfered with. As a precaution, Jennings told the NSU to stay clear of the target car. This would reassure those watching the car that nothing was wrong. The ruse worked. When 'Jones' was satisfied that nothing untoward was happening, he ordered McNamara to move the car once more.

* Taken from statement made by John McNamara to gardaí

'There was a key left over the sun visor. I took the car and had it serviced.

'"Jones" told me that the springs had to be re-enforced. And "Padraic" done it. "Jones" also told me this was going to England. I knew it was going over on a bombing mission. I saw the work being done on the springs,' said McNamara later.* The shock absorbers 'Padraic' fitted to the car were designed for a Mercedes. Their purpose was to disguise the weight of a bomb.

Then something happened that no one anticipated. The beacon stopped transmitting within minutes of McNamara delivering the car. This caused panic in the NSU who assumed 'Padraic' had located the device. There was nothing they could do but wait. As a precaution, the gardaí located Dixon should they have to take him into protective custody.

McNamara in the meantime had driven to a garage situated three miles away on the Dunboyne to Trim Road in County Meath. He purchased two five-gallon drums of diesel for the car's planned journey to England. 'Jones' had given him the money for the fuel. When he returned to 'Padraic', he filled the car with fuel. The entire process took three hours from start to finish.

The decision to wait and see what happened by the NSU proved correct. When McNamara took possession of the car again, the beacon began transmitting, much to the relief of those monitoring the conspiracy.

The car was moved between different locations. On 20 March, Dixon visited 'Jones' and saw the car with false registration plates attached. The purpose of the meeting was to say he was satisfied with the car and to inform Dixon he would not be getting paid for it because it was a special order, but Dixon didn't care one way or the other, though he did panic when 'Jones' said he wanted a private meeting. Dixon did not like a word of what he was hearing, but maintained his composure and agreed to attend.

THE MEETING TOOK place over lunch on 24 March at the Coachman's Inn beside Dublin Airport. Dixon arrived on time and was greeted in a friendly fashion by 'Jones'. Among the thoughts

---

* Taken from statement made by John McNamara to gardaí

that crossed the spy's mind was that he was going to be kidnapped or interrogated.

He was half-right. 'Jones' wanted to discuss how the gardaí had intercepted the Pajero. 'Jones', who still did not suspect Dixon, said the explosives had been delivered to the shed shortly before the raid. He attributed blame for the capture to someone close to Campbell; it was not his problem.

But 'Jones' had more news. The RIRA, he said, was planning to bomb Britain. Dixon listened to the bravado and said nothing; he enjoyed the lunch and discussed other business. After leaving the meeting, Dixon listened to his car radio where he heard more news of the RIRA. The RUC base in the village of Forkhill in County Armagh had been attacked with a mortar. The device missed the main base but landed in the barracks's compound where it exploded. The topic of conversation between Dixon and 'Jones' was relayed to Jennings within hours. The RIRA threat to bomb Britain was fast becoming a reality.

In the meantime, the NSU continued to monitor the BMW. The car was moved on 31 March to a storage facility previously unknown to Crime and Security. 'Jones' was being careful.

One man had driven the BMW to a yard near Kilcock village where it remained for two hours. During this time 'Jones' and others loaded bags into the vehicle. This was one of the RIRA's engineering teams. They were building a bomb. This time the smallest details were taken into account. 'Jones' put in place a series of good counter-surveillance measures. There were two lookouts: one man sat outside the gate in a County Galway registered Mercedes: another man sat outside in a County Louth registered Cavalier. His car was parked further up the road; they were watchouts.

When the BMW left the yard, it was escorted by the two scout cars. The convoy drove in a round about route, with both escort-vehicles conducting counter surveillance. Each vehicle would drive in front of the BMW, then double back and approach the stolen car from behind. The NSU watched the exercise from a spotter plane that flew above the cloud line.

The BMW was then driven to the car park of the Spa Hotel in Lucan village in County Dublin. The vehicle was followed by three NSU cars that kept their distance in case the RIRA was still keeping the car under visual surveillance.

The BMW remained parked at the hotel for 24 hours. It was then collected and driven to McDonald's Pub in the village of Clonee in County Meath on the night of 1 April.

Crime and Security believed the car was destined for Northern Ireland. 'Jones', however, had flown to Aintree in Liverpool that same morning to attend the racing festival. Dixon suspected that 'Jones' was going to collect the car himself. The informant's analysis was on target.

When it was collected at Clonee, the BMW was driven to Dun Laoghaire in south Dublin as part of a three car convoy. The driver parked the car in a small cul-de-sac that same night, much to the disbelief of the NSU. However, Jennings was correct in assuming the RIRA had tightened up its internal security. A short distance away from the car, gardaí noticed two men sitting in a parked car; they sat there all night watching the stolen BMW.

THREE MONTHS EARLIER, former Irish soldier Larry Keane had emerged from prison. Keane was a hardened criminal who was penniless and in need of cash. He was destitute.

One of 'Jones'' associates offered him £500 to drive a car to England. Hard up on his luck, Keane agreed to participate although he didn't know—and didn't ask—what the car contained. He privately suspected contraband tobacco, cannabis at worst.

He was desperate for money and he readily accepted the offer of work. Before he left to collect the car at Dun Laoghaire, he visited his former wife, Theresa Fennel. The couple was in the process of divorcing and had arranged to meet. After they had completed the necessary forms, Keane wished her the best. And said he was sorry if he ended up in trouble for drugs. She was struck by the remark.

Keane collected the bomb car at 5.30 a.m. on 3 April and drove to Dun Laoghaire Ferry Terminal where he attempted to board the HSS Stena Explorer. He never made it onto the ramp.

Armed detectives surrounded the car and pulled him from the driver's seat. An army bomb disposal team was called to defuse the bomb. When the car was searched, it was found to contain 500lbs of explosives. A full technical examination of the bomb, however, revealed that it was incapable of exploding because the detonator had not been constructed properly.

Theresa Fennel was listening to the news on the radio when she heard about the security operation.

'I don't know what it was, something in my head, but I said to myself, I have an awful feeling who it is. I was shocked,' she said later.

To protect Dixon and other informants, four people parked in a white BMW beside the bomb car were also arrested. Crime and Security wanted to give the impression that the gardaí were searching for stolen BMWs. By a stroke of good fortune, two of the female passengers in the second BMW were married but having affairs. The confused information released by the Garda Press Office had the desired effect. The media announced the bomb had been destined for the Grand National Races at Aintree in Liverpool. This was untrue; 'McGuinness' had decided to target London in the hope of destroying the political talks at Belfast.

One of the RIRA's Army Council said, 'Of course it wasn't meant for Aintree, people just said that because of the warning the year before. The plan was to bring it down to London and use it to cause havoc. There was a list of five targets where it could be used. These were places that would cause the utmost disruption. One of the targets was a busy motorway junction, which had a flight path overhead. That would have meant paralysing the roads and the skies around London.'

The primary aim of the bomb though was to collapse the peace negotiations and talks in Northern Ireland. Sinn Féin was in the throes of intense negotiations with the British and Irish governments. The political party was trying to finalise the Heads of Agreement document for the Peace Process. If the bomb had exploded, it would have collapsed the delicate process.

'JONES' SEEMED ANAESTHETISED by shock when the car bomb was intercepted; he didn't know how to interpret the capture. When the Pajero was seized, he figured it was unlucky. The counter-insurgency measures used by Crime and Security were working. Distrust now engulfed 'Jones' and everyone around him. He simply didn't know what to believe though he trusted McNamara more than anyone else and confided in him.

'"Jones" told me that there was somebody squealing and that I would have to find out. After this one was found, "Jones" told me to go out with the lads that were stealing the cars and make sure the gardaí weren't bugging them,' McNamara later told gardaí.*

Nine days later, on the morning of Tuesday, 10 April, 'Jones' met Dixon to tell him the RIRA was holding an internal inquiry to find out what had happened. It was their first conversation since the bomb's capture. 'Jones' began by asking some informal questions about the car but then lowered his guard. As far as he was concerned, the seizure was just one in a series of coincidences. He thought it was a miracle that the car had been stopped at Dun Laoghaire.

In his opinion, the gardaí could not have been watching the car for long. If they had, the bomb team would have been arrested—a remark that made Dixon wonder exactly what was going on. Keane was a no one. The bombers had escaped.

At the end of their informal chat, 'Jones' proclaimed that his IRA would not be beaten, before asking for another special order. That same night, the Irish and British governments, as well as most political parties in Northern Ireland, signed the Good Friday Agreement, setting out a plan for a devolved government in the North. The agreement provided for the establishment of Human Rights and Equality Commissions, the early release of republican and loyalist prisoners, the decommissioning of paramilitary weapons and far-reaching reforms of criminal justice and policing in Northern Ireland.

McKevitt and the RIRA Army Council were enraged. Sinn Féin and the IRA were never supposed to get this far. The RIRA

---

* Taken from statement made by John McNamara to gardaí

campaign had been a disaster, though the RIRA Army Council refused to admit defeat.

The details of Dixon's discussion with 'Jones' were relayed to White, who in turn passed the information to Jennings. He asked White to arrange another meeting. Like before, they met secretly in the house in Porterstown.

When Dixon walked into the house, Jennings was waiting there. He praised the informant for his valuable work, then handed him another a brown paper envelope filled with cash. It contained £10,000. The informant counted the money and returned £1,000 to cover his loan.

WHILE 'JONES' MAY have deluded himself into thinking that his brigade was impenetrable to the security forces, McKevitt and Campbell were not so sure. The RIRA Army Council decided to establish other bombing units to run the military campaign. The ruling body did not consider it prudent to depend on 'Jones' alone; subsequent events would show they made the right decision.

Campbell organised more attacks. These were successful and were executed without any problems. The second offensive began on 30 April when the town of Lisburn in County Antrim was attacked with a 600lbs car bomb. The car was left parked on Market Square which caused the RUC to evacuate hundreds of people while bomb disposal teams carried out three controlled explosions on the device. Miraculously no one was injured.

6

THE FIRST MARTYR

PASCAL BURKE WAS in trouble. Like Dixon, he needed money, but unlike the car thief, the Real IRA's Director of Finance was faced with not raising a few thousand pounds, but hundreds of thousands; enough funds to underwrite an effective bombing campaign that would replicate the bloody war fought by the Provisional IRA.

At 34 years of age, Burke was the second youngest member of the Army Council—'McGuinness' was the youngest. His youth, however, didn't insulate him from the pressure his colleagues were putting him under to carry out fundraising robberies. The RIRA needed hundreds of thousands of pounds to fuel its nascent campaign. Burke knew he couldn't raise that sort of money in a short time frame. The cash crisis was not helped by the natural consequences of the Garda successes against the new group. Thanks to the various seizures and interceptions, fear and paranoia now gripped the RIRA. Volunteers had developed a pathological distrust of their own organisation. The black operations mounted by Crime and Security had sown the seeds of mistrust and loathing in the tight knit organisation. Volunteers no longer trusted each other; paranoia gripped the Dublin Brigade; everyone was suspected of being a spy. No one wanted to risk getting involved in an operation for fear of being arrested.

Despite the problems, Burke could not afford to ignore the needs of his Army Council and began devising ways of making money. He began by putting out feelers for soft—but lucrative—targets. Burke was already well acquainted with the mammoth task confronting him. The Dubliner had been a trusted member of the IRA's Dublin Brigade. The brigade rarely engaged in military operations, but acted as a vital cog in the IRA machine. Dublin volunteers provided support to the Engineering and Quartermaster's Department, but their most important function was to raise money and cash. It was Dublin's raison d'être. Few Dubliners, if any at all, participated in attacks north of the border. Instead they gathered intelligence on banks, financial institutions, and post offices in the city for the IRA to rob.

Many targets were assessed by regional command and discounted. More often than not, potential targets were turned down because the risk of arrest or an armed shoot-out with gardaí was considered too high. The IRA's Green Book, its internal regulations, strictly forbade any member from attacking the gardaí or Irish soldiers. The RIRA Director of Finance was aware of several projects his former colleagues in the IRA had examined. The most lucrative of these involved hijacking a Securicor cash delivery van that collected hundreds of thousands of pounds from banks and post offices in the southeast of Ireland each week.

The van left Dublin each Friday morning and made towards small provincial towns in County Wicklow. The van would then return to Dublin where it would drop off the money at a Securicor depot. The van usually travelled without a garda or army escort. Organising an armed robbery is a massive and risky undertaking. It requires serious planning, preparation, and rehearsal. IRA Command had drafted plans to hijack the van but abandoned these for valid reasons. The van travelled on the N11 road between Dublin city and Wicklow town. If the van were hijacked on this route, volunteers would almost certainly be arrested because they would have to drive at least 30 miles to reach the relatively safe environs of Dublin city.

The IRA high command thought it was a suicide mission because patrol cars working in sync with the Garda Air Support Unit would almost certainly intercept the getaway car. Not everyone in the Dublin Brigade accepted this analysis however. Burke thought the heist was possible to execute if the unit was given a safe house in south Dublin, therefore reducing the drive time to the city after the raid.*

Now that he was in the RIRA, he had the perfect opportunity to test this analysis, and he was willing to take a chance. He assembled a five-man gang for the operation. The line-up was Danny McAllister, a 43-year-old volunteer from Ballybrack in south Dublin. He was a ruthless republican, whose dedication to the IRA was beyond reproach. He was born in Belfast but had moved to Dublin where he set up home in the suburb of Ballybrack.

The second team member was 23-year-old Stephen Carney from the Dolphin House flats complex in inner city Dublin. Carney was primarily a community activist in the inner city and had joined the IRA in his youth, helping the republican movement in anyway he could. He was an ideologically driven man who didn't succumb to the inertia of heroin abuse but got heavily involved in the anti-drugs movement.

Philip Forsythe was the third gang member. He came from Sallynoggin, also in south Dublin. At 25 years of age, he had little or no IRA experience. The fourth member was 24-year-old Saoirse Breatnach, also from Ballybrack.

The fifth man was Rónán Mac Lochlainn. He was 27-years-old and lived in Ballymun, one of the most deprived working class areas of Dublin. He was born in Belfast in 1971 two years after Northern Ireland exploded into near civil war. He had impeccable republican credentials; his mother was Róisín Mac Lochlainn, the infamous honey trap killer.

She is still a wanted woman in Northern Ireland where she stands accused of murdering three British Army soldiers in March 1973 when she and another woman lured four sergeants out of a bar to a flat by offering sex.

* Interview with member of the Provisional IRA

The flat was stocked with beer and food. When the women walked out the door, an IRA ASU entered and murdered the soldiers. His mother escaped by travelling across the border. She became the subject of a protracted extradition battle, which failed on the grounds that the killings were political offences.

She settled in Ballymun where she resumed her IRA operations, this time working for the English Department. Mac Lochlainn was reared in the most deprived area of Dublin. He attended the local national school but failed his exams at secondary level. He joined the IRA's junior wing—the Fianna—when he was 14-years-old. When he turned 18, he joined the IRA. He stayed away from drugs and crime; he trained to be a chef but left in his final year at college. He next worked as a courier and as a builder's labourer.

Like Carney, he got heavily involved in the city's anti-drugs movement. Mac Lochlainn was not considered a hard-line republican by the gardaí. He had only one conviction, for demanding money with menaces. He met his partner Gráinne Nic Gibb at a republican commemoration near Limerick in 1990. He was a severe romantic who could not live without the woman he loved. They moved in together and started a family. The two were inseparable.

The Director of Finance completed the picture. He would provide logistical support for the gang but would not take part because he was an Army Council member.

THE OPPORTUNITY TO mount the fundraising venture presented itself on 1 May when rank and file members of the Garda organised a de facto strike to protest over low pay. The strike was christened the blue flu. Gardaí aren't allowed to strike, so thousands of officers called in sick at the same time. Burke thought it would be to the gang's benefit that garda stations across Ireland would be severely understaffed during the industrial action. He thought the Garda's difficulty could be the RIRA's opportunity. Mounting a successful, daring raid on a cash delivery van would also embarrass the Special Branch and Government.

The gang prepared the groundwork for the heist meticulously.

They would strike on a stretch of remote motorway near the Cullenmore Hotel, near the village of Ashford, when the van was returning to Dublin city around 5 p.m.

The plan was as follows; Burke would oversee the hijacking. He would drive to Cullenmore alone and park on a lay-by located about two miles away from where the raid would actually happen on the Dublin side of the N11. He would communicate with the gang using a mobile phone and walkie-talkies. Forsythe, McAllister, Breatnach and Mac Lochlainn would hijack the van.[*]

They would travel to County Wicklow early that afternoon and set up a bogus road works on the hard shoulder of the N11. They would stop the Securicor vehicle when it arrived by blocking off oncoming traffic with a van. Carney's job was to tail the cash delivery van on its route in County Wicklow. When the van got near Cullenmore, he would call ahead to alert the main gang. He would also stop oncoming traffic, by force if necessary. The gang knew the security guards would not hand over the money voluntarily. They would have to use force, or the threat of it. Once the security van was stationary, they would cut a small hole in the vehicle, pour petrol in the hole and threaten to set the vehicle ablaze to frighten the security men out. If this didn't work, they would threaten to blow the van up with a rocket launcher. When they got the money, the two vehicles would drive to Dun Laoghaire, where they would park up the van and vanish with the cash.

Burke had sourced several weapons for the job. The armoury included an AK47 Kalashnikov assault rifle, a Mossberg 12-gauge pump action shotgun and a Smith and Wesson .357 Magnum revolver.[**] Burke could not source a real rocket launcher so he got a fake one. Ammunition was supplied for the arms including 18 shotgun cartridges, six rounds of .357 Magnum ammunition and 28 rounds of 7.62 mm ammunition for the assault rifle.

On the night before the raid, the plan was fine-tuned. There would be no mistakes. Burke didn't want any shots being discharged under any circumstances. No one was to be killed, least of all innocent bystanders.

[*] Interview with member of Special Branch
[**] Evidence presented to the Special Criminal Court

INITIALLY, EVERYTHING WENT according to plan on the day of the raid. Burke drove to Cullenmore in a white van while McAllister and the others set up bogus road-works hours in advance of the Securicor van's arrival. They noticed nothing unusual. Burke scanned the airwaves for signs of any garda activity. The 'council workers' pretended to carry out essential repairs to the road, ushering oncoming traffic past their blue transit van. No one suspected anything it seemed.

The Securicor van arrived on schedule minutes after 5 p.m. Carney was following four cars behind in a Toyota Carina. When the cash van reached Cullenmore he called ahead.

McAllister and the others prepared to mount the most daring raid of their lives. All four pulled balaclavas over their faces and grabbed their armoury of military weapons. McAllister jumped into the van and pulled out in front of the oncoming traffic. Breatnach was armed with the AK rifle, McAllister had the angle grinder, Forsythe had the imitation rocket launcher, and Mac Lochlainn was armed with the .357 Magnum revolver. Further down the road, Carney stepped from his car and produced a pump-action shotgun. The hijack was underway.

McAllister ran towards the Securicor van with an angle grinder. He attempted to cut a hole in the side of the security van while the others dragged the van's driver, Aidan McGauran, from the vehicle.* In the melee, another one of the gang used a lump hammer to smash the security van's windows.

The scene was one of utter chaos. Many motorists driving in rush-hour traffic on the main Dublin to Wexford road were caught up in the raid.

Breffni Earley, an innocent eyewitness, was parked immediately behind the Securicor van. When he saw the armed gang approach, he jumped out of his own vehicle and made off along the cars behind him, only to be confronted by Carney. He made no attempt to tackle the gunman, fearing he could be shot any minute.

And then he saw them. Through the corner of his eye, he noticed what he thought was a SWAT team weaving through the traffic. They were clad in black combat fatigues and they moved in military

---

* Evidence presented to the Special Criminal Court

formation, guns at the ready. Carney saw them too. He raised the shotgun to his shoulder and warned them to get back while shouting at his accomplices to run.

The NSU and Emergency Response Unit were moving in. Further up the road, Mac Lochlainn also saw what was happening. Armed gardaí were coming in his direction. Earley in the meantime dived into the undergrowth as between six and eight shots rang out. There was pandemonium.

Mac Lochlainn was overcome by fear. He panicked and made straight for a car, which contained an elderly couple. They were driving south to the village of Avoca and had tried to escape when the shooting broke out. He produced his Magnum and ordered the driver out of the car. The driver's wife pleaded with him to leave them alone. 'I said, "Go away, my husband has a heart condition," but he was shouting at us to get out,' she said later.*

They both struggled out of the car as detectives roared at them to get down on the ground. Mac Lochlainn turned towards the gardaí and pointed the Magnum in their direction as the elderly couple jumped into a ditch. The gardaí opened fire. Mac Lochlainn was hit in the chest and fell to the ground. He died as the gardaí tried to resuscitate him.

The remaining gang members panicked when they saw what happened. Breatnach dropped the rifle and ran away. He tried to hijack another car and was arrested after a violent struggle. McAllister and Forsythe also tried to hide in hedgerows but were surrounded and arrested. Burke was arrested simultaneously two miles from the scene of the robbery.

Carney was the man who nearly got away. When he saw the commotion, he sat back into his car and attempted to drive away, but collided with a Renault car parked behind him. A member of the NSU drove this vehicle.

Determined to escape, he reversed and drove off again but collided with a garda jeep, and his car ended up in a ditch. He was arrested at gunpoint.

In their initial reports, the Garda Press Office released inaccurate information about the sequence of events, saying Mac Lochlainn

* The Irish Times

had fired on the ERU and NSU first. He had not. The gang had obeyed Burke's orders.

MAC LOCHLAINN'S DEATH was a monumental event in the development of the RIRA. In some ways it was inevitable. McKevitt was stepping up the campaign to such a degree that the new army was either going to kill someone or suffer a casualty. The operation's failure was a serious blow; he had lost a valuable member of the Army Council and a volunteer. The death, however, afforded the RIRA with an opportunity to present itself to the public.

At the time the RIRA was still an unknown organisation. Only the Garda, MI5 and the IRA really knew about the dissidents. McKevitt and Óglaigh na hÉireann now introduced themselves to the Irish public.

Rónán Mac Lochlainn was given a republican burial. He was waked at his own home in Sillogue Gardens in Ballymun. His body was laid in an open coffin in the darkened front room of his home. A black beret and gloves rested on a tricolour, which was draped across the coffin. His home was a hive of activity. Mourners came and went. His children—still too young to comprehend how their father had died—made cards. On one card were the letters IRA. On the inside was a simple message: 'Bye bye, Daddy'.

His comrades gathered outside. They dressed for the street. They wore bomber jackets, jeans, runners, and baseball hats. They all covered their faces.

The funerals of IRA volunteers killed on active service are rare occasions in the Republic and no one knew the protocols. When the coffin was lifted into the hearse, one of the contingents from Northern Ireland ordered the pallbearers to remove it at once. IRA volunteers are carried through the streets to their final place of rest. By the time the order was given, the tradition had already been obeyed. The coffin was lifted to shoulder height by Mac Lochlainn's friends and carried through the littered streets of Ballymun.

The republicans had arranged a colour party and piper. These walked ahead of the coffin as detectives swarmed everywhere. Ballymun was saturated with gardaí and detectives. Unmarked vans surrounded the funeral while a helicopter flew overhead. The scene resembled Belfast in its worst days. His body was taken to Glasnevin cemetery, the State's national graveyard. A grave had been dug in the republican section of the cemetery.

McKevitt, McGrane, and 'McGuinness' walked with the crowd watched by the gardaí. They never spoke to anyone. They realised the enormity of their error when journalists started noting their presence and tried taking photographs. McKevitt, and not Mac Lochlainn, became the real focus of attention. He pulled a baseball hat down over his face and stared at the ground to avoid the incessant media glare.

The world had changed for McKevitt. He was now public property and his face was instantly recognisable. A BBC camera crew was at the funeral and caught the elusive Quartermaster on film. When he realised what had happened, he made off with McGrane, but it was too late. The image of him walking through the graveyard with the cap pulled down low would later haunt him.

AS MAC LOCHLAINN'S coffin was lowered into the ground, he received the traditional rituals for a republican killed on active service. The Irish tricolour that covered his coffin was folded. One of the colour party took his gloves and beret; these were handed to his six-year-old son Killian. A bugler played the Last Post.

The little boy cried as he clutched his mother's hand. Nic Gibb was overcome with grief. She was pregnant with her fourth child. The Sovereignty Committee had nominated Francie Mackey to give the graveside oration. His speech was politically charged. Mac Lochlainn, he said, was a 'true republican.'

'As a true republican, Rónán remained loyal and true to the constitution of Óglaigh na hÉireann when others used and usurped that constitution,' said Mackey. The message was aimed at the IRA Army Council and Sinn Féin. Mackey noted that there was no shortage of gardaí.

Bernadette Sands, Mackey, and the dead man's family gave interviews further catapulting the RIRA into the national consciousness. Until now the group remained an unknown entity in

Britain. Newspaper articles sometimes called the RIRA the True IRA. At other times, McKevitt's men were simply called the dissidents.

The volunteer's mother, Róisín, also used the death to give interviews about her son's decision to join the RIRA. This was good propaganda for the new group.

'Rónán was born in Belfast. At a very early age he became aware of the problems when he was searched as a child in his pram. He saw rioting. He was with me in the New Lodge Road in 1971 when Scottish soldiers ran amok, entered a bar, drank the contents, and then all hell broke loose,' she told *The Guardian.*

'I was wheeling Rónán in a buggy. I was thrown from one side of the road to the other, and I had a miscarriage a few weeks later. Rónán was very aware that "those bad men", as he called them, were the enemy.

'Rónán did not believe the lines that were being fed to him. There was no mention of British withdrawal,' she said. 'They (the Adams leadership) accepted a revamped Stormont, which they said they never would. They accepted too many things, which they said they never would.

'Rónán believed the IRA was fighting not for peace but for independence. Peace comes after that. Rónán believed he had not left the IRA, the IRA had left him. He rejected the Good Friday Agreement.

'Rónán did not need a mandate for his opinions. I remember well, when I was in the order of youth in the IRA, being told we did not need a mandate from anyone. The men of 1916 did not need a mandate to go out and fight on Easter Monday. Well, if they were right, then, they (the Adams leadership) do not have the right to tell anyone who wants to continue, that they were wrong.'

MATTERS HAD NOW reached a desperate stage for McKevitt. Crime and Security frustrated virtually every operation undertaken by the RIRA south of the border. He was deeply concerned about 'Jones' but he found it hard to imagine that he was the spy.

However, he guessed that someone close to 'Jones' was the agent. His training taught him to err on the side of caution. He knew Crime and Security operated by cleverly sowing dissension and mistrust.

'Jones' found himself in an impossible position. He could not contemplate the notion that Dixon was the informant. That would be admitting stupidity on his behalf. After he returned from Britain where he had attended the Aintree Racing Festival, he called Dixon. The two men arranged to meet on 5 May at The Deadman's Inn, near Lucan.

'Jones', aware that he had escaped arrest by the skin of his teeth, confided in Dixon as if he trusted him emphatically. He was sailing to the edge of the abyss.

He said that he had personally loaded the bomb into the BMW and wired the detonation device with six others. If the car were under surveillance, surely the bomb team would have been arrested. With this in mind and other information at hand, he was certain that the informant was not close to him. This was the only consolation he had. Hence he asked Dixon to deliver another special order. There was one stipulation. He required an ignition key for the car. Dixon said 'no problem.'

TWO DAYS LATER, Dixon called to say he had a car. His gang had stolen a Fiat Punto from Clonsilla in north Dublin. He also had a key. Dixon had sold the car two years previously and had kept a spare key. He arranged to pass the car to McNamara at the Grasshopper Pub in the village of Clonee.

His mistake was not to inform Crime and Security. Dixon was covering himself. He didn't think the car was going to be used in a bomb attack. He thought 'Jones' planned to park the car outside a house and light it on fire to intimidate the occupants. By the time Jennings learned about the Punto, it was too late. Crime and Security did its best to improvise. Plainclothes officers drove past the car and walked around Kilcock but they could not blend in. Days later, the car vanished without trace. Subsequent events would show the vehicle was used to attack an RUC base in the town of Belleek in County Fermanagh on 9 May.

Two mortar tubes aimed at the station were discovered in the garden of the Carlton Hotel where the wedding of a Tyrone Gaelic footballer Damian Gormley was taking place. The area was sealed off. RUC officers and gardaí, who were called to help, evacuated over 250 guests and 100 villagers.

One device exploded at 11.50 p.m. as RUC officers led people living in holiday homes past the area where the mortars were found. The attack was a disaster. The mortars failed to reach their target. But it did convince 'Jones' that his operation was watertight. The move also restored the RIRA Army Council's faith in 'Jones', who was rapidly falling under suspicion.

On the same day, 'Jones' ordered another special order. The car ringer sounded anxious to Dixon, almost as if he suspected something. 'Jones' explained that he was tightening up security. From now on, only four people would know anything about their work for the RIRA. He named himself, 'Bull', McNamara, and Dixon. This time 'Jones' sounded more brusque than usual.

He instructed Dixon to choose his most competent car thief. This person had to be able to steal cars with keys; he wanted a cat burglar. From now on McNamara and 'Bull' would accompany the thieves to ensure they were not passing the cars to the gardaí. If they were, McNamara would deal with them. Not alone would 'Bull' and McNamara accompany the thief at night-time, they would also drive them home afterwards.

From now on, 'Jones' proclaimed in no uncertain terms, Dixon didn't need to know anything. He told him that he still trusted him; if he didn't he would be dead but the less people who knew the better. 'The person who is responsible will pay with their life,' he added.*

The informant held his nerve. He said Vinny was the best thief. 'Jones' agreed with his choice but told Dixon to make sure the thief knew that any loose talk would be detrimental to his health.

---

* Information provided by Detective Sergeant John White to Northern Ireland Police Ombudsman

WHEN NEWS OF 'Jones" change in attitude was relayed to Jennings, he ordered the informant to notify him at once of all developments. If Vinny was asked to steal the cars, he would tell Dixon, who would in turn relay the information to Crime and Security through White.

McKevitt needed no fortune teller to tell him that an informant had penetrated his army. He had never found himself in such a dangerous position. The only consolation was that the informant was close to 'Jones'. If some additional information came his way, he could unearth the spy, but until then, he had to trust his instinct.

'McKevitt didn't trust anyone. He trusted his wife and Séamus McGrane. If he was forced to trust a third, maybe Campbell,' explained a Crime and Security analyst.

In reality, McKevitt found himself doing things that he would never have considered when he was in the IRA. The internal inquiry had concluded that the informant was probably one of the car thieves. But due to manpower shortages, they still needed 'Jones" assistance until the informant was found.

'Jones' had worked for the Quartermaster's Department of the Provisionals. In this capacity, he had often manufactured HME. In the ordinary course of events, he would not have been asked to provide HME while his unit was under investigation. But these were no ordinary times.

McKevitt and Campbell were already making plans to relocate the bombing teams into South Armagh. 'McGuinness' had by this time began training local republicans in the art of bomb making. The move served two useful purposes. The first would be to deter Crime and Security who could not operate north of the border. More importantly, Campbell would not be compromised so easily on his home patch.

IN THE MEANTIME, 'Jones' and his unit manufactured HME for transport to Dundalk and South Armagh. The explosive material was made in a farm shed near Carbury in County Kildare. 'Jones' personally oversaw the operation, according to McNamara.*

* Statement made by John McNamara to gardaí

Right: Michael McKevitt, the Quartermaster General of the Provisional IRA and founder of the Real IRA.
© *Garda Intelligence*

Left: Liam Campbell, photographed by the National Surveillance Unit (NSU). Campbell was appointed Real IRA Director of Operations for Northern Ireland in 1997.
© *Garda Intelligence*

Right: Séamus McGrane. The key member of the Provisional IRA Executive resigned in solidarity with McKevitt after the Falcarragh Convention in County Donegal. McGrane was McKevitt's most trusted advisor and a key figure on the Real IRA Army Council.
© *Garda Intelligence*

Left: Marion Price at a republican commemoration service in south Armagh. Price was a convicted IRA bomber who joined the 32 County Sovereignty Committee in December 1997. She remains one of the most high profile dissident republicans in her home town of Belfast.

© *Courtesy of the 32 County Sovereignty Movement*

Above: Francie Mackey and Joe Dillon. The two men were the driving force behind the 32 County Sovereignty Committee.

© *Courtesy of the 32 County Sovereignty Movement*

Left: Sinn Féin President Gerry Adams with Joe Dillon. The dissident republican was a seasoned campaigner with Sinn Féin until he was suspended from the party for opposing Sinn Féin's acceptance of the Mitchell Principals.

© *Courtesy of Joe Dillon*

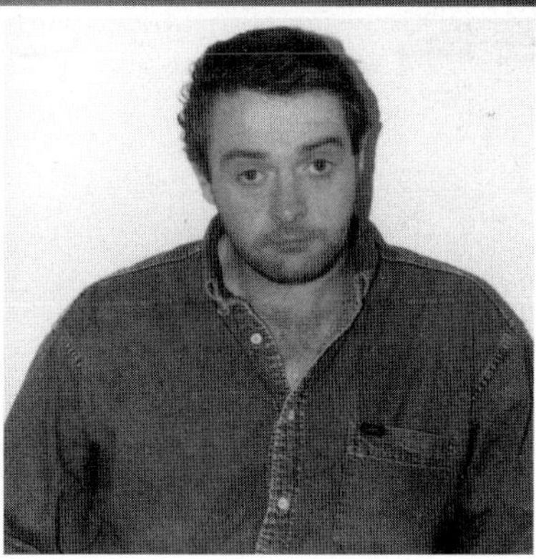

Above: The BMW was fitted with a tracking device by the National Surveillance Unit before it was delivered to the Real IRA by the informant Paddy Dixon. The BMW was later intercepted at Dun Laoghaire ferry terminal.
© *Photocall Ireland*

Left: John McNamara, who was later convicted for helping to build the giant car bomb. McNamara was a member of 'Jones" Real IRA unit.
© *Garda Intelligence*

Right: Detective Sergeant John White. The County Donegal based garda handled the Real IRA informant Paddy Dixon. Intelligence provided by Dixon allowed gardaí to intercept a string of Real IRA car bombs throughout 1998.
© *Declan Doherty*

Above: Taoiseach Bertie Ahern in conversation with his special advisor, Martin Mansergh. Ahern authorised Mansergh to engage in secret negotiations with the Real IRA. Mansergh held a face to face meeting with McKevitt four months after the Omagh bombing of August 1998.
© *Photocall Ireland*

Right: Fr. Alec Reid. The Redemptorist priest acted as a channel of communication between the Real IRA and the Irish government.
© *Pacemaker Press International*

Below: Dermot Jennings (left) pictured with former Garda Commissioner Pat Byrne and John O'Donoghue, the former Minister for Justice.
© *Photocall Ireland*

Oifig an Taoisigh
Office of the Taoiseach

24 July 1998.

Fr. Alex Reid C.Ss.R.,
Clonard Monastery,
Clonard Gardens,
Belfast,
BT13 2RL.

Dear Fr. Reid,

I attach our response based on discussions with our legal advisers in relation to the case submitted to the UN by the 32 County Sovereignty Movement.

The argument is taken strictly from our own legal and constitutional perspective, as it relates to current international law. Other legitimate arguments could be put forward from other perspectives, if we were to proceed on the basis of the likely validity in international law of Agreements freely entered into between the Irish and British Governments from 1925 to 1985.

In either case, in our opinion, no breach of international law existing at the present time can be established that would in the terms of the Memorandum now justify further on continued armed insurgency.

Yours sincerely,

Dr. Martin Mansergh,
Special Adviser to the Taoiseach.

Enc.

Oifig an Taoisigh, Tithe an Rialtais, Baile Átha Cliath 2.
Office of the Taoiseach, Government Buildings, Dublin 2.

Above: The funeral of Rónán Mac Lochlainn, the first Real IRA member killed on active service. Mac Lochlainn was shot dead by gardaí in Ashford in County Wicklow while trying to hijack a cash delivery van.
© *Photocall Ireland*

Left: Róisín Mac Lochlainn. She is wanted by police in Northern Ireland for the murder of soldiers.
© *Courtesy of the 32 County Sovereignty Movement*

Left: Francie Mackey and Bernadette Sands attending the funeral of Rónán Mac Lochlainn. Mackey delivered the graveside oration at Mac Lochlainn's funeral.
© *Photocall Ireland*

Above and below: University student Anthony Hyland was the leader of a Real IRA Active Service Unit instructed to bomb targets in London city. The conspiracy was betrayed by an informant. Hyland was monitored by Crime and Security and MI5 who filmed the republican on his travels around London.

Above: Video footage of the Omagh bombing. The bomb claimed the lives of 29 people, including a woman pregnant with unborn twins.

Left: Prelude to a massacre. This photograph was taken by a tourist on Omagh main street minutes before the bomb exploded.
The bomb car is seen to the right of the photo surrounded by men, women, and children.

'When we were mixing the explosives in the mixer for the bomb in the shed in the yard, 'Jones' came up to the yard to see how things were getting on and because we had not the job done—he got mad and took the shovel off us and mixed it himself,' McNamara later told gardaí.

'We mixed 15 bags of white sugary stuff and six to seven bags of brown stuff. There was probably over half a tonne of stuff. It was the only stuff we mixed for a bomb. We spent two bits of days at it.'

They would use an orange coloured cement mixer with cogs on the outside of the drum. It had a petrol engine. When finished, the mix always consisted of a brown substance that was like half mixed cement. This was then mixed with a sugary powdery substance.

The bags were hidden in the corner of a field near 'Bull's' home. A stranger driving a white Peugeot van collected the first consignment from 'Jones'.

'We went over to 'Bull's' place, again the same way, one car in front and one car behind. We got the explosives in the same place, at the corner of the ditch, about seven bags, each bag was about the size of a bag of cement. I knew then that it was explosives that he was shifting.'*

The van driver took the second consignment. McNamara escorted him through Kilcock village and onto the Dunboyne Road where he headed off alone. When the first consignment was transported without hindrance, they moved the second. The unit used three cars for the operation though.

'Jones' travelled in his jeep. 'Bull' drove ahead scouting the route for garda patrols. McNamara drove behind.

'The three of us loaded 15 bags of explosives into 'Jones'' jeep. We then brought these explosives to 'Jones'' yard. There they were hidden in an overgrown ditch.'

IN THE WHIRLWIND of paranoia, 'Jones' continued to make disastrous decisions. He kept in contact with Dixon. On 12 May, he called the informant and asked him to have Vinny ready for another special order. Dixon was cautious. He offered a Toyota Corolla, which he had stolen earlier and hidden in Clane. Dixon took it for

---

* Statement made by John McNamara to gardaí

granted that 'Jones'' business premises were under permanent surveillance by the NSU. He had no idea how many detectives or cameras were watching but figured the watch was continuous. Trying to find out more about the new plans, he decided to visit 'Jones'.

When he entered his yard, he saw the Corolla was missing. The car had been used to transport the first shipment of HME. The NSU had watched the car and followed its journey. Crime and Security were unsure as to whether it was carrying a bomb, so allowed it to travel. The car headed towards Northern Ireland. When it crossed the border, the RUC took over the surveillance operation but lost the car. It was found burned out days later. The spare wheel was missing. This indicated that the vehicle had been used to transport something. If the thieves had removed the spare wheel, space had been at a premium.*

'Jones' arranged for McNamara and 'Bull' to collect Vinny at the Spa Hotel in Lucan on the night of Wednesday, 13 May to steal another car. Until now Dixon had refused to pay his thieves for any cars that fell into the special order category. The boss ordered Dixon to pay Vinny £300 for his night's work; this would make him think they were ringing the car. The plan seemed reasonable.

'Jones' was slightly more confident and trusting than the previous time they spoke. The Punto Dixon had passed to McNamara in Clonee had been used in the mortar attack on Belleek. The fact that one of Dixon's cars had been used in a successful attack relaxed him somewhat. It was a chance piece of good fortune; the focus of suspicion was shifted elsewhere.

Although Dixon appeared to be part of 'Jones'' inner circle once more, he was not. The new security measures in place remained. Dixon now relied on Vinny to tell him about what was happening. Dixon would wait on calls from the young car thief. On Thursday, 14 May, the informant called White to say Vinny had stolen a Toyota Carina GTI the night before from a housing estate in Navan in County Meath. The burglar broke into a van to get the vehicle's keys. Vinny drove the car to Maynooth in County Kildare.

---

* Intelligence collated by Crime and Security

McNamara followed from behind and when he parked the car, dropped him home.

The news was relayed to Jennings immediately. The NSU was ordered to wait for the Carina, which was driven to Clane the next morning. The car was moved 24 hours later to Dundalk after being fitted with false registration plates. The NSU tailed the car, which was driven into the side of a house where a lorry container was left. The doors of the container were then closed and locked. The NSU moved into position and waited.

FOR A TIME, Dixon appeared to be treated with a degree of trust. 'Jones'' operation was up and running again. There had been no interceptions by the gardaí. But this confidence was misplaced. Bad luck and a lack of manpower within the Garda had enabled the RIRA man to deliver two cars to the Army Council.

On 19 May, 'Jones' asked for another special order. He wanted a powerful car with the keys for the ignition and door. McNamara and 'Bull' would accompany Vinny. Crime and Security considered it far too risky to attempt to follow. They found themselves caught in a moral dilemma. If they were unable to track the stolen cars, they would be used for bombings, the outcome of which was loss of lives.

Dixon had been asked to get a car. Jennings suggested offering Dixon more cash. White agreed and urged Dixon to take this course of action.

Three days later, Dixon reported back to his handler, calling him at 2 a.m. in the early hours of 22 May. Vinny had just called. He had stolen a purple BMW in Malahide, north County Dublin. As before, McNamara had accompanied him. The car was parked behind a fast food take-away in Maynooth. The NSU raced to the scene and attached a transmitter.

The car entered 'Jones'' yard at 9 a.m. the following morning. McNamara collected it. 'I knew this was going to be used for a bombing as well,' McNamara said later.* Once inside 'Jones'' compound, the car was fitted with new registration plates. A

* Statement made by John McNamara to gardaí

number of men had travelled in the Carina. One of these took possession of the BMW, and drove off followed by the Carina.

THE CAR WAS intercepted the next day at Carrickaneena in County Louth. When gardaí moved in, it had been fitted with 938lbs of improvised explosive mixture, a booster tube and detonating cord, making it a giant car bomb. It was being driven into the north to explode on the day of the referendum on the Good Friday Agreement. One of the two men arrested was Patrick McDonagh, a 36-year old market trader and father of four children from Dundalk. His cousin Kieran McDonagh, a father of three, drove behind.

The ERU stopped the car 80 yards from the border after a high-speed chase on a remote road leading to the village of Jonesboro in County Armagh. The bomb car had been chased at speeds of up to 70 miles per hour before the ERU jeep got in front of the BMW.

When the bomb was stopped, McDonagh tried to run across the border. Armed detectives had to drag him to the ground before he was arrested. The Carina, which had been following the BMW, reversed at high speed but was blocked by a garda car. Gardaí found 437lbs of the mix in seven bags in the boot of the second car.

As the two prisoners were being handcuffed, another vehicle approached, this time from the northern side of the border. It slowed down on seeing the unmarked patrol cars and jeeps. There were four people inside—one of them was Campbell. He was supposed to collect the bomb car but had escaped by the skin of his teeth. The gardaí couldn't touch him—he was in another jurisdiction.

Despite having to watch, powerless, as one of their main targets simply drove away from a bomb find, the operation was a success for Crime and Security. The ERU had arrested two prisoners and stopped a bombing that would have influenced the historic referendum taking place.

THE ARRESTS ALSO marked the beginning of the end of Dixon's career as a RIRA informant. Within hours, 'Jones'' operation was closed down. Campbell was not a man who would leave himself open to risk. 'Jones' himself also realised his mistake. He warned McNamara and the others not to talk.

'"Jones" talked to me and told me that I was probably going to be lifted and keep my mouth shut while in the barracks,' McNamara later said.*

For his reward, Dixon received another cash payment from Crime and Security. This was made on 27 May when he was handed another £10,000 from the Secret Service Fund. The black operation was now over having run its course.

* Statement made by John McNamara to gardaí

7

CLANDESTINE DIPLOMACY

THE IRISH GOVERNMENT chose to ignore the very existence of the Real IRA in the belief that the underground organisation could be contained by the gardaí. The coalition Government of Fianna Fáil and the Progressive Democrats did not want to engage in any secret diplomacy with the breakaway faction of the IRA. The arguments advocated by McKevitt and his rebel entourage were nothing more than the dying gasps of militant republicanism, according to Crime and Security.

The dissidents were simply intent on causing trouble for Gerry Adams and Sinn Féin. The Government accepted the advice without question and took the view that the RIRA was nothing more than a temporary phenomenon that would implode sooner or later.

The Department of Justice received weekly reports on the dissident group. These reports focused largely on the strengths of the RIRA, which did not amount to much—the most generous estimates gave the RIRA some 200 members. And few recruits wanted to join. Never before had the gardaí been so successful in destroying a republican organisation. The Irish government was content to treat the RIRA as a thorn in the side of the security services rather than a politically driven organisation. This attitude changed in May for two equally important reasons. The first was the upsurge in RIRA violence, which coincided with Campbell's decision to formalise links with the CIRA and take personal charge of all military operations; the second reason was firmly political and involved the 32 County Sovereignty Committee.

On 22 April, Rory Dougan and Bernadette Sands travelled to New York to formally lodge a submission to the United Nations headquarters. Francie Mackey was the third member of the delegation but was unable to enter the United States after immigration officials at Dublin Airport refused to issue him with a visa. Mackey had been convicted for assaulting an RUC officer in the early 1990s. Mackey urged the other two to travel without him.

The mission received no media publicity in Ireland but its purpose was noted by the Department of Foreign Affairs. The Irish office at the UN did not discount the importance or purpose of the republican deputation. Faithful to the protocols of the UN, Sands and Dougan were well received by officials from various countries, much to the disbelief of the British and Irish officials.

Joe Dillon had personally formulated the submission, which was based on the teachings of Seán McBride, the Nobel laureate. The document was 19 pages long and contained copies of the 1919 Declaration of Independence, the Proclamation of the Republic, and a letter from the Irish Republican delegate to the French Premier Clemenceau seeking admission to the League of Nations.

The chairperson of the 32 County Sovereignty Committee, Michael Ahern, had also written a covering letter urging the UN to consider Britain's involvement in Irish affairs.

'We contend that the Government of Great Britain denied Ireland the right to national sovereignty through the colonisation of our country; its partition; the continued occupation of the six north-eastern counties and the manipulation of a veto on national self determination through the fostering of a national minority. This has resulted in continuing cycles of oppression /domination /resistance /oppression,' wrote Ahern.

Much to the surprise of the UN, Dillon had constructed a watertight argument that questioned the legal issues surrounding the Good Friday Agreement. While the 32 County Sovereignty Committee failed to raise the same issues in Ireland, they enjoyed more success in New York. If left to their own devices, it was only a matter of time before the issue would be raised on an international platform. The UN would make an excellent springboard to launch a debate that could not be easily influenced by Sinn Féin and the IRA. The Irish office at the UN reacted with a combination of horror and astonishment. Of course, the Irish question had been raised at the UN throughout the Troubles, which was the essence of the problem; Britain and Ireland had proclaimed to the world that the Troubles were over. The key question for the Irish government was not whether it should engage in secret dialogue with the RIRA, but how?

SUCCESSIVE IRISH GOVERNMENTS had sanctioned clandestine diplomacy with the Provisional IRA, which culminated in the 1994 and 1997 ceasefires. The IRA had always held Fianna Fáil* in higher regard than Fine Gael** for historical reasons. The IRA took the view that most Fianna Fáil supporters deep down secretly supported the war against Britain, although they would never condone violence. If young republicans did not join the IRA, or Sinn Féin, they usually did the next best thing and joined Fianna Fáil.

This meant that Fianna Fáil was the political party that succeeded in drawing the IRA into constitutional politics, because the IRA did not trust any other political party. However, to enter into tentative talks with the RIRA was unchartered territory. No representative of the Irish government had ever engaged in discussions with the dissidents.

Crime and Security had drafted successive reports for the Department of Justice on McKevitt and his army, based on accurate information gleaned from the awesome intelligence apparatus now dedicated to combating the RIRA.

Dublin officials were also in communication with the IRA, which gave more insights into the workings of the RIRA—indeed, the secret information passed by the IRA sometimes surpassed and

* Political Party in Government
** Main Opposition Party

usually equalled the Crime and Security reports in accuracy. When the Taoiseach* Bertie Ahern finally sanctioned discreet negotiations with the RIRA, the organisation was in the throes of stepping up its campaign of violence. This gave a sense of urgency to the covert discussions, which were conducted behind the backs of the Progressive Democrats and, of course, the British government.

The problem that Ahern faced was how to talk to a faction of the IRA that was vehemently opposed to any dialogue that entertained the notion of consensual politics.

The most unsettling and politically dangerous aspect of the plan was the possibility that the RIRA would cause a massacre while the contact was ongoing. The truth was that Ahern had no choice but to engage the dissidents.

In the first week of May, the Irish government sent a secret message to the 32 County Sovereignty Committee through Fr. Alec Reid, a Redemptorist priest who lived in Belfast.

Fr. Reid was born in County Tipperary and fully understood the intricacies of the republican movement. The Redemptorist opposed violence but understood why young men in west Belfast joined the IRA. At every juncture in the violence that engulfed Northern Ireland, Fr. Reid remained in the shadows from where he worked for peace. He began his secret peace work in 1982 when he commenced dialogue with Adams. The two men soon developed a fireproof relationship.

His experience and sincere efforts to achieve peace endeared him to many IRA activists. He was granted permission for his secret work by his order, and the Church authorities in Rome. Therefore he came with a moral authority that perhaps no one else possessed. Ahern would not personally participate in the planned talks for obvious reasons, but appointed his special advisor Dr. Martin Mansergh to speak on his behalf.

Mansergh was an important emissary. Born in County Tipperary, Oxbridge educated, he acted as Ahern's special advisor on Northern Ireland. His English accent belied his republican credentials and strong beliefs in a United Ireland. He was effectively a republican intellectual who not alone was capable of arguing for reunification, but openly endorsed it. By instructing Mansergh, the Taoiseach was sending a clear signal: the Government considered the RIRA to be a serious organisation.

Although the RIRA was undergoing a rapid transformation in its military structures, the Army Council welcomed the news that Fr. Reid wanted to talk. Members of the Army Council would later say it gave the RIRA a certain validity.*

Fr. Reid arranged a venue for the first meeting. He secured a room in the Redemptorist Monastery in Dundalk and invited the 32 County Sovereignty Committee to send representatives. The republicans sent four delegates: Francie Mackey, Rory Dougan, Bernadette Sands, and Joe Dillon. The Taoiseach sent two: Mansergh and a middle-aged civil servant, who avoided introducing himself by name. Fr. Reid chaired the talks, which began with Mackey introducing the republican delegation to Mansergh and his aide.

The talks were cordial. There were no tensions and both sides adopted a friendly manner when dealing with the other. Each side listened attentively to the other. Fr. Reid made no interjections. Dressed in black, he sat motionless with his chin resting on his hand and his eyes closed.**

'It was as if he was asleep, but, of course, he wasn't,' noted one of the republican negotiators. Mansergh gave the impression that he understood the sovereignty position.

'He used the language of understanding our position and repeatedly nodded his head, but that was probably him being clever. There were some frank moments when we put our side and he countered it—but there were no rows. It was quite civilised.'

Dillon espoused the committee's view that the Good Friday Agreement gave legitimacy to what he called the illegal presence of the British in Northern Ireland. The delegation passed copies of their literature and submission to the UN. Mansergh promised he would reply and give his opinions on their arguments.

Bernadette Sands was notably silent and took notes at the meeting like a secretary. Her only contribution was to ask why Mackey had been refused a visa to the United States. Mansergh skirted around

---

* Interview with member of the Continuity IRA
** Interview with member of 32 County Sovereignty Movement

the question. He said the matter was one for the US government and not him.

Mansergh is highly intelligent and more than capable of directing a conversation. Towards the end of the discussions, he indicated that he was talking to the RIRA.

The remark caused Mackey to interject and proclaim that the 32 County Sovereignty Committee was there to represent itself and nobody else. According to one of the delegates, Mansergh was equally swift in his response.

'Bombs along the border don't help. If there is somebody here who can pass the message on, then fine.'

The Government representatives knew full well that the RIRA Army Council would be briefed on the night's discussions. The republican side felt Mansergh was more interested in getting the RIRA to cease its military campaign than listening to their notable arguments. This, of course, was true.

Although the meeting lasted several hours, the republicans left the monastery grounds under the cover of darkness wondering what the true purpose of the talks had been. They felt Mansergh was there to size them up.

'We felt he was there in one way to try to tease out what level of intellect there was in the Committee. We also felt he was trying to see the calibre of person who was joining up. I am sure he was also trying to find out the calibre of recruit to the army. It was an intelligence gathering exercise.'*

If it was, it was part of a dual strategy. Crime and Security had become aware of the planned negotiations. The NSU had monitored the entire event and reported back to Crime and Security. Garda Headquarters had their own reasons for monitoring the secret diplomacy. Given the series of successes against the RIRA, the Government would have expected nothing else. The information obtained by the intelligence operation provided Crime and Security with a complete overview of the RIRA and McKevitt's strategy. It was another part of the jigsaw. There were more pressing worries for the Army Council than political chats with Mansergh, however.

* Interview with member of 32 County Sovereignty Movement

THE ARRESTS ON the border were concrete proof of a double agent. Campbell had never come so close to arrest since joining the IRA some 15 years earlier. The incident panicked him. The Director of Operations was personally shaken by the experience. When the RIRA Army Council for Northern Ireland gathered to conduct an autopsy of the failed operation, he outlined the gravity of the situation. If he had arrived at the scene ten minutes earlier, he would be facing ten years in prison. In no uncertain terms, he warned McKevitt to disband the Dublin Brigade or face the consequences.

The Quartermaster knew he was right but manpower shortages within the RIRA meant he needed every member it could get. To disband the Dublin Brigade—the second biggest unit in the organisation—would be foolhardy. He rejected the notion out of hand, but he made a conscious decision to trust no one with the notable exception of his deputies, McGrane and Campbell.

Perhaps for the first time in his life, McKevitt began doubting the motives of those around him. Throughout his adult life, he had displayed nothing but raw nerve and when it came to republicanism, he had nerves of steel.

He possessed a steadfast dedication to the RIRA, and nothing had ever stopped him from carrying out his militant republican activities. His liberty had often been under threat in his long republican career; the difference was that this time the threat was immediate. Although he had been a senior member of the Provisional IRA, there were others in the organisation who bore the brunt of public odium and security force attention. As IRA Quartermaster, he was able to work largely in the shadows.

Times had changed. A day rarely passed without his name being mentioned in the national newspapers. He was also the Garda Síochána's number one target; this made him even more cautious.

More than anything, he did not like the way some members of his Army Council shrugged off the successes of the gardaí. The blanket assumption that such interceptions were to be expected unnerved him further.

McKevitt was a disciplined student of the security services and could see Crime and Security was running a black operation. He knew the purpose of the project was to terrorise him, spread dissension and fear, and ultimately force the organisation to implode. The gardaí were operating in a way like never before; they made no mistakes. They struck with surgical precision. Every time the RIRA mounted a strategic attack, volunteers were compromised. There was obviously an agent in the Dublin Brigade. McKevitt privately assumed there were possibly handfuls, but not even the highest-ranking volunteers in Dublin knew the overall workings of the organisation. There had to be someone else; the question was who?

THE ARMY COUNCIL had ordered various internal investigations into the Dublin Brigade and 'Jones'. A businessman from west Dublin led the mole hunt, but soon admitted that he could not identify the informant. This man compiled a list of suspects, debriefed them all, yet he could not identify any one person that could be executed with certainty. At every juncture in the plan to bring down the Peace Process, the Dublin Brigade had failed miserably. Not alone did it appear there was an informant in Dublin, it was increasingly clear that the entire brigade in the capital city was compromised.

Given that most of the attacks organised by 'Jones' were intercepted en route to a target, it was logical to assume the security services had watched the Engineering Unit build and assemble the bombs. If this were the case then it was logical to assume the gardaí had decided not to act in order to continue thwarting the organisation; the highest distinction granted to an enemy of the State. Or had they decided not to act because one of the bomb-makers was a double agent. McKevitt could not tell. He was overcome with paranoia.

This was a nightmarish scenario for McKevitt. If Crime and Security had penetrated the inner sanctums of the RIRA, how much did they really know? It was only now that he began to fully examine the successes and failures of his military operations. When he studied the manner in which the bombs were intercepted, he could see the hand of the security services at work everywhere. The facts spoke for themselves.

Not one of the large bombs had exploded properly. The same thing happened to mortars, which either misfired or failed to reach their target. Although McKevitt was struck by the absolute certainty that someone senior in the organisation was working for Crime and Security, Special Branch, or MI5, he said nothing. He decided open confrontation would not be a wise course of action. Everyone around him was a suspect.

Some on the Army Council opined that the spy was a Trojan horse; a Provo who sided with the RIRA for espionage purposes. During this time—in the throes of uncertainty—McKevitt took nothing for granted and suspected those who made the suggestion of being the traitors. The truth was that no one knew for certain what was happening. It was impossible to distinguish between the line of truth and fiction. But McKevitt knew one thing for sure —a car thief alone was not undermining the entire campaign. The black operation had the desired affect. The RIRA did not know what to believe.

The situation had become so desperate by the month of May that the Army Council overhauled their entire strategy. Time was against them. The referendum on the Good Friday Agreement had been supported by ninety eight per cent of the electorate in Ireland despite vehement opposition from the 32 County Sovereignty Committee. The message articulated by Sands had fallen on deaf ears. Not alone was the 32 County Sovereignty Committee ignored by the Irish public, republicans gave little or no consideration to the arguments it fought to uphold. After the initial flurry of interest in the pressure group, which mobilised some political interest, their name had disappeared from the headlines. This state of affairs disgusted McKevitt.

The RIRA was an abject failure. Not even the Quartermaster General could ignore that. The name Óglaigh na hÉireann did not strike fear into the hearts of the British government; it was greeted with ridicule. This grated his nerves. The RIRA needed to make a powerful impact. The time was right to strike back; to go beyond what the gardaí and MI5 would expect. They decided to attack London once again.

This idea was born out of a desperate need to restore confidence in the organisation. Campbell, McKevitt, and 'McGuinness' had the absolute conviction that an attack on London was the best course of action. 'McGuinness' played the role of warmonger. All agreed that a car bombing would be foolhardy; too many people would be required. The preliminary discussions ruled against any operation that could be compromised. It was imperative that nothing would go wrong this time.

The RIRA was not known for the accuracy of its bomb attacks but for the abysmal level of its internal security. The fewer people involved the better. The Quartermaster was specific in his instructions to the Chief of Staff. If successful, the attacks would turn out to be a masterful move.

McKevitt laid down specific security measures aimed at guaranteeing success. The Active Service Unit would comprise volunteers drawn from three different brigades. McKevitt said they should be lily-whites; men with no criminal records. These would answer to one single person appointed by 'McGuinness'. They would not talk about the RIRA or politics. This was to be policy; there were to be no mistakes.

The plan was to reconnoitre London city. The first bomb would be planted at Charring Cross Tube Station. The RIRA had decided on a 'no civilian deaths' policy. To ensure no casualties, there was to be a long warning. Then days later, the unit would plant a bomb at a telephone box in the city centre. Once the two bombs had exploded, the RIRA would phone in telephone warnings every ten days. The Army Council wanted to cause a summer of chaos.

'McGuinness', who was still Chief of Staff, was warned to make sure that nothing went wrong. Other safeguards would come into play. Those chosen for the operation would be unknown to each other.

The three volunteers chosen to bomb London were Anthony Hyland, a 26-year-old student from County Meath, Liam Grogan, a 22-year-old from the town of Naas in County Kildare, and Darren Mulholland, a 22-year-old from Dundalk in County Louth.

Grogan had just gained a degree in commerce from University College Dublin. He had met Hyland through the debating society and playing football. Hyland also attended UCD where he studied economics. Mulholland was in the second year of a theoretical physics degree at Queen's University Belfast. They were all intelligent, young, and had bright futures.

Each one was assigned a definitive role in the operation. Hyland was charged with overseeing security; Grogan was ordered to assist in the attacks and help transport the explosive devices; Mulholland's role was to reconnoitre potential targets.

None were previously known to the gardaí. Campbell and 'McGuinness' hoped this would ensure the operation ran smoothly. If there were a mistake, all three would pay. The bitter truth was that someone had betrayed the three from almost the moment of the plan's inception.

THE FIRST PERSON to have definite knowledge of the conspiracy was Jennings. Crime and Security had begun watching the three students from the moment of their instruction. He calculated that the RIRA would try to strike as soon as possible. This assessment was based on the prevailing political climate in Ireland and Britain. And with that as a starting point, he deployed the NSU to watch the three round the clock. Meanwhile, MI5 and Scotland Yard were formally notified of the pending attack. The intelligence obtained by Jennings suggested the attack would involve the detonation of several incendiary bombs at various locations in London.

Jennings' cunning in agent handling knew no bounds. Crime and Security had specific information on the entire plan. Hyland, Grogan, and Mulholland were followed everywhere. Their private telephone calls and post were intercepted. The surveillance operation was difficult and consumed huge resources and manpower. However, Jennings did not wish to arrest the three, to protect the source of his information.

The Chief thought it would be desirable if they were arrested in Britain. His strategy was to disguise his sources of information, even if it required other police forces taking the credit for his work. He knew McKevitt had ordered internal inquiries into the previous captures. It was paramount that he protect the informants.

The agencies agreed to cooperate. Crime and Security would obviously handle the investigation in the Republic. Once the suspects entered British jurisdiction, Box and Scotland Yard would take care of apprehending the suspects and prosecuting the case.

All sides accepted that Scotland Yard could arrest the three if they posed an immediate threat to civilian life. Even Jennings accepted the logic of this but he insisted that it would be better if the three were caught carrying explosives to guarantee court convictions.

As the students prepared to bomb London, 'McGuinness' instructed the engineering department to begin building incendiary devices for the attack. The devices—built inside lunch boxes—contained a small timing device, a detonator, and plastic explosives. They were manufactured in safe houses in the working class area of Ballyfermot in west Dublin under 'McGuinness" supervision. When constructed, they were collected and delivered to Hyland. The tactic employed by Crime and Security was to watch everything. This tactic was not a new technique in police methodologies. Even the most ardent critics of black operations accepted that to protect informants, terrorist conspiracies had to be allowed run. There was no point in arresting the three unless they could be caught with bombs.

Hyland was considered more extreme than the others, showing himself to be a cold and calculated operator. Mulholland likewise showed no emotions. Grogan, however, spoke about the IRA when drunk, often bragging about his membership of the RIRA.

For the NSU, the operation was soul-destroying. The detectives had to watch the suspects 24 hours a day as they lived the lives of young men, not terrorists. The only part that interested Jennings was their travel arrangements. When the students began to make plans, he called a conference in Garda Headquarters. Pictures of all three suspects were sent to MI5 and Scotland Yard when it became clear that an attack was imminent.

If more proof was required, it came from Hyland. He had made a telephone call to a young Irish woman living in London. This had special significance for the operation. The three students had planned to travel separately to London. Hyland took the lead and used a fellow student to arrange a safe house. This student's name was Robert Moore and his sister Elaine was living in London.

Hyland was a brilliant republican operator. He showed no outward support for the IRA. If anything, he pretended to be apolitical. On UCD campus, he was considered a harmless business student, certainly not a bomber. Because of his indomitable sincerity, Robert Moore didn't hesitate in passing on his sister's telephone number and suggested that he give her a call if and when he visited the city. Moore had no idea that Hyland was a RIRA bomber. Hyland did just that. The perfect operation base, he concluded, would be Elaine Moore's flat on Parkhill Road in London.

Crime and Security monitored Hyland's movements with microscopic attention. Every shred of intelligence was passed to their counterparts in London. Calls made from pay phone kiosks were traced. The NSU sifted through his household rubbish for incriminating evidence. His letters were intercepted in the sorting office and read for secret codes. Casual acquaintances were followed until their identities were confirmed.

His telephone calls to Elaine Moore ensured that she came under suspicion. MI5 took the lead in monitoring her. When Hyland began making frequent trips to London, MI5 watched his every move. It was at this point that MI5 overstepped the mark.

When Hyland re-entered Dublin after one of his recent trips to London, NSU again picked up the surveillance. The operation was running as normal when the undercover gardaí noticed that others were also tailing Hyland. They immediately suspected the RIRA of running a counter-surveillance operation but the gardaí quickly learned that this was not the case.

It was MI5. Box had decided to run its own surveillance operation tailing Hyland from Dublin to Holyhead. T-branch had sent agents into the Republic. These agents began tailing Hyland but were quickly noticed by the NSU.

Crime and Security contacted MI5 and demanded an explanation but none was forthcoming. Having denied all knowledge of the operation, Box could hardly further exacerbate the problem through an admission of guilt.

The NSU were uncertain as to whether Hyland realised he was under surveillance. For the sake of the operation, Jennings gave the order to ignore the agents. His wishes were obeyed.

HYLAND WAS BLISSFULLY unaware of the surveillance and returned to London on 22 June. He made his way again to Elaine Moore's front door. He stayed no more than an hour, explaining his presence by saying he was passing through the area. MI5 eavesdropped on the conversation. The true purpose of Hyland's visit was to gain her confidence. And it worked. Moore told him to call by any time.

Hyland and Mulholland were next observed taking separate flights from Dublin to London on 3 July. From the moment they arrived, they were put under surveillance by MI5. They spent the night at separate addresses in London and returned to Dublin the next day. While he was in London, Mulholland visited furniture shops in Fulham in west London.

Hyland called Moore once more. This time, he asked if he could stay the night. She was on her way out to a social gathering but said she would leave a spare key under the mat. When she returned home, he was there. He slept on the couch.

MI5 watched round the clock. They gave Hyland the code name *Wheat Bran* and Moore was called *Delicious Food*. Hyland left early the next morning dressed like a city worker. He flew home to Dublin that night.

Like most Irish people, Moore held nationalistic beliefs but was not a militant republican. She displayed an open love of Irish history and was affectionate about Michael Collins, the legendary leader of the IRA. From MI5's perspective, this was more proof than they needed of her involvement in the unfolding conspiracy. Worse yet, they formed the opinion that she was playing a role in the planned campaign. The truth was that she knew nothing. She was innocent.

Then an unexpected opportunity presented itself. Moore's house-mate moved out, leaving the Irish woman with a spare room and in desperate need of a paying tenant. MI5's Irish Desk, knowing this would open a direct channel to Moore, instructed a female agent to respond to the advertisement. Every type of listening device and eavesdropping equipment had been used to monitor the republican suspects, but legitimate access to the flat was a new situation. The agent introduced herself as Nicky and she said she was Welsh. On introduction to Moore, she made remarks about Celts having to 'stick together'. Moore paid no attention to the comments. Nicky was in her late twenties and was attractive with shoulder length hair. She said she had just come out of a relationship. Moore immediately offered her the room.

The possibility of gaining a foothold in Hyland's operational base would have seemed impossible a month earlier, but this is exactly what transpired.

On 9 July Hyland returned to London again. This time he travelled by ferry to Holyhead. On arrival in London, he spent the day buying mobile telephones using different names. He met the other members of his bombing team in central London. They took anti-surveillance measures to make sure they weren't followed. They didn't work.

The RIA had smuggled the incendiary devices into Britain. The devices had been wrapped in plastic film and covered with talcum powder to avoid detection by sniffer dogs.

As usual, Hyland called Moore and asked if he could stay. He told her that he would call at 7 p.m. that evening. She wasn't at home when he arrived but he resurfaced later. Hyland was carrying a bag, which he left in Moore's flat. He was briefly introduced to Nicky. He left the next morning to begin planting the devices. As soon as it became apparent that he intended arming the small bombs, Scotland Yard moved in.

Hyland was arrested with six devices in his rucksack. He had planned to plant them in a nearby furniture store. Moore was arrested at her place of work. When her flat was searched, detectives found a kilo of Semtex in Hyland's bag. She was arrested and charged with conspiracy to cause explosions and possession of explosives. Her case became the subject of a lengthy legal campaign that eventually secured her freedom. Hyland, Mulholland, and Grogan, however, were all convicted. They were jailed for more than 20 years each. The young men who had such intellectual promise would spend the best years of their lives behind bars. In 2001, they won the right to be transferred from Britain to Portlaoise jail in Ireland, where they are serving their sentences.

8

THE BORDER CAMPAIGN

THE CONTINUITY IRA had watched the fortunes of McKevitt and the Real IRA with more than a degree of passing interest. Although the dissident leader had chosen not to join Republican Sinn Féin and the CIRA, McKevitt maintained a policy of communicating in secret with the rival leadership. To the outside world, neither republican group officially recognised the other, with both claiming to be the true IRA. This was a logical position for each side to adopt, as they didn't want the world to know they were interacting—they wanted people to think they were separate entities.

The truth was entirely different. Those at the top of each paramilitary organisation often met to discuss politics and strategy and to share intelligence. The meetings were kept a closely guarded secret from volunteers in each organisation.

'There was a floating membership between Continuity and the RIRA. Sometimes we didn't know who was in what group. Lads from Continuity would often be asked to take part in an operation for the RIRA. I suppose they took the attitude that they were fighting the British and it didn't matter what organisation they belonged to,' said one RIRA Army Council member.*

*Interview with Real IRA Army Council

In the summer months of 1998, the secret alliance grew even stronger. CIRA needed weapons and they believed McKevitt was the man to give them what they needed. After the failed efforts at amalgamation, the leadership of the CIRA decided to try other avenues of informal cooperation, and they could think of none better than arms acquisition.

McKevitt was an expert smuggler. His credentials spoke for themselves. He had a proven track record in arming the IRA. He was in his mid-thirties when, in the mid 1980s, he was appointed Quartermaster to the Provisionals' Northern Command. At the time, the Libyan government had offered the IRA what amounted to enough weapons to keep them in the war business for 20 years. McKevitt accepted the task of smuggling the weapons into Ireland on one condition—that he personally oversaw the operation from beginning to end. On that occasion, the weapons were smuggled from Libya through the Irish Sea, first on board the Casamara, a vessel laden with machine guns and rocket launchers, then the Sjarmar. The escapade will forever be remembered in republican folklore.

The Casamara sailed to Malta in July 1985 where it collected an IRA team and sailed off into the Mediterranean Sea, where it rendezvoused with a Libyan ship that off loaded several tonnes of weaponry. McKevitt and his most trusted men later landed the arms at Clogga Strand in County Wicklow. Full of fire, young and ambitious, McKevitt showed himself to be a logistical genius. He oversaw every stage of the plan.

His keen sense of internal security made him stand out. He told the Army Council in general terms what was happening but not the exact times, locations and dates because he didn't trust them. He secretly realised from the start that he could rely on no one but himself.

McKevitt went on to arm the Provisionals with virtually every bullet they had at their disposal. In fact, McKevitt himself had not been aware of his own importance in the IRA until his resignation, 12 years after Clogga Strand and the Libyan arms.

Many of the men who sat on the CIRA Army Council were aware of his capabilities. They had been in the IRA when McKevitt pulled off the Libyan masterstroke. They now hoped he could carry out a similar feat for the dissidents.

A senior member of the CIRA from Limerick was tasked with making the approach to the RIRA. This happened in late May 1998.

The CIRA representative didn't know McKevitt personally although the two knew of each other by reputation. The project was presented to McKevitt as a gift. The Limerick man told McKevitt the CIRA had opened up an arms route to the Balkans. However, they did not have the capabilities, or the contacts to smuggle the weapons to Ireland. This was an embarrassing admission but McKevitt figured it was an honest one. He considered the CIRA and RSF as a virtually extinct organisation. Other republicans had nicknamed them 'Dad's Army' because they were made up mostly of older republicans. But McKevitt was now presented with a real chance to open an arms smuggling route from Eastern Europe. This was the precise moment he had waited for.

ALWAYS MINDFUL OF security, McKevitt did not discount the possibility that the whole thing was an elaborate sting operation by MI5. But he felt more assured when he heard that 'Bob' had brokered the deal. Several years earlier, at the age of 35, 'Bob' had been appointed Chief of Staff of the CIRA. For years he had been regarded as the best operator in the organisation. He was cordial and domineering at the same time, a ruthless man who was wholly committed to armed republicanism. A friend once described him as the most committed republican he ever met. He hated the IRA for recognising the legitimacy of the Irish government.

McKevitt was aware that 'Bob' had left Ireland in the mid 90s to work in Bosnia. The general assumption was that he volunteered to work with aid organisations for charitable reasons. But there were others. He needed no encouragement to leave Ireland because he thought he was about to be charged. Ironically, the Irish government financed his trip.

He had worked around Newry town in County Down and neighbouring South Armagh as an engineer and electrician. His real skill, however, lay in bomb making. McKevitt knew 'Bob' of old. He liked him, even though 'Bob' had sided with Ruairí Ó Brádaigh when the latter left Sinn Féin in 1986. 'Bob' had helped build up political support for Ó Brádaigh in County Armagh, which was traditionally a Provisional stronghold. This was a stubborn, possibly life threatening move, but one which generated a grudging respect from the IRA.

In Bosnia, 'Bob' made it his business to make contacts on the ground. At the time, Kosovo and Bosnia Herzegovina were awash with guns from the civil war. Many of these guns were seized by United Nations troops, however, thousands of unregistered weapons and munitions remained in the hands of the civilian population. The Balkans became a centre for illegal trafficking in military weapons. Former soldiers and paramilitary types controlled the bulk of the trade.

'Bob' immersed himself in the Eastern European underworld and ingratiated himself with arms dealers, some of whom were Catholics and sympathised with the man they perceived to be a true Irish patriot.

Since its inception, the CIRA had been unable to arm itself sufficiently, but 'Bob's' decision to relocate to the Balkans changed that. He must have realised immediately that he had made a good move. He found himself in a position to buy weapons at half price: Kalashnikovs at £320 and M-84 machine guns at £800. He started buying. He revelled in the deal, which included rocket-propelled grenade launchers, or RPG18s, manufactured by Yugoslav Defence Industries.

The benefit of the arms to the two dissident groups was almost beyond calculation. In his role as IRA Quartermaster General, McKevitt had sourced weapons from firms in South Africa and the Libyan government but the end of Apartheid and Colonel Ghadaffi's decision to come in from the international cold meant those two possibilities had been closed down.

The fall of Communism in Eastern Europe had also disrupted potential arms sources. At one stage, the IRA could have purchased tonnes of small arms from Czech companies but no longer. Irish America, which had traditionally provided weapons, was also a reluctant supplier of arms and munitions, given the support for Sinn Féin and the Peace Process.

The RIRA was now presented with a golden opportunity to arm itself. McKevitt had no compunction about doing business with Croatian and Albanian Mafiosi. He could also use his logistical expertise to ship an arms consignment from one of the small ports on the Dalmatian coast. Smuggling weapons from this region would also be easier than importing guns from America. Once a shipment crossed the border into the European Union, there was a clear route back to Ireland by road and ferry with a reasonable chance of evading detection.

'Bob's' main contact in the Balkans was Ante Cubelic. He was a farmer who lived across the border from Bosnia, just inside Croatia.

The deal the two men put together cost $30,000. In return for money, the republicans would obtain AK47s, handguns, lunch-box bombs, and rocket launchers. CIRA wanted to split the consignment 50-50, conditional on McKevitt smuggling the weapons back to Ireland and investing in the shipment. McKevitt took the CIRA up on the offer. Despite the fact that he would be helping to build the CIRA—something he was vehemently opposed to—McKevitt was completely behind the deal, which he privately considered a bargain.

LIAM CAMPBELL'S STYLE of republicanism brought about a much more direct and concentrated liaison with 'Bob' and the CIRA. The arrests of the student bombers in Britain had left the RIRA struggling to regroup. Campbell had been the most clear-sighted about the prevailing situation. He wanted to start from scratch. He didn't trust anyone; he certainly didn't trust those on his own Army Council whom he secretly viewed with suspicion. Impatient to the bone, like McKevitt, Campbell had an intense and passionate feeling for power. If he ever talks about his life in the

RIRA, he would likely admit that he hadn't liked 'McGuinness' from the inception of the violent organisation. The young Chief of Staff was motivated by republicanism. Campbell was a firebrand republican, but he was also heavily involved in smuggling. After years of commanding the Armagh Brigade of the IRA, he had been stood down at a court martial because he wouldn't stop smuggling. Little by little, Campbell had ostracised himself from the IRA.

When McKevitt set up the RIRA, it turned out to be Campbell's salvation. It was hard for him to envisage a life outside militant republicanism. McKevitt had thrown him a lifeline, which saved him. Now he planned to return the favour.

Campbell and 'McGuinness' had argued from the moment they met. There is no doubt that Campbell held 'McGuinness' personally responsible for the predicament of the army. In spite of everything, all the security precautions and internal inquiries, the RIRA Army Council still did not know who was working for Crime and Security, nor how the gardaí appeared to possess precise information on their activities. Whoever was the traitor, as far as he was concerned, it was the job of the Chief of Staff to hunt them down. In his eyes, 'McGuinness' was an abject failure; his time had come. He also privately blamed McKevitt for the situation they all found themselves in. 'McGuinness' may have been Chief but McKevitt was boss.

Despite the setbacks, Campbell still thought the situation could be rescued if control of all military operations was passed to him. His first priority was to make an impact. He didn't want to make the mistakes of the past. What Campbell was planning was a frightening, nihilistic onslaught. The strategy was to mount attacks purely for the sake of mounting attacks. There would be no subtle armed politics—it was time to blow the heart out of Northern Ireland. Campbell didn't particularly care where the bombs exploded once they exploded. It was a desperate plan but one which McKevitt had no issue with. The Quartermaster's treacherous and ruthless personality caused him not to flinch. He gave Campbell permission to launch a counter offensive of his choosing. Campbell was given a free reign. He didn't have to tell the Army Council where the next target was; he was in complete control of prosecuting the war. He started from scratch. It was at this point that 'Bob' entered the complex equation.

TO PROTECT THE position of the IRA from any suspicion of demise or disintegration, 'Bob' and others in the CIRA had forged an alliance with Campbell while the Provisional IRA ceasefire remained intact. The two sides would pool resources and intelligence in an effort to protect the very existence of the IRA. It was republicanism in its purest, simplest form: the continuation of the war against the British presence in Northern Ireland.

In reality, the move was a last throw of the dice by the dissidents. The CIRA had failed to make its presence felt since its formation in the late 1980s. 'Bob' knew the IRA faction to which he aligned himself had been a failure. He was desperate for his organisation to be taken seriously, not laughed off as old men who could contribute nothing to republicanism. Successful attacks, even if carried out with the RIRA, would make his organisation much stronger—and the IRA would have to take notice.

The dialogue between Campbell and 'Bob' was a serious threat to the entire peace process. The talks were informal. In the beginning, intermediaries delivered messages between the two sides. They then started talking face to face. 'Bob' is credited with making the initial moves, according to one member of the RIRA.

'The CIRA lads kept making overtures to us. They wanted to get involved. They really wanted to get stuck in.'

Neither Campbell, McKevitt, nor 'McGuinness' had any issue with the proposition that the CIRA should come on board. If 'Bob' was saying he would offer his services to launch a fresh wave of bombings, then they were only too happy to embrace the offer as it dovetailed with their new strategy. The two sides were always mindful of security and did not discount the possibility that everything they said and did was being monitored. Or worse again, someone was a spy. MI5 had tried to recruit 'Bob' when he travelled abroad on holidays before so he figured that Box would use the same tactics on other volunteers.

Faithful to the new security measures, they agreed only to meet in places where they felt safe. The safest place was the Emerald Bar on Church Street in Dundalk.

The bar was a watering hole for republicans; strangers stood out among the clientele and they were not made feel welcome. The gardaí constantly watched those entering the bar, but it was a fruitless exercise. Sometimes on cold nights, when the gardaí were watching outside, the clientele would pull hoods over their heads to stop detectives from making positive identifications. The Emerald Bar was a republican haven. It was a place where they could meet to drink, eat, be merry, and discuss republican politics without fear of infiltration.

The RIRA met in the Emerald in the absolute knowledge that it was safe. That Colm Murphy owned the premises was another bonus.

When he was young, Murphy had joined the Provos' Armagh/Louth Brigade, working alongside an IRA man who would later become the IRA Chief of Staff. McKevitt had also been central to the Armagh unit. Rough and ready, small in stature and feisty by nature, Murphy became one of the brigade's most ruthless volunteers.

For almost 25 years, he remained under constant Garda surveillance. The Armagh man was arrested and convicted twice in the Special Criminal Court. The first occasion was in 1972 on firearms charges and the second was four years later in 1976 for similar offences.

When he was dismissed from the IRA, he joined the INLA. It was only natural for him to commit himself fully to the organisation. The biggest obstacle faced by the leftist republican group was lack of arms. In 1982 Murphy attempted to solve the problem by travelling to the United States to source weapons. The intelligence services learned of the conspiracy from an informant and Murphy was arrested. He served his sentence at the infamous Terre Haunte Prison in Indiana. He returned to Ireland on his release in 1985. When he came home, he started his own construction firm, which he named Mountakean Construction. The venture was profitable and made him a millionaire.

Murphy's dedication to republicanism was noted for its migratory nature—he didn't care which organisation he belonged to, as long as it was fighting the British. With a fierce dedication that few have shown, he pledged himself personally and financially to several new paramilitary groups over the years. The prospect of arrest and incarceration did not seem to perturb him. Those who know him were not surprised when he joined the CIRA when it came into being.

Murphy was one of those who backed the IRA faction and helped get the organisation on a military footing. He seemed prepared to do what was expected of him.

CIRA began their operations around the border in the autumn of 1994, several months after the first IRA ceasefire, and around eight years after RSF was formed. At the time, Garda intelligence had received numerous tip-offs reporting suspicious movements at Murphy's home—which is strategically located near the border at Ravensdale in County Louth—in particular around sheds near his house.

On the 18 October, his home was searched and a jeep stolen in Dublin earlier that day was found. 'Bob's' home near Dundalk was simultaneously raided and bomb-making equipment was found. The gardaí had tailed the jeep to Murphy's home having observed another CIRA volunteer, Michael Hegarty of Knockmore Gardens in Tallaght, Dublin, driving the jeep earlier that day. Hegarty was subsequently arrested and charged with the theft. This didn't stop Hegarty.

He was later caught with a van bomb at Donaghmoyne a year later, on 10 November, along with Robert McGilloway, a Derry born volunteer who lived in Swords, Dublin.

The van was located at a derelict house near Longfield in County Monaghan. The bomb weighed 1400lbs. McGilloway would later be seen by Crime and Security, meeting with Murphy.

Murphy was a wealthy man. He owned 30 acres of land and had extensive savings in various bank accounts. The Emerald Bar, however, was his nest egg. He owned 50% of the pub. His wife owned the other 50%.

Because Murphy pledged his support to any republican group, it was in the Emerald Bar that Campbell began building his new RIRA. Although the factions opposed each other politically, they did agree on the need to continue a military campaign.

'They [Continuity IRA] kept asking us if there was anything that they could do to help us—they were eager to be involved. So we would meet them and say, "Well, we've got this bomb, why don't you do something with it?"'

The two organisations needed each other. Campbell sidelined the RIRA engineering department, however, the mere sign of cooperation between Campbell and 'Bob' encouraged others to join.

The group was distinct because there was no visible command structure. Everyone answered to Campbell because he provided the materials from RIRA arms dumps. The system worked on the basis that different people were assigned various roles and jobs. All involved were content just to see the resurrection of the IRA on the border. Politics would come later.

CAMPBELL'S STRATEGY WAS to destabilise the ongoing negotiations in Northern Ireland through the work of the INLA, CIRA, and RIRA. When the CIRA joined the border rebellion, the INLA got involved. The strategy had three components. The INLA would provide stolen vehicles, which the RIRA would transform into car bombs. A mixture of RIRA and CIRA men would oversee the third stage of the strategy by delivering bombs to targets. The decision would serve a number of useful purposes.

The most important aspect of the plan was that it would frustrate Crime and Security. Recruiting informants in County Dublin and County Kildare was one thing; enlisting a spy around the border would prove to be far more difficult. The new allegiances changed the fortunes of the RIRA immediately.

The first attack came on 22 June in south Armagh where a huge landmine exploded on a remote road between Newry and Forkhill, near the village of Drumintee. The CIRA planted the landmine, which blew a huge crater in the road making it impassable.

The bomb served as a warning to the RUC and British Army, who had begun using the road since the IRA ceasefire. The Provisionals had used similar tactics to keep the security forces off the roads in south Armagh during their war against the British.

The RIRA soon found itself caught up in a whirlwind of violence. This bomb effectively forced the army and RUC to begin using helicopters as the only means of transport in the area. This had a detrimental effect on the Peace Process because regular policing and detection suddenly became almost impossible.

McKevitt and the RIRA were now exerting their authority. On 24 June, two days after the landmine attack, the town of Newtownhamilton in County Armagh was bombed. The RIRA constructed the bomb and loaded it into a stolen car supplied by the INLA, which delivered the car bomb into the town. The device contained a Semtex booster and a 300lbs charge.

The INLA unit involved came from Dundalk and was led by Nicky O'Hare, a ruthless criminal and murderer. A caller gave a 50-minute warning, but the area had not been fully evacuated when the bomb exploded. As a result, six people were injured as the RUC tried to clear the area.

There was little Crime and Security could do. Analysis of the upsurge in RIRA attacks showed that McKevitt was no longer operating out of the Republic. 'Jones" operation had been shut down. And so began a new chapter in the development of the RIRA. Apart from the physical damage caused by a fresh bombing campaign, the attacks were a disaster for the Irish government because Campbell and McKevitt proved they were capable of bringing dissident republicans together.

The INLA was by far the most volatile paramilitary group to emerge from Northern Ireland. Their involvement came as a complete surprise to Garda Headquarters. No one had anticipated that the INLA would join the RIRA. The organisation was never known to have Semtex or even bomb-making capabilities. The group had planted booby-traps and landmines in the 1970s and early 1980s but never a car bomb aimed at widespread damage.

McKevitt's strategy was a grandiose one. He wanted to gain political strength through bombings, continue the underground war until he forced the British out of Ireland. He was determined not to compromise his republican position.

The attacks continued. A week later, on 2 July, the RIRA blew up the Dublin-Belfast railway line at Carnagat outside Newry. The next attack was overtly political and caused fear among the security services.

The unit built a 1,400lbs bomb, which they attempted to drive into the centre of either Portadown or Armagh city at the height of the Drumcree crisis. The intense levels of military and RUC activity on roads in the north Armagh area foiled the bombers and the device was abandoned near the sleepy village of Moy.

The republicans though made a grave mistake. A British Army team disarmed the bomb, which enabled the RUC to recover the device and detonator intact. Although the forensic detectives that sifted through the component parts found nothing conclusive, the construction techniques gave them an indication as to who was involved. The police withheld the bomb parts should scientific developments make it possible to extract evidence at some future time.

THE MAIN THEME of the military campaign was devastation. The republicans sought to make an impact. The bombs were designed to topple buildings and create scenes of mass destruction and havoc. The RIRA wanted the world to know that Northern Ireland was still ungovernable: that nothing had changed despite the endorsement of the Good Friday Agreement. On 21 July, they attacked Newry RUC station using Mark 15 mortars, each weighing about 200lbs. The mortars misfired. Each device only travelled 5 yards. The devices were similar to the type used by the IRA to attack British Army soldiers stationed at Osnabruck in Germany in July 1996. Nobody was injured.

Most people agreed that the RIRA was now a major threat. Crime and Security found it difficult to monitor Campbell despite the vast array of technical devices at their disposal. The bombs continued exploding.

Other developments helped the cause. 'McGuinness' had trained two members of Campbell's unit in the art of bomb making. The recruits proved themselves to be more than capable of building simple but effective bombs. Always mindful of the possibility that either MI5 or Crime and Security could infiltrate his cell, 'McGuinness' made sure that everyone played a role in the attacks. Direct participation in attacks remained a prerequisite for everyone in his team to ensure they were not agents. In any case, there were never any problems with his bombs and explosive devices.

The devices were cleverly built. When putting the TPUs together, the engineers would wear yellow or gold marigold gloves to prevent fingerprints being left behind. 'McGuinness' would travel to Dundalk and onwards into south Armagh where he oversaw the construction of the larger bombs. He taught at least four republicans how to construct TPUs and bombs.

The principal components of the TPUs were a toggle switch, a Couchpan mechanical timer with a red warning light, and a metal clip connector, which he used with a PP3 battery. He taught his students to insert the devices into plastic Tupperware containers, which he would seal using household glue. His trademark was to burn the logo off the Tupperware box using a hot knife. This was another attempt to frustrate the security forces and their quest to find any identifying evidence.

The team who delivered the bombs to chosen targets was comprised mostly of RIRA and CIRA volunteers. The more astute and experienced republicans on the RIRA Army Council had reservations about the campaign.

They certainly were delighted to see the bombing campaign run like clockwork but there was a subconscious fear that something could go wrong. Whether the new Army Council were simply powerless to control Campbell, or chose to turn a blind eye to his loose operations, is unclear. The possibility of carnage should have been considered, given the size of the bombs and those involved, but it wasn't. On the ground, the feeling amongst the ASU was entirely different. Those who planned and executed the bombing campaign saw themselves as making history, being part of a new IRA uprising, similar to the inception of the Provisional IRA in 1969.

The most important feature of Campbell's ASU was that the main players knew each other and spent long periods of time among themselves. They travelled to work together, socialised, and drank amongst themselves. The result of this was that Crime and Security found it impossible to recruit an insider.

Campbell promised to detonate bombs every week. Caution was not at the forefront of his mind. For the previous two months, the unit had mounted several strikes that avoided wounding civilians and bystanders. On those occasions, accurate warnings giving the precise locations of the car bombs were phoned through. Frustrated by their failure to murder a member of the British security forces, Campbell gave an order to disguise the precise location of bomb cars. The callers could give the general vicinity of the bomb once it did not specify exactly where the device was concealed.

This was not aimed at hindering evacuations. Its true aim was to cause casualties amongst the RUC and British Army. Inaccurate warnings would also help prevent British Army bomb disposal experts from disarming explosive devices, and by default gathering intelligence or evidence. The effect of the new order soon became apparent.

ON THE AFTERNOON of Saturday, 1 August, the town of Banbridge in County Down was devastated by a car bomb that exploded in the main shopping area at 4.30 p.m. The bomb was concealed in a red Vauxhall Cavalier that was parked in Newry Street. It contained 500lbs of explosives and was capable of killing anyone standing in its vicinity.

The car was delivered into the town around 4 p.m. Once the unit was safely on its way back to Dundalk, a 20-minute warning was phoned to the police. The caller did not give the precise location of the bomb, nor when it would explode.

The confused warning caused chaos. The RUC were in the process of evacuating the town when the car bomb exploded sending shrapnel and debris flying in all directions. Some 33 people and two RUC officers were seriously injured. Scores of others were shaken having seen large chunks of metal flying through the air. Forensic experts who mapped the scene afterwards found metal from the bomb car up to 600 yards away. Protestants and Catholics reacted with horror to the near carnage. Banbridge was left in ruins. Businesses and shop premises were badly damaged, some had to be demolished.

By coincidence, Martin Mansergh, the man who met with dissident republicans on behalf of the Irish government, was travelling near Banbridge that day. He took a detour to view the damage. He was horrified by the attack and amazed there were no fatalities. The attack reverberated around Northern Ireland. The message though was lost on the RIRA and Campbell. From his home south of the border in Upper Faughart, he was pleased with the news. Two injured RUC men were better than none.

9

PRELUDE TO A MASSACRE

THE SECRET DIPLOMACY between the Government and the Real IRA continued as the latter stepped up its campaign of violence. Mansergh only attended the first meeting—Fr. Reid was the conduit for the rest of the talks. The Sovereignty Movement, as it was now known, refused to be drawn on the issue of insurgency. Instead they demanded the talks confine themselves to political issues and the Peace Process. The republican side had little experience in any form of official negotiations. Each time Fr. Reid raised the issue of insurgency, he was silenced. The republicans would not acknowledge—even through innuendo—that they spoke for McKevitt.

The lack of any agenda made a mockery of the discussions. Not alone did the Sovereignty Movement, refuse to talk about the RIRA, they ruled out the possibility of discussing anything other than their own campaign. In effect, what they demanded was the same type of treatment afforded to Sinn Féin and the IRA. This was out of the question for as long as bombs continued to explode, and was the main reason why Mansergh didn't meet them. Although it was apparent that the dialogue was a waste of time, Mansergh, through Fr. Reid, persevered.

Part of the strategy to create a cohesive relationship that could bring about a RIRA ceasefire involved treating the dissidents and their opinions with the most seriousness. The Government would accept all literature and documentation in good faith. This policy was aimed at building mutual trust. In reality, this was part of a well thought out strategy for fighting terrorism through dialogue. The Department of the Taoiseach was of the opinion that republicans in the long term could never be contained by the security services. But they could be drawn into politics through the back door if the seeds of democracy were planted in their minds. In accordance with this procedure, Mansergh had accepted a copy of the UN submission from Francie Mackey and forwarded the document to the Attorney General, David Byrne.

The purpose of this was to again reaffirm to the republican side that the Taoiseach was sincere in his dealings. Byrne drafted a three-page response, which acknowledged the merits of the legal arguments formulated by Joe Dillon. These, the report suggested, were important and worthwhile but they did not excuse the use of violence.

Mansergh dispatched an official response to Fr. Reid. He did not write to Dillon seeing that as too dangerous given that he was facing charges before the Special Criminal Court. His communication to Fr. Reid consisted of a cover note printed on official Government notepaper with a gold harp emblem embossed and a copy of the three page report from the Attorney General. The note read:

> Dear Fr. Reid,
> I attach our response based on discussions with our legal advisors in relation to the case submitted to the UN by the 32 County Sovereignty Movement. The argument is taken strictly from our own legal and constitutional perspective, as it relates to current international law. Our legitimate arguments could be put forward from other perspectives, if we were to proceed on the basis of the likely validity in international law of agreements freely entered into

between the Irish and British governments from 1925 to 1985.

In either case, in our opinion, no breach of international law existing at the present time can be established that would in the terms of the memorandum now justify further or continued armed insurgency.

Yours sincerely

Dr. Martin Mansergh,

Special Advisor to the Taoiseach

The letter and the attached report made no mention of the IRA. Fr. Reid sent a copy of the response to the Sovereignty Movement, whose executive discussed the paper at length. By this time, a further two meetings had already taken place with Fr. Reid. It was at this point that relations began to strain.

The first reason was that the dissidents did not fully trust Fr. Reid. They considered him to be too friendly with the Sinn Féin leader, Gerry Adams. The priest's sole motivation, of course, was to halt violence and stop the bloodshed. The second greatest obstacle to the success of the negotiations was the Sovereignty Movement itself. The dissidents did not understand that the Government had to protect itself from any suspicion of illegal activity or unethical dealings with dissident republicans. Although they refused to confirm they were the political division of the RIRA, they turned a blind eye to the fact that just about everyone knew they shared the same views as McKevitt. The self-denial on the Sovereignty Movement's part ensured the talks ended in failure.

The third defining factor that had a detrimental effect on the clandestine discussions was the recent success of the RIRA's campaign. The RIRA Army Council didn't want a ceasefire. If McKevitt and 'McGuinness' were to enter into any form of constitutional politics after criticising Adams and the IRA for doing the same, they would bring ridicule on themselves. They chose to commit themselves to war. Crime and Security had monitored the meetings and assessed the mood among the dissidents. In the reports sent to the Department of Justice, the security advisors had maintained a common belief that McKevitt did not want to engage in any political process but remained focused on the goal of collapsing the Good Friday Agreement. This forced the Government to concede they were misguided to have entered into indirect talks in the first place.

The Sovereignty Movement had four meetings with Fr. Reid, Mansergh only attended the first one. The last of these took place in the aftermath of the Banbridge bombing at the Redemptorist Monastery in Dundalk.

The mood was glum. Fr. Reid spoke little and made no secret of his dismay. Those in attendance concluded that he believed his efforts had been in vain. The Sovereignty Movement knew the same. It had taken the arrest of 30 volunteers to get them this far; the RIRA Army Council had no intention of turning back now.

Dillon earlier concluded that Mansergh was more interested in talking to the RIRA than listening to the Sovereignty Movement's arguments. He was right.

'That was noticed. Some people in the army got the impression that, because the Government was concentrating on ending the war; that was all that counted. It made some army people believe that war was the only thing the Irish government would listen to,' said one republican.

'JONES' KNEW WHAT betrayal meant. His efforts to unmask the mole ended in failure every time. He tried everything to uncover the agent. He told lies and untruths to different people in the beleaguered hope that he might hear the same information from an official source; thus unmasking the traitor. The plan was a complete waste of time.

'Jones' was a ruthless operator in his own right but any credibility he once possessed had now vanished. Even he accepted the order that he play no further role in the military campaign. In any case, Campbell would have nothing to do with him. 'Jones'' pursuit of the mystery informant was as much for the benefit of the Army Council as his own criminal enterprise. He was obviously under suspicion like everyone else involved in the operation. He was also eager to prove to the Army Council that he was no informant. Unmasking the real informant would significantly improve his standing.

Some volunteers in the Dublin Brigade developed a pathological fear of doing business with him. It was not hard to see why. Scores of RIRA men had ended up in jail or facing charges as a direct result of 'Jones'' participation in the RIRA. The black operation mounted by Crime and Security could not have been more successful. Everyone suspected everyone else.

Where Crime and Security inserted an agent into a criminal enterprise, they usually inserted more than one in order to verify the intelligence received. It was more likely than not that there was a second or third informant within the Dublin Brigade. But who?

'Jones' knew the finger of suspicion was pointed in his direction. To a deeply suspicious Army Council, nothing seemed too absurd.

McKevitt had vouched for 'Jones' when he had joined the new army. That 'Jones' was hated and despised in his own community because he consorted with drug dealers did not seem to matter. According to one IRA source, if it were not for his brotherly relationship with McKevitt, 'Jones' would have been abducted and tortured as part of the mole hunt.

THE UNLIKELY SPY at the heart of 'Jones'' operation remained securely in place. Dixon never fell under suspicion. Jennings and the intelligence analysis department at Crime and Security used him to monitor the intricate workings of 'Jones'' operation in County Kildare. Dixon never came into contact with more senior officials in the RIRA, although they occasionally visited 'Jones'. He knew they visited from time to time because he was told so.

The arch criminal's actions of the time would suggest that he felt untouchable. Even though it was clear that his gang had been infiltrated he continued to engage in car theft and crime despite his compromised situation. On the morning of Monday, 10 August, 'Jones' sent a coded communiqué to Dixon asking him to instruct Vinny to steal a car the following night. 'Jones' named a time and place—11 p.m. outside a Shell garage on the Clonsilla Road in west

Dublin. He did not specifically say he wanted the youth to steal a special order but Dixon figured this was the case because McNamara and 'Bull' would accompany Vinny. The conversation was brief and without pleasantries. He had no option but to agree to the request. The only thing he did not think of was that this was a trap. If anything, suspicion was now focusing on Vinny.

An unexpected problem presented itself the next day. In the throes of the internal inquiries hastily organised by the RIRA, Vinny had had a change of heart. He wanted out. He figured it would only be a matter of time before he was accused of being the informant. His concern was not unfounded. Dixon ordered him to do as he was told but he had stopped listening. Dixon would later tell White that Vinny was panicked; the pressure had become too much.

Stealing cars was one thing; bombing England and Northern Ireland was something else. The true informant felt some degree of responsibility for the predicament in which Vinny found himself.

If Vinny refused to obey 'Jones'' instructions, it would be tantamount to signing his own death warrant. If some other thief was to provide a car which was used in a successful attack, 'Jones' would put two and two together and come up with four—Dixon and Vinny would almost certainly be murdered. He had no choice. Dixon's simple argument made absolute sense. Once Vinny considered the potential consequences of his actions, he agreed to do the job, albeit reluctantly.

Then something happened that no one expected. Vinny failed to make the collection the next night. He vanished without a trace. No one could find or contact him. He also powered his phone off which left Dixon in an unenviable position. When 'Jones' telephoned Dixon wanting to know if something had happened, he had no answer. It took a further 24 hours to locate the car thief. When Dixon did finally catch up with him, he discovered Vinny had gone off alone and got drunk.

'Jones', however, kept demanding that Vinny steal a car with McNamara. At 10 a.m. on the morning of Thursday, 13 August, he instructed Dixon to have Vinny prepared to work late that same evening. By now Dixon was able to tell when the boss meant business. The information was relayed to White, who in turn notified Crime and Security.

White met the agent that same evening. He told Dixon to monitor everything. It was of utmost importance that he obtain specific information about what was happening. To do this, White suggested that he urge Vinny to stay overnight in his house. That way, Dixon would hear the full story. Dixon did as he was told and delivered Vinny at 11 p.m. to Clonsilla.

Jennings had considered it too risky to deploy the NSU. Given the high state of anxiety and distrust in the gang, it would be almost impossible to observe the rendezvous without compromising the entire operation. If McNamara or 'Bull' were to notice anything untoward, Vinny would certainly be murdered. Dixon, the real informant, would inevitably fall under suspicion if this were to happen.

The hours passed slowly that night. Dixon feared for Vinny. He was worried that 'Jones' had really abducted the car thief and was interrogating him. He could only wait and hope. He felt powerless. The informant was working the late shift that night when he got a call at 3 a.m. from Vinny. Dixon felt the weight of the world lift from his shoulders. The two men met an hour later. As instructed, Dixon brought the thief back to his house, where he learned about the night's events.

'JONES' HAD WANTED Vinny to take a car and McNamara had collected him as arranged. The two men went about their business as normal. They searched for a family saloon or a small car to steal but couldn't find one. They had, of course, found suitable cars but none at houses that Vinny felt safe entering to retrieve the keys. Because they didn't want to return empty handed, the two had travelled as far as Mullingar town in County Westmeath as part of the search. It was a futile exercise.

However, neither of the two men were really interested in putting their necks on the line for 'Jones'. McNamara would later say, "'Jones" told me to go meet Vinny at some bus yard on the Clonsilla

Road. My instructions were to bring Vinny down the country somewhere, to get a hatchback car and a [Nissan] Micra for the following Monday. When 'Jones' told me that he wanted a hatchback, I knew he wanted it for a bombing. I knew that Vinny didn't want to get a car that night. I didn't push him nor was I interested.'

To keep 'Jones' happy, the two arranged to meet the next day, Friday, 14 August. But at 2 p.m. that same Thursday afternoon Dixon was called by McNamara to say the collection was off. He gave no reason. This was good news. Up until now, when he cancelled a job he always made another arrangement. He guessed that 'Jones' was putting distance between himself and the car thieves.

News of the message was relayed to White at his home in County Donegal. Neither White nor Dixon suspected anything untoward. White casually informed Crime and Security of the news. They would all realise that the arrangement had been cancelled to keep them from knowing how the conspiracy would end.

WITH A DEGREE of ease that not even McKevitt had shown when he smuggled tonnes of weapons from Libya, Campbell single-handedly changed the fortunes of the RIRA. His attention to detail and security revamped the campaign. He made the RIRA into a force to be reckoned with in the space of a few weeks. For some time, he had been thinking his IRA should do something that would shake the entire republican movement—eventually deciding on a series of car bombings mounted by a coalition of republicans drawn from the CIRA, INLA, and the RIRA.

His controversial decision to cut all links with 'Jones' and the Dublin Brigade had proved itself to be the most judicious decision made by a member of the Army Council. Campbell's absolute conviction that someone high up in the organisation was an informant also played to his advantage. He knew 'Jones'' operation was compromised but his senses told him there was another agent. The RIRA Army Council had not paid too much attention to his irreverent suspicions but now they did. His track record over the previous weeks spoke for itself. The RIRA was now a force to be reckoned with.

Campbell found himself in a position where he could do no wrong. He operated independently of the Army Council and did not consult anyone except McKevitt on his operations. This went against the rules. The founders of the RIRA had devised a chain of command that mirrored the Provisionals when they first set up the organisation. The modus operandi adopted by Campbell rendered this obsolete. This was noticed by some at leadership level but they chose not to raise the matter.

'They nearly killed scores of people in Banbridge. The goal posts were being moved. Banbridge was a disaster yet no one said anything. I think they were just happy to be in charge of something,' said one source.

Working in absolute secret with the tight knit band of dissidents, Campbell went about the business of terrorism. He had never felt so lethal. It was clear that the team was trustworthy and reliable, and he gambled on none of them being open to recruitment.

Campbell was an experienced IRA man. Most people living along the border would never cross him out of fear. Others treated him as a folk hero and talked about car bombings he organised as if they were courageous acts of rebellion. More often than not, they ignored the violence, suffering, and grief he caused.

BY THIS TIME, the campaign was running like clockwork. For the first time since its inception, the RIRA was enveloped by optimism at volunteer level. The mood was decidedly different at leadership level, though no one would admit it. There were deep divisions on the Army Council.

'McGuinness' was no longer in control, though he was still Chief of Staff. Campbell consulted nobody; the Director of Operations for the North established a new rhythm. This was the beginning of what the analysts at Crime and Security would call the doomsday period. This time their strategy did not work.

The problem was that Crime and Security used uniform techniques to counter the RIRA. The clandestine operations were directed towards a short-term law enforcement objective with an immediate impact in mind—putting terrorists behind bars and disrupting the organisation. Dixon's role as a spy had run its course and the security forces now had to adapt. Once Campbell overhauled the workings of the RIRA, the intelligence gathering system fell apart. It was much harder for the Garda to infiltrate Campbell's unit. The effect of this was to have deadly repercussions for the Peace Process and the people of Northern Ireland. Campbell's reckless and overconfident approach to the war would soon become apparent.

ON THE NIGHT that 'Jones' sent McNamara and Vinny to Mullingar, the border gang sent their own team of car thieves off into the night on a similar mission. Convinced that acquiring stolen cars was the most dangerous part of the bombing campaign—in terms of infiltration by the security forces—Campbell's ASU sourced their own cars from a gang that operated out of Dundalk.

The leader of the gang never had any dealings with Campbell, or any senior member of the RIRA for that matter. He took his instructions from an INLA commander who occasionally helped McKevitt.

They had attended the same school and had grown up together. As adults they remained friends. The two would often meet to do business.

One of the gang had sourced a string of cars for the RIRA through the INLA. Some were stolen while others were purchased for sums of less than £100. For example, he bought the Cavalier used in the Banbridge bombing from McGuigan's Garage in Forkhill, paying £100 in cash the day before the bombing took place. Educated on the streets, the leader of the gang did not consider himself a republican. His involvement with the RIRA was financially driven. He was a thug.

On the night in question, the car thieves went to the quiet market town of Carrickmacross set in the low hills of County Monaghan just south of the border. The gang travelled in a maroon coloured Mazda, which belonged to one of their friends. The chief thug didn't use his own car for criminality.

The gang members knew Carrickmacross well. They were regular visitors to the town, which lies 15 miles west of Dundalk. They often drank in the Fiddler's Bar on the main street. On arrival in Carrickmacross, the thieves began patrolling the town's small housing estates looking for a suitable car to steal. It was after midnight and their movements were quickly noticed.

Patrick Conlon saw the gang cruising very slowly past his home on Pearse Avenue around 1 a.m. and figured they were up to no good. Because it was a dark night, he mistook the Mazda for a Peugeot, but he did catch a good look at the occupants. He clearly saw three men in the vehicle.

The town of Carrickmacross is relatively small. Around 10,000 people live there and the gang had difficulty locating a suitable car to steal. They ended up driving around for more than an hour before eventually making their way to Macartan's Villas. The entrance to the estate is situated on a hill, which is protected by speed ramps. These forced the gang to drive at a snail's pace.

It was here that they saw a maroon-coloured Vauxhall Cavalier L. The car bore the registration 91 DL 2554 and belonged to Paul Ward from nearby Tullynacrunnat. He was staying overnight in his girlfriend's flat.

The car was seven years old and this made it relatively easy to steal. The driver stayed in the Mazda and kept the engine running should the gang need to make a speedy escape while one of the thieves forced the driver's door open.

Once this man gained access to the car, he set about removing the plastic covering from the steering column. This exposed the ignition keyhole and four wires going into a square shaped box. The wires were red, black, yellow, and a blue and black striped wire.

The thief was expert at hot-wiring cars. He connected the wires, then inserted a screwdriver into the ignition slot and turned it clockwise. In a rehearsed manoeuvre, he next broke the steering column by pulling hard on the wheel leaving the car ready to drive away.

Once the driver heard the Vauxhall's engine start, he drove away. The Cavalier followed his direction. The two cars left Carrickmacross in convoy. When the car thief was sure that no one was following, he called his INLA contact using his mobile phone.

The INLA man was waiting on the call. The conversation lasted no more than 60 seconds. Less than a minute later, the INLA boss called a member of Campbell's RIRA unit. This man was ready and waiting to collect the car at a pre-arranged location. The gang made their way back to Dundalk. They parked the stolen car in a council estate. It was left parked under a lamppost. The RIRA collected it some time before dawn. The gardai were not on the lookout for the stolen car because its owners were unaware that it had been stolen.

A key factor in the success of the ASU was its ability to operate on both sides of the border. Campbell saw this as imperative. South Armagh was still a no-go area for the RUC. The security situation gave the RIRA a number of safe bases from where to operate in terms of making explosives, constructing bombs, and building mortars.

The ASU operated from a number of locations in this regard. One was a building off the main Dublin to Belfast Road. HME was secretly manufactured here in hired cement mixers. This location was perfect. It was centrally situated and close to the border. This gave 'Bob' and the other members of the unit with engineering skills quick access to the Cooley Mountains where they often tested explosives and detonating devices. Local farmers on the Cooley Peninsula often reported hearing loud explosions at night and finding huge craters on tracts of remote lands.

The second operation base was situated in County Monaghan in an old farm shed situated near Cullaville. In accordance with the new security measures in place, the Cavalier was driven across the border into south Armagh. The journey took little more than 20 minutes. It was here that the car was transformed into a bomb the next day.

SOME MEMBERS OF the team had already started mixing the necessary explosives. The bombers used a recipe called co-op explosive mix. The compound was made from ground down ammonium nitrate fertilizer and icing sugar. It had the power of 50% nitro-glycerine dynamite.

While the explosive was being mixed, other members of the engineering team made structural changes to the car. The vehicle was fitted with heavy-duty shock absorbers similar to those used in trucks. The attachment of these is standard in car bombs: the shock absorbers keep the car rigid by concealing the weight of the explosives on board. When the HME was prepared, the mixture was shovelled into sacks, which were loaded into the boot. Inserted into the explosive mix were steel tubes packed with Semtex. These would boost the bomb's velocity on detonation.

Campbell himself oversaw the construction of the bomb at every stage. One of 'McGuinness'' students wired the detonation device into the bags of HME. With the precision of a surgeon, he next inserted a TPU inside a small plastic lunch box, which was positioned in the front passenger seat. This was wired to a black plastic knob and two metal switches designed to activate a time-delay device. When the procedure was completed, the ASU had constructed a 500lbs bomb that was hidden in the family car. The whole process took no more than 48 hours and cost about £500 to build.

WHAT NO ONE knew was that Campbell had asked 'Jones' to deliver a car for the following week in order to send Crime and Security on a wild goose chase. The false registration plates affixed to the Cavalier were registered to a man called Bernard McGinn. The actual owner of the plates was an innocent party but years earlier another man of the same name had betrayed the South Armagh IRA of which Campbell had once been O/C. He was now on a war footing and wanted to send a message to the security forces. The secret message was in part to satisfy his own craving to let Garda Headquarters know his ASU was watertight and partly to frustrate their intelligence operations. He wanted Special Branch and Crime and Security to know they could recruit informants in

Dublin and elsewhere, but not on the border, the birthplace of true republicanism.

AT DAWN THE next day, Saturday, 15 August, the RIRA prepared to bomb Omagh town in County Tyrone. The bombing was to have special significance. Omagh is situated in the centre of County Tyrone and lies in the heart of Ulster.

Situated at the foothills of the Sperrin Mountains, where the Camowen and Drumragh rivers merge to form the River Strule, Omagh is 70 miles from Belfast and 34 miles from Derry city. This made the town a strategic target. If the RIRA could strike against the British presence in Omagh, it could strike anywhere in Northern Ireland.

The Director of Operations was doing no more than flexing his muscles. That Francie Mackey, a leader of the Sovereignty Movement, was an elected member of Omagh District Council, was irrelevant.

The bomb car was moved to the farm shed in County Monaghan overnight. The ASU now came together at this shed where further work was carried out on the car. The bombers arrived together in a car they planned to use to scout the route into Omagh.

At the workshop, the ASU rechecked the timing device and went over the plan. The car was to be delivered to a location near Omagh Court in the centre of town. Once in position, they were to call Campbell who would phone in the warnings. There was some concern that the bomb could explode whilst in transit. The explosive mix had been laced with diesel but they were assured it was stable. One of the bombers was fearful of being accidentally killed. He was anxious about the operation going wrong. The drivers were also concerned about being arrested or stopped.

Campbell reassured them, saying the route would be scouted and if they really felt threatened, they could abandon the car and detonate the bomb on a remote roadway. This relaxed the bombers.

Everything was in place. Campbell returned home to await news of how the operation went. When they had completed the essential procedures, the bombers took possession of the car and headed north towards Omagh. They left shortly after noon.

The first vehicle scouted the road for Garda or RUC checkpoints. The unit believed the RUC had no intelligence forewarning them of the attack, however, there was always the possibility that they could stumble upon a traffic checkpoint. The scout car drove two miles ahead of the bomb car for this reason.

The two-car convoy remained in constant contact using two mobile phones. The bombers made 24 telephone calls before the afternoon was out. The first part of the journey took them along the main road to Monaghan town. This route brought them through the villages of Castleblaney and Clontibret in County Monaghan, which they passed through without incident.

THEY PASSED THROUGH Castleblaney around 12.41 p.m. They were 48 miles from Omagh town. For security reasons, they bypassed Monaghan town, diverting through the village of Stranooden. The risk of being noticed by the gardaí in the bustling town was too high.

At 1.29 p.m. the first mobile called the phone in the bomb car. This call was relayed through a mast at the border crossing at the village of Aughnacloy. The scout car was giving instructions to the bomb car. The call concerned which of the several border roads was safe to cross. This call was logged at 1.39 p.m.

Omagh was a relatively short distance away. The scout car arrived on the outskirts of Omagh first and waited at a beauty spot called Pigeon Top Mount for several minutes while the bomb car went into the town centre.

A call relayed to a nearby mast at 1.57 p.m. put one of the mobile phones at Bridge Street, just yards from where the car bomb was later abandoned. At 2.10 p.m., one of Campbell's men in the scout vehicle spoke by mobile phone to the boss, who had stayed south of the border. The Director of Operations for the North had borrowed a phone from another member of the ASU, a businessman from Dundalk.

The conspiracy was unfolding. The bombers had reconnoitred the journey prior to the day of the attack. They did their best to choose a route allowing them to travel unnoticed. However, when they entered Omagh, they were filmed on some CCTV systems.

At precisely 2.18 p.m. a CCTV installed at a petrol station filmed the bomb car heading into Omagh. The film showed the car's front suspension raised from the weight of the heavy load in the boot.

One minute later, a call was made from the bomb car telling the scout car it was about to park. The time was 2.19 p.m. Omagh town was thronged with shoppers, tourists, and workers. Several people going about their daily routine noticed the bomb car. One witness saw the Cavalier crossing a traffic junction. The bombers spoke every few minutes almost as if they were using a radio system to communicate. At the same time, the bomb car contacted the scout vehicle to say it was in the town.

Omagh Court House was the bombers' target. Despite all the planning that went into the attack, the ASU did not know it was a festival weekend. The market town was filled with hundreds of shoppers and visitors.

When the bomb car drove into the town, the driver of the bomb car could not find a parking space near the court. In a moment of panic, he continued driving and pulled up outside SD Kells draper shop at 35-37 Market Street. It was nowhere near Omagh Court.

Shoppers thronged the street. Mothers were helping their children try on school uniforms for the new term.

The bombers paid no attention to the risk of causing mass murder and set the timer to detonate in 40 minutes. One of the two men in the bomb car flicked two switches to activate the timer and the detonator. The two men then stepped out of the bomb car and walked towards Campsie Road, which leads out of the town.

The driver inadvertently drew attention to himself by easing the door of the car into a closed position. He appeared to be afraid of the bomb going off if he closed the door firmly. The scout car had by this time driven into Omagh town and was waiting. The bombers sat into the scout car and made good their escape.

THE BOMB WAS now armed. The ASU contacted Campbell to say the device was in place. This was news he desperately wanted to hear. The call was also a signal for the issuing of the bomb warnings.

At 2.29 p.m., the first of three warning calls was made from a telephone box at McGeough's Crossroads in Forkhill. The warning call was made to UTV. The caller spoke in a ruffled voice that made him hard to understand.

'Hello. Newsroom. Bomb. Courthouse in Omagh. Main Street 500lbs. Explosion 30 minutes. Martha Pope. IRA. Óglaigh na hÉireann.'

There was a flurry of calls from the bomb car whose occupants were trying to give the precise details of where the bomb car was parked. Campbell had ordered that no precise time be given. This was to deter the security forces from trying to disarm the device. The result of all this was utter confusion.

Two minutes later, the Samaritans in Omagh town were called but the line was diverted to Coleraine. The caller repeated the warning. When asked to clarify the location, speaking in a 'quiet, gentle voice', he said, 'Two hundred yards up from the courthouse'.

The third warning came at 2.31 p.m. and was made from New-townhamilton. The message was 'Martha Pope. Fifteen minutes. Bomb. Omagh town.'

Three different people had dialled through the bomb warnings. Campbell made the last call.

The RUC believed the bomb was about to go off at Omagh Court House. The policemen on duty ran towards the shops in the area and rushed people to a cordon they set up further down the street beside SD Kells. There was pandemonium. A tragedy of imaginable proportions was unfolding. In trying to get people to safety, the police inadvertently shepherded men, women, and children towards the bomb.

10

AUGUST 15

THE BOMB EXPLODED at 3.10 p.m. and wiped out all human life in its immediate environment. The explosion sent a fireball into the air causing the Cavalier to explode and disintegrate into flying shrapnel. There were 20 people standing near the police cordon. Flying shards of metal tore through their bodies, ripping off their arms and legs, as flames engulfed them and consumed their lives. The bombing of Omagh town was an atrocity of unimaginable carnage. The scene was one of hell on earth with burning and charred bodies lying everywhere.

The bomb itself caused a shockwave that struck the nearby buildings. The entire front wall of SD Kells exploded into the building, while the roof collapsed into the top floor. The roofs of adjoining buildings were blown off simultaneously. On the opposite side of the road, the bomb blasted out the shop fronts. A thick cloud of dust descended on the street blinding the survivors. Those standing a further distance from the epicentre of the explosion found themselves caught in a storm of glass, rocks, and metal which punctured their bodies, killing some of them by inflicting multiple injuries.

Body parts littered the road. Arms, legs, hands, and pieces of flesh were strewn everywhere. An unforgettable smell of charred flesh hung in the air. Those who survived the initial explosion could hear nothing. Their eardrums were burst by the supersonic noise from the blast. The people who paid witness to the atrocity went into immediate shock.

The scene was one from the bowels of hell. The survivors, wounded and bloodied, wandered around the wreckage nursing their own injuries in a semi-conscious state. Many stared at the remains of the dead. People screamed for help. Others lay on the ground, collapsed and unable to comprehend the scene. The dead and dying were everywhere.

A water main under the road burst open and pumped out hundreds of gallons of water. The effect of this was to wash body parts down the sloping street.

Pat McElhatton arrived on the scene within minutes.

'The first thing I saw was a shoe in the middle of the street. There was dust everywhere. No one could really see more than a few feet ahead. I looked at the shoe again. There was an ankle inside the shoe. The shoe was standing on its own in the street.'

He saw charred arms, legs, and torsos strewn among the debris. The dead suffered the ultimate indignity of having their clothes burned off their bodies. The bomb had left them naked. The lifeless bodies were covered in dirt and blood.

Some of the dead lay on the ground with their eyes wide open. Time almost stood still.

McElhatton went into shock. He was unable to comprehend the sight. He had driven into Omagh to film a cycle race and was carrying a video camera. He began documenting the scene.

'There was just panic. They were all running about looking for their kinfolk, running into shops to see were they there, turning over bodies. You don't think at all, everything goes black. It was bedlam. You would hardly know where you were. The smell of the bodies and everything was terrible. It was rotten.'

He continued walking, not really knowing why he was filming or even where he was going.

'There were a lot of things that just made me switch off. There were legs and arms on the ground. There were dead people everywhere. There are no words to describe it. It was hell on earth. The scene wasn't one of this world.'

McElhatton continued to document the atrocity. 'There were people screaming everywhere. People were digging through the rubble with their bare hands. Then someone roared at me.'

He switched the camera off after recording 12 minutes of footage.

THE TRUE STORY of the Omagh bombing is one of mass murder, but also one of bravery. The survivors began to help the dying. The street was saturated within seconds with ordinary people trying to help their loved ones, neighbours, and friends. With blood flowing from open wounds, they began searching for survivors in the rubble.

People who lived nearby ran to the scene to offer help. Those who could not offer assistance stood with their hands in their pockets looking at their murdered kin in disbelief. Some walked away from the carnage not knowing what to do.

John King was one of the first people on the scene. He worked as a local carpenter.* The first thing he noticed was what he thought was a shop dummy lying in the middle of the street. After he passed the first shop dummy, he saw what he thought were more dummies. These had no arms or legs. It took him several seconds to realise he was stepping over dead bodies.

Rosemary Ingram was the traffic warden on duty in Omagh town that fateful afternoon. She had been standing near the bomb car but miraculously survived. When she got to her feet after the blast knocked her to the ground, someone handed her a tiny baby whose body was black and charred. The baby was the dying 20-month-old Breda Devine.

Ingram was one of the few people standing near the bomb car to survive. But survival came at a price. Shrapnel had embedded in her torso, legs, and arms. She looked down at the tiny baby. She had an open wound across her torso and had suffered the most excruciating pain for a small child. Ingram was beyond grief and despair; the pain of her injuries made no impact. The baby was still but Ingram could feel a faint heartbeat. In a deep state of shock, she could not find the words to summons help and so scrambled to her feet and began

---

* Omagh bomb Inquest

walking towards Tyrone County Hospital. She managed to make it to the hospital where her legs gave way and she collapsed. The baby was taken from her but died not long afterwards.

Some survivors woke to find themselves trapped in a living nightmare with their loved ones dead beside them.

Kevin Skelton was standing in the shop next door to SD Kells when the bomb exploded. When he regained consciousness, he scrambled to his feet and began searching for his wife and two daughters. He found them in what remained of SD Kells.

His wife Philomena lay on the ground covered in dust, dirt, and rubble. Her clothes were blown away; her body lay pierced with shrapnel. He checked for a pulse but could find none; he knew she was dead. His battle to save his family was not over.

He began to search for his daughters, Tracey and Shauna. Tracey emerged from the rubble and began taking her mother's pulse. Kevin found his other daughter Shauna lying under his wife's body.

THE EMERGENCY SERVICES took no more than ten minutes to reach the scene. Members of the British Army Medical Corps stationed at a base in Omagh were among the first on the scene. Dr. Samuel Potter rushed to administer first aid to the injured and dying.*

The first two bodies he saw were two men lying almost crossed over in a crucifix. He continued to sift through the wreckage, all the time trying to remain calm, despite the horrific scenes assailing all his senses.

He found the body of a young, heavily pregnant woman carrying a little baby. This was Avril Monaghan and her 18-month-old baby Maura. She had died while trying to protect her precious baby. The two were dead. She was also carrying unborn twin girls who died before they were of this world.

Stunned and horrified, he continued searching for any signs of life but there were none. He did find another body; that of an elderly woman lying at the entrance of the shop. The body was that of Mary Grimes, Avril Monaghan's mother-in-law, the grandmother of

* Omagh bomb Inquest

Maura and her two unborn sisters; three generations of the one family dead.

Potter went on to pronounce life extinct on 20 bodies and a body part within 20 minutes, or one person every 60 seconds.[*]

Local people took it upon themselves to help the soldiers and policemen in anyway they could. The sheer scale of the carnage put the emergency services under mammoth strain. A fleet of ambulances ferried the dying and wounded to Tyrone County Hospital, which lies on the outskirts of the town. It was not enough; there were too many wounded.

Rescuers flagged down two passing buses and dozens of cars to take the remaining people to hospital.

The wounded queued to get on the buses. Blood streamed from their foreheads and shrapnel was embedded in their skin; they consoled themselves with the fact they were still alive. Men and women lifted survivors who could not walk because they had lost one or two limbs. The helpers used blankets as makeshift stretchers. The injured were even bundled into the boots of passing cars for transportation to hospital.

Everyone did what he or she could. Shop assistants in the town's pharmacies dispensed medical supplies to anyone who needed them. The women at Nicholl and Shiels drapery store handed out blankets to cover the dead and keep the injured warm. The rescue operation was not over yet. Dozens of people dug through the rubble with their bare hands in the hope of finding someone alive.

MINUTES AFTER THE bomb exploded, the death toll stood at 20. The RUC staff in charge on the day knew this figure was rising steadily and issued an appeal on local radio stations for all medical staff to make their way to Tyrone County Hospital as soon as possible.

The call was answered. Nurses and doctors drove to the hospital not knowing the true scale of the horror that awaited them.

Dr. Dominic Pinto was the first surgeon to arrive at the hospital, which was now guarded by armed soldiers.[**] 'When I came to the front of the hospital, it was absolutely quiet. What greeted me when

[*] Omagh bomb Inquest
[**] Omagh bomb Inquest

I got into the main corridor was sheer pandemonium. This was not a major incident, but a major disaster of battlefield proportions. There were people lying in corridors of the Accident and Emergency Department, overflowing into the Radiology Department.'

Blood streamed down the steps that led into the hospital's Accident and Emergency room. The presence of extra staff made no impact on the delivery of treatment services. The hospital had neither the facilities, nor bed spaces to sufficiently deal with the crisis.

This forced the authorities to start ferrying the victims to hospitals in neighbouring counties—Belfast, Tyrone, Derry, and Fermanagh. Other victims were transferred to hospitals south of the border. There were more deaths to come. One of the ambulances collided with a car on the way to Belfast city and killed the driver, Gary White. His death was a consequence of the Omagh bombing.

BACK AT THE scene of the explosion, the work continued to locate survivors buried under the rubble and collapsed buildings. Firemen, police officers, and soldiers sifted through the debris with their hands. No one was found alive; all they could find were more bodies and body parts. The death toll continued to rise.

Omagh had been thronged with shoppers that Saturday afternoon. The school term was due to begin and many mothers were buying new school uniforms for their children. There was also a contingent of Irish and Spanish children visiting from County Donegal as part of a school tour. Omagh town centre was also a place of employment and many people had been at work.

That evening, when all hope had faded and when the end of the world seemed to have arrived for the families of the dead and missing, RUC and medical staff began compiling a list of the dead. The bomb had murdered men, women, and children of all faiths and creeds. The bomb was not sectarian. It killed Protestants, Catholics, and a Mormon.

The dead included Breda Devine, the 20-month-old baby that Rosemary Ingram had tried desperately to save. The baby was born three months premature but had clung to life. Her mother Tracey had taken her into Omagh while she shopped for a wedding present for her brother. The baby's mother was left fighting for her life with 60 per cent burns.

Aidan Gallagher, 21, should have been working that afternoon at his garage and panel beating business. The Gallagher family lived on the Circular Road in Omagh and Aidan had taken the day off to buy a pair of jeans. He was murdered.

Five people from the tour group of Irish and Spanish children died. Four boys were killed. They were Seán McLaughlin, 12, Oran Doherty, 8, Fernando Blasco Baselga, 12, and James Barker, 12; their team leader Rocio Abad Ramos, 23, also perished.

The Irish boys came from the village of Buncrana in County Donegal. Ramos and Baselga both came from Madrid. The tour party had visited the Ulster American Folk Park, which is situated close to Omagh town. The party chose to end the afternoon with a shopping trip to Omagh.

Ramos had heard the bomb warning and moved to protect her young charges. She died instantly, as did Oran Doherty and Fernando Baselga when the car bomb exploded. Seán McLaughlin was pronounced dead on arrival in Tyrone County Hospital.

James Barker battled to survive. He fought against his injuries and pain for two hours while surgeons performed an operation in an attempt to save his life. He died in the operating theatre. Half of the young tour group did not return home to County Donegal that night. They either died or were seriously injured.

Julie Hughes, 21, was killed after she was evacuated from the Image Xpress photographic shop and directed towards the police cordon. She was a student at Dundee University and had decided to spend her summer holidays at home in Omagh town.

The bomb claimed the lives of two best friends Samantha McFarland, 17, and Lorraine Wilson, 15. The two teenagers had given up their Saturday afternoon's to work in an Oxfam charity shop situated in the town centre. The two girls were directed towards the bomb when the RUC evacuated the area. Ironically, the charity shop was not damaged in the explosion; they would have been spared if they were left alone.

Geraldine Breslin, 43, and her best friend Ann McCombe, 48, worked in Watterson's clothes shop. The two were on a tea break when told to evacuate. Like many of the victims, they were standing close to the police cordon when the bomb exploded.

Their colleague Veda Short, 56, was in the throes of a celebration when she died. She also worked in Watterson's clothes shop but was on her break at the time and had gone for a walk down to Market Street. Earlier that day, she had witnessed the birth of her grandchild.

Deborah-Anne Cartwright, 20, was another victim. She worked in a beauty salon on Market Street. The bomb exploded seconds after she left the shop, killing her instantly.

Gareth Conway, 18, was another student murdered in the bombing. He had been shopping for a pair of jeans when the RUC directed him to the police cordon seconds before the bomb detonated.

Esther Gibson, 36, was a Sunday-school teacher from the village of Beragh. She worked in Desmond's clothes factory. She had just finished shopping and had left her belongings in her car, which was parked outside Dunnes Stores. The bomb claimed her life.

Brenda Logue, 17, had left her mother and grandmother momentarily to see why people were running down the street. She caught the full force of the bomb. She was a sixth-year pupil at Saint Theresa's high school in Carrickmore and played for the school's Gaelic football team.

Olive Hawkes, 60, was also murdered by the RIRA. She lived a few miles outside Omagh and was due to celebrate her ruby wedding anniversary in a few days time. She was killed by flying shrapnel. Jolene Marlow, 17, also died in the atrocity. Jolene and her younger sister Nicola had taken their grand aunt into Omagh to go shopping.

Another shopper murdered by the RIRA was Brian McCrory, 54. He came from Ballinamullan Road and had gone into the town centre to buy paint. He had seen the commotion and headed to the RUC cordon where he died.

Alan Radford, 16, was a schoolboy from Castleview Park. He was in the town shopping with his father and mother when the bomb exploded. He was due to start training as a chef the next month. The bomb claimed his life.

Elizabeth Rush, 57, was serving customers in her shop on Market Street across the road from where the bomb car was parked. The blast destroyed the building causing it to collapse, killing her and several others instantly.

Bryan White, 27, was a horticulturist from Knockgreenan Avenue who died alongside his father Fred, 60. He had returned from University in England and was due to start a job with the council two days later. The two men were wandering around the town when they were directed towards the police cordon. Another man, Seán McGrath, 61, would die later as a result of wounds he sustained. He was from Omagh town and left behind four children.

OMAGH LEISURE CENTRE was transformed into an incident centre to deal with panic-stricken families that heard of the bombing by listening to news reports. Hundreds of people from the surrounding towns rushed into Omagh searching for their missing loved ones. So many people tried ringing the centre that the phone system collapsed.

Only five bodies were identified immediately. Many relatives had to wait for hours for news. Among them was Donna Maria Barker, whose young son James had been fatally injured.

Donna Maria received the news of the bombing from her mother who had heard about the carnage on a radio bulletin. She called every hospital in Northern Ireland looking for news of her eldest son. She was certain that some terrible harm had come to him. Her family reassured her but she believed nothing but her own instincts. She prayed and prayed silently for God to intervene but somehow she knew James had perished. Three hours later, three hours of turmoil and unbearable anguish, her worst fears were confirmed. Overwhelmed by grief, her heart in a state of inconceivable turmoil, she drove to Omagh to identify her young son in the mortuary.

She went into shock when she was shown his body on a mortuary table. Her son lay lifeless covered by a blanket. The doctors advised her not to look because of the nature of his injuries. She insisted. She was beyond grief and despair. Summoning all the powers of strength she had left, she slowly lifted the blanket.

Her boy's eyes were wide open. He had suffered serious internal injuries and a substantial head injury. The body was still swathed in bandages, dressings and strips. In the deepest grief, she held her son in only a way that a mother can and privately prayed that he had felt no pain. When all hope had gone, she looked into his eyes and was struck by their brilliance. Afterwards she would recall that she had never realised how stunning her son's eyes were. It was an image that etched itself in her memory.

THE FAMILIES OF the local people murdered by the RIRA had heard the explosion from their homes. Mark Breslin was Geraldine Breslin's husband. He heard the blast from his garden and panicked when he saw a helicopter hover towards Omagh town and descend in a spiral manoeuvre that he considered dangerous. It was the tightest spiral he'd ever seen. He knew something terrible had happened.

He immediately tried calling Watterson's, the shop where his wife worked. He was glad when he heard a voice on the other end of the phone line. He interpreted this as a good omen, a sign that his wife was safe and well.

Geraldine had been evacuated and had not returned, he was told. He walked into his sitting room, switched on the radio, and waited.

When she didn't phone, he made the decision to call the shop again. But the town's phone system had collapsed. He interpreted this as another positive omen, a signal that she was unable to contact home. Time went slowly. After an hour, he decided to go to the hospital to see if she was there. He left two notes, one on the front door and one on the back door, just in case she came home in the meantime.

The town was enveloped in a blanket of chaos. Traffic was bumper to bumper. He abandoned his car and began walking.

The radio stations were broadcasting messages urging anyone who needed information to go to the leisure centre, but the need to locate his wife overrode everything. When he arrived at Tyrone County Hospital, he saw blood flowing down the steps of the entrance.

People were everywhere. There were blood soaked towels strewn in the waiting room. Injured people sat in wheelchairs. The hospital porters tried in vain to mop up the blood. There were dozens of people waiting for transport to other hospitals, people with superficial injuries.

He was filled with a nervous energy. He asked a nurse for a towel to dry himself off because at this stage he was soaking. He could see the panic on the faces of the nursing staff.

'There were nurses down there and one of the nurses said, "We just got a call from Enniskillen—they're not taking any more casualties."'

For some reason, the comment shocked him. He felt like fainting. 'I felt the blood just down at my feet. I'm not injured or anything like this. I don't want to pass out when there are people worse off than me.'

He started searching the hospital himself. He walked around the wards. He eventually made his way to Ward 6 where he met a nurse standing with a clipboard. He asked about his wife but the nurse was trying to bring herself up to speed.

He glanced at the list. Midway down, he saw his wife's name, address and telephone number jotted down in untidy handwriting. He interpreted this as another good omen, figuring that she must be conscious. His spirits lifted. He asked to see his wife but this prompted more questions from the nurse who tried to check his own identity.

'She says, "Well what's her date of birth?" and I said, "I can't remember", as all good husbands do. At that stage I was just lucky that I knew her name because I was in such a tizzy. So I kind of convinced her that I was [who I said] and she says, "Geraldine has a number of injuries—back, front injury. She's now down in the Intensive Care Unit, in the theatre."'

Relieved and exhausted, he walked in the direction of the intensive care unit. He sat outside the operating theatre. He felt blessed and lucky. He saw other people desperately searching for missing family members and thought his wife had been spared.

Around 7.30 p.m., a nurse approached him and asked if he wanted to see his wife. The nurse told him the doctors were trying to stabilise Geraldine before they operated.

He took the opportunity. She was semi-conscious. There was a patch over burns she had suffered. He also noticed she had lost teeth, but these injuries were superficial and didn't matter. She was alive.

'She was on drips and she probably didn't recognise where she was. But she did recognise me and she said a couple of words. Then I left.'

She emerged from surgery a few hours later. A nurse came and told him they were evacuating Geraldine to Belfast by helicopter. He followed his wife to the heliport where he said good-bye. He stood back as the aircraft took off, turned on his heels and went back into the theatre to ask the duty nurses how the operation had gone. Geraldine had lost a foot, he was told. He didn't care once she was now safe from harm.

Mark followed the helicopter in his car. He arrived in Belfast about 11.30 p.m. and inquired about his wife's condition. The nurse asked him to step into a waiting room.

'Then the doctors came in. I thought they were going to warn me about all the beeps and buzzes and wires, you know the usual things. But my sister clocked first that they were coming in to cushion the blow. So they said that she had died. That they had fought to keep her alive. Just as I arrived, they gave up the battle.'

A priest accompanied him back to his home where he broke the news to their son Gareth and his mother-in-law.

'Gareth was sleeping in the front room and Geraldine's mother was in it gathering up the bed or something. So the priest broke the news to her mother and I broke the news to Gareth. And that was it.'

This was the story of the Omagh bombing.

WHEN NEWS OF the attack reached Dublin, Jennings was notified immediately. He was personally sickened. Crime and Security dispatched all its agent handlers seeking information on who was responsible.

The ASU learned about the carnage by listening to news reports on the radio, as did the Army Council. The realisation that something had gone disastrously wrong circulated quickly. Panic set in.

Those who sat on the Army Council heard about the atrocity on the news that night. One Army Council member recalled, 'I was at home when the first reports came on at around 3.20 p.m. or 3.30 p.m. My first thought was, "That's interesting, that's the first time they have brought the war over to Tyrone."

'Then the news said there had been casualties and I knew straight away it was bad. Then it came through that there were three dead, then five, then seven, then 10. Then 13. The death toll kept rising. I knew we were fucked. I knew there and then the entire army was fucked.'

11

CEASEFIRE

THE REAL IRA became the most notorious terrorist group in the world at dawn the next day when the true toll of the massacre became apparent. The scenes of the bombing filmed by McElhatton were broadcast on television and spread outrage across the world. The image of murdered people lying dead on rubble-strewn streets ignited a wave of criticism against the RIRA and the 32 County Sovereignty Movement. The stories of how the ordinary people of Omagh found their children, sisters, brothers, fathers, mothers and grandparents dead amongst the rubble touched the hearts of the public. It was evident that savage August weekend that the RIRA had brought about a situation of the worst circumstances imaginable.

Since 1969, when the Provisional IRA began its campaign of guerrilla warfare against the British Army, Ireland had experienced all kinds of horrendous acts, including sectarianism and state sponsored murder and assassination by agents of the British government. But Omagh was different. There was peace in Ireland in August 1998. People thought violence was a thing of the past; the republicans proved everyone wrong.

Among the many atrocities that convulsed Ireland throughout three decades of civil strife, the Omagh bombing stood out as the worst, the most virulent and cruel. The death toll the next morning stood at 28 people with 220 injured. In time, the number of dead would rise to 29 people. The true figure was 31 dead given that Avril Monaghan was pregnant with twin girls. The RIRA, the group that claimed to uphold true republicanism, had caused the single biggest loss of life in the history of the troubles.

As the heart-broken families of Omagh prepared to bury their dead, McKevitt summoned the Army Council to a secret meeting in County Louth. The gathering was attended by approximately four members of the Army Council in the darkest of subterfuge. Remarkably, there were no recriminations, no fights or accusations although they were all sickened.

Campbell, whose careless attitude to life was directly responsible for the massacre, wasn't formally reprimanded, though questions were asked as to exactly what went wrong. In typical form, he blamed the RUC for not evacuating the town properly.*

'It was very glum. We were all quiet because we knew how serious things were. There was a debate about what we should do next, after this disaster. We knew we were in a deep hole and some people said we could and should bomb our way out of it. But in reality there was only one thing we could do—call a ceasefire,' said one RIRA Army Council member. However, not one member of the Army Council wished to abandon the campaign.

In their opinion, the IRA had been responsible for similar atrocities but had survived intact. Although they didn't express any opinions on the bombing, privately Campbell and McKevitt thought the anger towards the RIRA would subside in time. Others agreed with them. 'Bad things happen in a war. Omagh was a tragedy. But the way to make sure there aren't any more Omaghs is for the British to get out,' one RIRA figure later stated.

Although McKevitt had seen mass murder in the past, the extreme loss of life that resulted from the Omagh bomb personally sickened him. As a member of the Armagh/Louth wing of the IRA, he had seen various operations that had caused mass fatalities. In January 1976, the unit murdered 11 Protestant workers near the village of Kingsmills in Armagh in a naked act of sectarianism.

* Interview with Real IRA Army Council member

McKevitt wasn't there for the massacre, but he was a member of the brigade behind the attack.

His unit also carried out the Narrow Water massacre in retaliation to the shooting dead of innocent Catholics in Derry on Bloody Sunday. That attack, which took place in August 1979, is now folklore in IRA history.

The ASU claimed the lives of 18 paratroopers and marines in a series of co-ordinated attacks. The attack made the IRA in south Armagh famous for its ingenuity and cunning. The attack came in two parts. The first involved blowing up a lorry carrying nine soldiers. The IRA had left a 700lbs bomb hidden in a hay trailer. The bomb exploded as they drove by. When rescuers from the Royal Marines arrived by helicopter, another bomb exploded, this time hidden in a derelict castle, killing 11 more.

The Provisionals had survived the public outrage. McKevitt and the Army Council were of the opinion the RIRA could do the same.

Although none of them wanted to announce a ceasefire, they all privately assumed they had no alternative but to make some sort of public gesture.

'It was to give us time to regroup. There was no way that we were interested in calling it a day. But we weren't going to make any decisions without first going to the volunteers, it was up to them to decide, not us,' later said a member of the RIRA Army Council.[*]

Despite the carnage, the horrendous suffering and the calamity of the murders at Omagh, the Army Council remained clear-sighted. The ceasefire, said one member, was not worth the paper it was written on. 'You could have written that ceasefire declaration on toilet paper. It was only a move aimed at stalling the inevitable crackdown.'

The truth was an entirely different matter. They were all running scared. McKevitt knew what inevitably lay ahead. The media had descended on his home. He now learned the true meaning of overt surveillance. Unmarked patrol cars sat outside his home. Detectives followed him everywhere he went. On one occasion, his car went into a ditch when gardaí were following him. The gardaí drove on.

[*] Interview with Real IRA Army Council member

Worse was yet to come. Anyone associated with the RIRA or the 32 County Sovereignty Movement became a target for the media. McKevitt became public enemy number one. Journalists and photographers sat outside his home. The Print Junction, the tee-shirt printing shop, run by Sands in Dundalk town centre was boycotted. Hundreds of people attended a peace vigil in Blackrock, McKevitt's home village.

'McGuinness' became a target. The engineer had spent his life living in the shadows; now he was fair game. He was photographed coming to and from his home in Dublin. The appearance of his photograph in the media, albeit with his eyes blacked out, caused more than a degree of friction between him and his brothers and sisters. At the time, it was generally accepted that he had built the Omagh bomb. His girlfriend threatened to leave him. One of his brothers announced that he would kill him if someone could prove his involvement.

Francie Mackey instantly became a figure of hate in Omagh town, where he was elected to the local Council. On the Monday morning following the bombing, the Council held an emergency meeting, which Mackey attended. He was the centre of a massive media scrum. Other councillors demanded his resignation forthwith. He was asked to condemn the bombing, which he did. But this made no difference.

The Omagh bombing—even before the full scale of the horror became known—had made a powerful impact on the people of Ireland. The calamitous deaths of the children and the shocking way they died ended any lingering support for militant republicanism for good. There was only one problem; the RIRA and Army Council could not see this.

Whether he chose to allow himself to understand the enormity of the horror the RIRA visited upon Omagh or not, McKevitt quickly decided to embrace the notion of dialogue. This was for his own benefit and those on the Army Council. Those around him may have thought that he was resilient to everything and incapable of fear, but he wasn't. He was running scared. This brought about a change in his frame of mind. He immediately let it be known to his closest advisors that he would try to open up contacts with the Irish government to inform them about the Army Council's intentions to call a ceasefire.

According to one Army Council member, McKevitt was uncertain about the reaction they would receive. He gave the instruction that from now on everything was going to be handled on a need to know basis.

The truth was that he didn't know what to do or who to trust. His first mistake was to allow himself to succumb to the belief that he was in a position to bargain. The fact was brutal and painful: the RIRA was in tatters. He refused to accept the notion of defeat, however.

McKevitt had never participated in politics or Sinn Féin, hence he had no idea of how such contacts were conducted. Until this time, McKevitt had distanced himself from all official dialogue; now he wanted his name stamped all over it. To McKevitt's own brand of self-importance, nothing seemed too absurd.

His first move was to send a message to the Redemptorist priest Fr. Alec Reid. The message was relayed in the strictest secrecy to Mansergh. But it was too little, too late. The opportunity for talks had long since passed. The Irish government signalled that it would not enter into any further dialogue with McKevitt or his band of republicans but intimated that it would be willing to listen if a ceasefire was called. Arrangements were made for Fr. Reid to meet McKevitt at Clonard Monastery as quickly as possible. Fr. Reid would act as a conduit for the Government.

WHILE THE RIRA leadership were busy trying to save their own skins, police on both sides of the border were preparing to hunt them down. The police investigation into the Omagh bombing took four distinct forms. The first was led by the RUC. This inquiry operated from Omagh Police Station and was led by Chief Superintendent Eric Anderson, the principle detective in the region. He was a much respected investigator who had put dozens of republican and loyalist terrorists behind bars in his long career.

RUC Special Branch ran the second investigation. This worked in tandem with the Omagh Inquiry, though in reality they remained separate. RUC Special Branch was a secret police force within a police force.

The problem Anderson's team faced was not how to find any evidence that could secure a charge, but rather how to find any evidence at all. The Omagh bomb had not alone wiped out all life but incinerated all the evidence.

South of the border, Garda Headquarters established their own inquiry room at the divisional headquarters in County Monaghan. The focus of the investigation was Carrickmacross, from where the Cavalier used in the bombing had been stolen. From the very beginning, the intelligence services on both sides of the border believed the bombers probably lived in the Republic. This was confirmed within days when Anderson's team collected enough fragments of the bomb car's chassis number to allow them to trace the vehicle's true identity. The number was sent to Garda Headquarters whose stolen car section traced it to Carrickmacross.

At the time, the garda commander for the Northwest Region was Kevin Carty. Gruff, abrasive, and fiery, Carty held the rank of Assistant Commissioner. He was a workaholic—a man who possessed a no nonsense attitude to life. He demanded that his subordinates apply themselves to their duties with absolute dedication and loyalty. Officially, the Garda were only supposed to run an investigation into the theft of the Cavalier but Carty had other ideas; he wanted the bombers.

His man on the ground was Tadgh Foley, the detective inspector in Monaghan Station. Foley was an easy-going Cork man who had a reputation as a problem solver. An affable man, he was struck immediately by the plight of the Omagh families. From the very beginning, the two gardaí didn't just set out to catch the car thieves; they set out to bring the bombers to justice.

THE FIRST PEOPLE to identify those responsible for the attack, however, were Crime and Security. When Jennings heard the first reports of the bombing, he knew the RIRA had changed tactic and moved their operational base from County Kildare. Crime and Security had prevented a string of RIRA attacks under his watch. Now there were scores of people dead. There had been no warning, no tell tale sign of premeditation.

The agents Jennings ran close to the RIRA's hierarchy had heard nothing of an imminent bombing; nothing that could have foretold the deaths.

The bombing stunned Crime and Security. Jennings dispatched his agent handlers to start gathering information on the attack. One of the first people approached was White, whom he instructed to talk to Dixon.

The detective sergeant met his informant on the Monday after the bombing. White drove to Dublin where he met with Dixon who told him that he hadn't heard from 'Jones' since the previous Friday. Like everyone else, Dixon had seen the news reports and footage of the bombing. He was shocked. The massacre was beyond his comprehension. The scenes he saw on television—the outrage he sensed amongst his friends and family—reinforced the notion that he was in serious trouble.

Jennings had feared that Vinny had double crossed Dixon and had, in fact, stolen the bomb car. But this was not true. Dixon knew that neither he nor Vinny were trusted by 'Jones'. Privately he interpreted the bombing as a sign that his career as an informant was over. He could help no more. White accepted his story and relayed the information to Jennings. There was nothing that anyone could have done.

Jennings began assisting Carty's investigation at once, though Dixon's role as an informant was withheld. Crime and Security sent every shred of intelligence to the incident room at Monaghan Station. Although Crime and Security had no specifics as to the identities of the actual bombers, they had a list of suspects.

Of more importance was 'Jones'' operation. Foley was furnished with enough information on 'Jones' and his modus operandi to allow his detective unit to hit the ground running.

AS EXPECTED, FOUR days after the bombing, the RIRA Army
Council announced its planned cessation of activities. It came in a
phone call to the Dublin Correspondent of the *Irish News.*

Perhaps for the first time in his career, McKevitt was afraid. The
pressure was so intense that it consumed all his energy. He was
wrong when he thought public anger would slowly fade. If
anything, it got worse.

In a desperate attempt to ease the tension, Sands moved publicly
to distance both herself and McKevitt from the bombing. Desperate,
isolated and alone, she called a local priest to say that neither she
nor her partner had anything to do with the bombing. The priest
went public with her denial but this didn't calm the storm.

Once the Army Council announced the cessation of operations,
she decided to address the Irish public on *Liveline*, an afternoon chat
show broadcast on RTE Radio One.

She introduced herself by name to the presenter Joe Duffy and
rang from her T-shirt shop. Duffy came straight to the point and
asked had she fled her home.

'No, I haven't fled my home. I came in here today, into the shop
to open because I, and I don't want this to be misunderstood and I
know people will probably say, "My goodness, why is she in
working?" but I am here because I have nothing to hide. I have
absolutely nothing to flee for and I am not prepared to run away for
something I did not do and that's why I am standing here.'

Again Duffy came straight to the point and asked if she
condemned the bombing. This was a deliberate ploy. Throughout
the history of the Northern Ireland Troubles, Sinn Féin had always
refused to condemn IRA murders and atrocities. Duffy wanted to
see if she would do the same.

'My goodness, how could anyone even condone it?' she asked.

'We have been on record, Francie Mackey has put it on record,
and indeed has had to come out several times and clarify it. Why it
has not been picked up, why people are continually ignoring what
we are saying, I don't know, I really don't know.'

She evaded condemning the attack, prompting Duffy to ask her
once again.

'We have, we have, we are on record.'

She wouldn't use the word condemn herself and tried to avoid the question. When Duffy asked if she used the word herself. She answered, 'Yes, yes, our chairperson Francie Mackey has.'

Sands had no great understanding of public relations. She desperately tried switching the subject and redirecting the question. Duffy asked her to clarify the situation.

'I have already condemned and we will not condone it, and the loss of innocent life could not possibly be justified.'

Duffy asked what she thought of the people who planted, organised, and directed that bombing. She wouldn't take the bait.

'I don't even think about them. I am not in a position to think at the minute and just agreed to talk to you at the moment to clarify things and, as I have said to you already, I don't wish this day to be . . . I just feel this is all inappropriate, I really do. I am being very, very serious here with you.'

Predictably, she used the opportunity to say she welcomed the RIRA declaration adding that she had been struck by the enormity of the carnage.

'I think it's just the whole overall thing, the fact that it's innocent children, women; I mean it's the whole human tragedy.'

The innocent remark caused Duffy to interject and ask, 'When you say innocent, who would not be innocent?' he asked.

She called the remark a figure of speech.

Duffy concluded by asking if she hoped the people who perpetrated the crime would be brought to justice.

'Well I'm sure they will, I'm sure they will. I'm sorry, I have to go now . . .'

She then hung up. The interview only managed to increase resentment against the Sovereignty Movement across Ireland.

IN THE THROES of the calamity, the RIRA Army Council moved to organise a Convention to ratify a permanent ceasefire. The Army Council had wanted to declare a full ceasefire rather than a suspension of military activities but didn't have the power. They had left the IRA for ignoring the Constitution, which stipulated that

a Convention must be held and the IRA membership balloted on
such a serious decision.

There was one problem, however. The massive security
crackdown on RIRA volunteers made it practically impossible for a
large group of members to meet.

The RIRA turned to Fr. Reid for help. McKevitt, who was himself
somewhat shocked at the public reaction to the massacre, wanted
breathing space to hold a Convention with the sole intention of
proposing a ceasefire.

The two sides met secretly at the Redemptorist Monastery in
Dundalk. In attendance that night were McKevitt, other members
of the Army Council and Fr. Reid.

According to a member of the RIRA Army Council present, there
was no negotiations and no secret deal.

'We told Fr. Reid what we were about to do. McKevitt informed
Fr. Reid that we were going to call a meeting of volunteers to argue
for a ceasefire. But we also told him that there could not be a
ceasefire without that meeting. The IRA constitution was clear
about this.

'We said there was no way we could hold a meeting of 60 or 70
volunteers with the current level of Garda harassment. It was so
intense that none of us could move. We asked for space to get all our
people together. That's all we asked for—space—nothing else.'

Fr. Reid relayed the message to Mansergh, who had been on
holiday in County Donegal at the time.

Unknown to all sides in the subterfuge, Crime and Security had
monitored the meeting as part of the intelligence operation. A high
ranking informant close to the Army Council had made them aware
of the meeting's time and location.

Overt surveillance did ease in the following days which allowed
McKevitt to hastily organise a Convention. The actual location for
the gathering was between south Armagh and County Louth.
Approximately 50 volunteers drawn from across the country
attended the Convention, which was addressed by the Army
Council.

'The meeting lasted all day and we explained the various options. But the only real option was to call a ceasefire. But, again, we stressed that this was only a temporary measure; that our war was not over.'

From a discreet distance, the NSU monitored the frantic activity within the RIRA. Their observations were relayed to the Government through Crime and Security, and latterly the office of Noel Conroy, the Deputy Commissioner in charge of operations. The analysis of the intelligence agency was that McKevitt was under immense strain but had not walked the road to Damascus. The RIRA still reserved the right to kill and murder despite its commitment to organising a ceasefire.

MEANWHILE, CARTY MADE no secret of the fact that he wanted to bring the bombers to justice. While the RUC made appeals for information, the Garda team led by Foley mounted dawn raids on the homes of every republican living near the border. The idea was to deny the RIRA a minute's peace. RIRA volunteers were dragged from their homes and questioned. Harassment and vigilance were the orders of the day.

Unknown to anyone, Crime and Security continued running Dixon inside 'Jones" operation. White would drive to and from County Donegal to rendezvous with the informant, who remained in place in the midst of the RIRA. Ironically, the agent would report on the activities of Carty's investigation and how it was proceeding.

At 8.50 a.m. on the morning of Tuesday, 25 August, Dixon received a call from Damo, a car thief who regularly supplied vehicles to 'Jones' and the RIRA. Foley's team had arrested his criminal partner. Damo was fearful.

By coincidence, later that same day, 'Jones' called Dixon and asked him to attend a meeting in Blanchardstown, in west Dublin. The pressure was getting to him. He feared for his own safety and wanted Dixon's opinion on which members of the gang would talk to the gardaí if arrested. 'Jones' asked Dixon to get the younger car thieves out of the country.

In an act of bravado, he warned Dixon that anyone who betrayed him would be killed. Portlaoise Jail, he said, would be the least of their problems. Dixon said nothing. He never argued with 'Jones' and always tried departing on good terms. In any case, Crime and Security were monitoring the events.

News of the crackdown on the dissidents spread like wildfire. 'Jones' figured that he would be arrested sooner or later. In anticipation of a Garda raid, his unit began issuing threats to those who knew too much. To 'Jones'' now paranoid and overheated fear, nothing seemed too absurd.

On 26 August, he met Dixon and issued warnings to him and the father of one of his car thieves. This time he was accompanied by a RIRA figure from Clondalkin called Francis. The businessman who had headed the RIRA's mole hunt also attended the meeting.

'Jones' quickly came to the point. He warned the car thief's father that his son would be executed if he spoke to the gardaí. By this stage it was clear the Government was about to introduce new laws relinquishing an accused man's right to silence.

'Jones' gave the following ultimatum. When the new powers were introduced, all those arrested were to answer every question with a denial. This was the instruction from the RIRA. 'Jones' was nervous.

JENNINGS DID HIS best to protect Dixon. On Thursday, 27 August, 12 days after the bomb, it became clear that Foley's team planned to arrest the informant at his home the next day. White said he wanted to talk to Dixon when he was in custody. Jennings told him to talk to Foley.

Dixon was arrested as predicted. News of the arrest was relayed to White who immediately drove to Monaghan Station. In such circumstances, gardaí will usually turn a blind eye if a fellow officer asks to speak privately to a prisoner. Foley duly obliged but took an immediate dislike to White. He simply didn't trust him.

As promised, Foley brought White to meet Dixon who was being interrogated. Foley then left. The pair opened a window in the interrogation room and spoke to each other out the window. The detectives investigating the bombing didn't know what to make of the strange behaviour. In any case, Dixon was released without charge the next day.

Foley worked his way through the investigation at speed. His inquiries inevitably led him to 'Jones' and his extended gang. They were all arrested. And every one of them—with the notable exception of 'Jones'—revealed everything. McNamara made a full confession, admitting to mixing explosives and building car bombs.

Foley's team didn't leave the matter rest. The garda investigation sought and obtained warrants to search 'Jones'' premises. The criminal had not seen this coming. The detectives began sifting through his business premises in search of incriminating evidence. This sent the godfather into a state of absolute panic. In the midst of the arrests, Dixon received a call on the following Monday morning. The person speaking, live and direct, was 'Jones', having been released without charge.

He was in no mood for conciliation and was engaging in a damage limitation exercise. Then he came out with an unexpected comment. He told Dixon not to worry because the RIRA had cut a deal with the Government. In return for a ceasefire, nothing was going to happen to anyone. Dixon did not know what to make of the bizarre claims. The truth was that 'Jones' had lied when he claimed there was a deal.

The Army Council had sought no guarantees in its dealings with Mansergh, via Fr. Reid. 'Jones' was trying to save his own skin and frighten his associates into non co-operation with the gardaí.

Out of mischief, Dixon asked about McNamara. He knew McNamara had implicated the boss in everything. 'Jones' said he was on his own. If he made a statement, there was nothing he could do for him. Not alone was his security now entirely compromised but Crime and Security concluded that 'Jones' had resorted to telling lies to frighten people from implicating him in any crime.

'He didn't know which way he was coming or going. He was desperate. He knew there was an informant close to him and he knew he was suspected of being an informant. He embellished what little information he had to make it appear that nothing could happen to him,' recalled one garda.*

* Interview with Crime and Security

ON 1 SEPTEMBER, the Government called a special session of the Oireachtas, the Irish Parliament, to pass the toughest security laws ever introduced in the history of the state. The legislation drafted in response to the Omagh bombing revoked the right to silence; created a new offence of directing terrorism; gave the gardaí more powers to hold suspects for longer and allowed for the forfeiture of property where it was used for storage of firearms or explosives.

The most radical element of the legislation concerned a court's ability to draw inference from the refusal of a suspect to answer questions. This was perhaps the most powerful weapon ever introduced against republican extremists. Throughout the years, IRA men and women who had been arrested and questioned refused point blank to answer any questions. Instead, they would focus their attention on a spot on the wall while in custody and refuse to speak. The IRA had trained volunteers in anti-interrogation techniques. In many parts of Ireland, prospective IRA volunteers were assessed on their ability to say nothing while in custody. The legislation changed all that. If they didn't speak, they could be found guilty. And if they did, they would inevitably have to lie, which would open further lines of investigation for their interrogators.

The RIRA had set out on their trail of terror with a simple aim: to destroy the power sharing agreement in Northern Ireland. But perversely, the bombing of Omagh actually strengthened the Good Friday Agreement.

It also allowed Sinn Féin and the IRA the freedom to move towards constitutional politics. On 1 September, Adams proclaimed that the 30-year war mounted by republicans had effectively ended.

As Adams was making his historic remarks, the IRA were getting ready to show the RIRA that they still had a sharp bite.

The IRA had become aware of the pending ceasefire announcement. They felt they could make some political capital out of the move and undermine McKevitt at the same time. To thwart the RIRA, the Provisionals decided to formally comment on the Omagh bombing. The mechanism for attack was a lengthy article, which appeared in *An Phoblacht/Republican News,* the Sinn Féin newspaper, on 3 September.

The IRA began by expressing its condolences to the families of those killed and injured.

'In human terms it was a disaster and a tragedy of enormous proportions. No one could fail to be moved by both the suffering of the victims of the bombing and the generosity of spirit of the families of those killed and injured in the explosion.

'The Omagh bomb had undoubtedly caused damage to the struggle for Irish independence and unity. We suspect that this attack and previous bomb attacks by this and other groupings have been aimed at the Peace Process, in general, and at Sinn Féin's peace strategy in particular. Irish republicans throughout the 32 counties have, both privately and publicly, made very clear their anger at the actions of those responsible for the bomb.'

That the Provisional IRA had mounted similar attacks and murdered in similar fashion was forgotten. Until this point, the IRA had remained silent about the RIRA, refusing to recognise the entity at all. The Provisionals now used the deaths to score points against McKevitt.

'The erroneous claim by these people to be Óglaigh na hÉireann is a good indicator of exactly what they are about and the motivation behind the actions. Prior to their defection they were given the opportunity at an Army Convention to put their analysis to delegates elected by and representing the entire membership of Óglaigh na hÉireann. Their views on future strategy and direction were rejected by the vast majority of those delegates. Having failed in what was essentially a bid for leadership, this small number of individuals then resigned from our organisation and, in a very deliberate and calculated way, set about trying to undermine both the duly elected leadership of Óglaigh na hÉireann, and the future strategy which had been agreed and endorsed by the Army Convention.

'Their lack of credibility among volunteers or our support base has caused them therefore to seek to gain legitimacy by trying to hijack the name of Óglaigh na hÉireann, and, by extension, trying to put themselves and their views in the proud tradition of 80 years of struggle.

'While they have failed on both counts, many republicans feel nonetheless aggrieved that they have tarnished the name of Óglaigh na hÉireann and many are justifiably angry at their use of the term "RIRA". The grouping have done only disservice to the republican cause. They have no coherent political strategy, they are not a credible alternative to the Irish Republican Army. In the immediate aftermath of the Omagh bomb they announced a temporary halt to their actions. This is insufficient. They should disband and they should do so sooner rather than later.'

The last sentence was telling. On 7 September, the RIRA announced their ceasefire in a coded call to Ireland's national broadcaster RTE at 11.50 p.m.

The Chief of Staff actually communicated the decision to RTE. The cessation came into effect 10 minutes later. By this stage, the IRA knew that a ceasefire was imminent. In an attempt to generate good publicity from the news, the IRA had sent threats to members of the RIRA and the Sovereignty Movement. This was nothing more than a stunt. Instead of simply sympathising with the victims' families, the IRA used the opportunity to consolidate their own power.

The article also appeared to have been drafted and scripted with such co-ordination that McKevitt and the others privy to the secret talks with the Government figured that the IRA had been made aware of the pending ceasefire announcement. There was more proof.

A few days before the ceasefire, the IRA sent volunteers to 40 houses, north and south of the border with warnings to the dissidents.

The IRA had clearly expected some sort of announcement and the RIRA believed the threats amounted to nothing more than a PR exercise.

In each case, the RIRA members were read out a 'comm' from the mainstream leadership. The same message was read out to all those targeted. It ordered the RIRA to disband and accused them of stealing IRA weapons.

Those who did the threatening included members of the IRA Army Council and senior members of Sinn Féin. Among those threatened was the engineer and Chief of Staff 'McGuinness'. He was the only member of the RIRA Army Council to receive a warning. He was approached as he sat in a pub.

'Someone arranged to meet him. They walked into the pub, produced a piece of paper and read out this statement. The bloke's hands were shaking. He made a complete fucking fool of himself,' said a member of the RIRA Army Council.

Not a man to panic, 'McGuinness' walked away, choosing to ignore the threat. In other parts of Dublin, RIRA volunteers adopted a more direct line of approach to the Provisionals.

'The Provos threatened some of the brigade in the north city. That was the straw that broke the camel's back. They got pissed off, went off and got tooled up and started looking for the guy who threatened them. They were going to kill him. Things had gone too far.'

The IRA decided against visiting McKevitt. When news of the earlier threats reached him, he reacted in a cool and calculated way. He sent messages to high ranking members of the IRA warning them to watch their step.

THE WITHDRAWAL OF overt surveillance on the Army Council lasted just a few days — enough for them to organise the ceasefire. After that, it went back to what it had been like before the meeting with Fr. Reid.

'The Special Branch was giving us a really, really hard time. They would be waiting for you outside the house and would follow you everywhere, a few feet behind the car. They used to run people off the road all the time. They were covert and very overt. They sat outside one volunteer's house in Cork for two months after Omagh. Two uniformed garda actually sat in a car outside the house all day and all night. They didn't move,' a member of the Army Council recalled.

While the Government and the security services proclaimed that the RIRA was now finished, the truth was that within weeks of the Omagh bombing they began regrouping.

Jennings' analysis had been correct. The ceasefire was a tactical move to give McKevitt and his army some breathing space. By the end of October, the dissidents had elected a new leadership and were preparing to unleash a new campaign in the name of Óglaigh na hÉireann.

THE OMAGH BOMBING had made a powerful impact on Ireland and the Government. Although Bertie Ahern promised the public that the RIRA would be hunted down with all the rigors of the law, in reality the Government took a more pragmatic approach. It hoped the RIRA would disband.

When the Government was warned that McKevitt was reorganising, the Taoiseach and Mansergh made a last effort to stop the violence. Mansergh was told to meet McKevitt face to face and push for disbandment.

The meeting was organised under a veil of top secrecy. Mansergh had met the 32 County Sovereignty Movement prior to the Omagh bombing but discontinued the dialogue when he realised RIRA was on a war footing.

The Government now hoped the RIRA would embrace some form of constitutional politics or dialogue. They were hopeful that some form of agreement could be reached because McKevitt had sought to enter into dialogue following the Omagh bombing. Mansergh had declined the invitation for ethical reasons: the political fallout would also have been beyond comprehension if the details of any such meeting were ever revealed.

Mansergh now had a change of heart. The RIRA ceasefire was four months old and the organisation had not engaged in any paramilitary activity although Crime and Security maintained that McKevitt had no intention of reneging on his promise to create a new IRA.

In mid December, Mansergh sent a secret communication to Fr. Reid. He said he wanted to meet McKevitt in person, face to face.

Fr. Reid didn't ask any questions and set about making the necessary arrangements. Working with absolute discretion, he sent a message to McKevitt asking him to attend a meeting in the Redemptorist monastery in Dundalk during Christmas week.

McKEVITT WAS ALREADY waiting for Mansergh when he walked into the room in the monastery. Although Mansergh travelled alone, McKevitt took no chances. He was accompanied by Séamus McGrane, the RIRA Director of Training for the South.

The RIRA were uncertain about the true purpose of the meeting. McKevitt, however, was astute enough to know that Mansergh meant business. The Government representative was one of the few people in Ireland that could speak on the Taoiseach's behalf. Mansergh caught him by surprise and dispensed with the pleasantries. He told McKevitt that he had a message; the Taoiseach wanted the RIRA to disband and disappear.

Ever the fool, McKevitt was incapable of reading between the lines. He dismissed the proposition out of hand. Even if the RIRA did agree to disband, he said, members would be left defenceless to attacks by the Provisionals. The IRA, he proclaimed, would kill them all.

Mansergh had no reason to believe McKevitt who twisted and bent the truth to suit himself. Once Mansergh was sure he was wasting his time, he concluded the meeting. McKevitt was more than taken aback at Mansergh's reaction, which was polite but sharp. The two men didn't arrange to meet again. The Government had been hoodwinked into believing it could negotiate a truce with McKevitt. Now it knew the only way of dealing with McKevitt and the RIRA was through the court system.

When Mansergh walked, he was unaware that the Carty investigation was about to embark on a line of investigation that would split the RIRA, result in the arrest of key players in the Omagh atrocity and by default strike terror into the paramilitary group.

Much of the evidence gathered through the garda investigations was compiled for the Director of Public Prosecutions. The evidence was used to prosecute a number of republicans accused of RIRA offences. What follows is the evidence presented to the judges of the Special Criminal Court and their judicial colleagues in Britain as given by police and state witnesses.*

* See Appendix

12

THE CONFESSION

THROUGH THE USE of sophisticated computer software and determined police work, Carty's team had identified two mobile phones that appeared to follow the route likely to have been taken by the Omagh bomb car. Crime and Security had traced all GSM traffic that had passed through mobile phone masts erected near the border. Analysis of calls made from the two phones showed they had called each other while they travelled from Monaghan to Omagh, then back again, on the day of the bombing.

When preliminary inquiries confirmed that Colm Murphy was the registered owner of both phones, Carty moved immediately. He was convinced they had stumbled upon the communications network used by the bombers. And he was right. Now the Garda had a rough idea about who was involved.

The first phone involved was Murphy's private phone. Murphy also owned the second mobile but it was used on a daily basis by Murphy's foreman, Terence Morgan. Murphy had taken the phone from Morgan, who was unaware of its intended use and was a completely innocent party.

Crime and Security needed no encouragement to compile lists of all the calls made from Murphy's phone in the weeks prior to the

Omagh atrocity. Careful scrutiny of the bills by the intelligence department opened up a Pandora's box of information.

Among the list of names that Murphy was questioned about were a Louth-based businessman called Oliver Treanor and a man called Joe Fee. The building contractor was also questioned about a Dundalk man called Derek Brady.

Carty and Foley both took the view that it was beyond the realms of possibility that Murphy's phone just happened to be present in Omagh prior to the explosion.

Identifying the telephone traffic was the result of a lot of man-hours and hard work. After six months of following bogus leads, tip-offs and false information, the investigation team had identified just eight short conversations, which could solve the riddle of who bombed Omagh.

To ensure they had as much information as possible, the team made the decision not to arrest Murphy immediately. Rather than race ahead and make a mistake, Crime and Security were asked to monitor his movements and begin intercepting his telephone calls. Jennings saw to the request without delay.

Carty's strategy involved surprise. He wanted to catch Murphy unaware. He wanted to know everything. If Murphy played a key role, the gardaí rightly suspected he would still be in regular contact with the conspirators. The decision seemed reasonable but the operation itself was called off in weeks. Murphy no longer spoke to the RIRA.

This became apparent to Crime and Security within weeks. The transcripts of his personal calls concerned his family and business life; there was no mention of the RIRA.

At that moment, when all the necessary background checks were completed, Carty gave the green light to arrest the republican.

COLM MURPHY WAS arrested at his home at Jordan's Corner in Ravensdale outside Dundalk shortly after 6 a.m. on 21 February 1999, almost six months after the bombing. Foley directed the operation, instructing his detectives to literally pull the suspect out of his bed.

Murphy was a seasoned republican, who had been arrested several times before. Foley told the investigation team they would only get one chance to get Murphy. There could be no mistakes.

When the search team entered his home, he was told to get dressed, frogmarched out the door, and put into an unmarked garda car. He was then driven at speed to Monaghan Garda Station for three days of interrogation. Murphy had been through the arrest process several times before but he noted the gardaí were acting slightly differently this time. There is no doubt that he anticipated he would be arrested, but he did not suspect the investigation team would have any hard evidence on him; this was his biggest mistake.

The interrogation of a suspect is the most important part of any investigation. Interrogators must watch an interviewee like a hawk. If a suspect shows the slightest sign of confessing, it must be seized. Foley and the investigation team had gathered the night before to discuss the interview.

The plan was simple. There would be three interrogation teams. They would have on average two hours to interview the suspect before he was entitled to take a break. Each would ask Murphy simple questions and try pressuring him into making a confession. The team could prove categorically that his mobile was present in Omagh at the time of the bombing. The phones also linked him to the Banbridge bombing of 1 August.

Once Murphy had confirmed that his phones had not been stolen or lost, he would then be confronted with the technical evidence and called to account. Whatever his reaction, he would face criminal charges.

AT 8.25 A.M. DETECTIVE Gardaí Liam Donnelly and John Fahy escorted Murphy into the interrogation room situated on the second floor of the Monaghan station. The room itself was small and contained a Formica table and three chairs.

Murphy took his seat and sat facing his two adversaries. The door was then closed. One of the detectives pressed a button, which switched on a red warning light to let others know the room was in use. And so began his interrogation.

Fahy asked the first question.

'Were you ever in Omagh?'

This didn't unnerve Murphy and he responded without thinking. 'Never in my entire life—never.'

These were the words the gardaí wanted to hear, although Murphy had no way of knowing he was preparing the groundwork for his own demise. Fahy asked if he had ever driven through the village of Auchnacloy. He said he had but only en-route to somewhere else.

Murphy appeared confident and self-assured, which led the two detectives to conclude that he had not planted the bomb himself. He had the appearance of a man who believed he could not be charged for the Omagh bombing; either because he was innocent, or he believed he couldn't be charged if he wasn't physically there. He was wrong on the second count.

Murphy was honest insofar as he told the gardaí he had spent the afternoon of 15 August drinking with friends in the Emerald Bar. Like many others, he learned of the bombing by watching news bulletins.

Donnelly remained silent while Fahy continued to ask questions which Murphy interpreted as innocent and meaningless.

The interrogators then came straight to the point. Fahy changed tact and began to mention the names of those who appeared on his mobile phone bills. The line of questioning was aimed at worrying Murphy, who had no information as to what the gardaí did or did not know.

Fahy asked if he knew Derek Brady from Dundalk. From this moment on, Murphy adopted a new policy of answering everything he could without saying anything.

'He used to work for me—I let him off four or five months ago. I last saw him about one week ago in the Emerald Bar.'

'Why did you let Brady go?' inquired Fahy.

'The foreman usually says who he wants to let go and keep. About five months ago the foreman at DCU, Dublin, wanted Brady let go.'

'Did Brady's departure coincide with the Omagh bombing?'
Murphy said it had.

Part of the strategy to get Murphy talking involved changing the
topics of conversation without notice. The aim was to hinder
Murphy's thought process. The strategy was reliant on throwing
Murphy off balance by introducing the topic of Omagh in terms of
a massacre rather than a republican attack.

As soon as he would answer one specific question, Fahy would ask
him to condemn the bombing.

'I'm not in the business of condemning. It's just a tragedy,' retorted
Murphy.

'Have you any remorse for Omagh?'

'No, I haven't. Omagh is just an awful tragedy.'

Once he started answering questions, he had crossed the line. Both
sides knew the constant stream of questions and answers back and
forth was a prelude to a confession. This was like a game of chess,
only the stakes were much higher.

The gardaí watched every expression on Murphy's face with
microscopic attention. His body language betrayed him. He had the
look of a man in serious trouble. Fahy kept asking questions.

'What about the Dalys?'

'They don't work for me but I know them and sometimes put work
their way.'

'What about Séamus Daly?,' asked Fahy.

'I got him a job in Dublin.'

Donnelly now spoke for the first time. He introduced the topic of
the Banbridge bombing. The detective made no mention of the
telephone evidence. That would be presented to the suspect later.

If the detectives were hoping the mention of Banbridge would
intimidate Murphy, they must have been disappointed. He
remained calm and focused.

In an attempt to keep the communication going, Donnelly raised
the current status of republicanism asking Murphy if he was proud
of his political beliefs.

'As proud as I have to be.'

IN THE DAYS prior to the dawn arrest, Foley had drafted an 11-page document on the Omagh bombing. The document outlined the sequence of events that precipitated the attack, including the theft of the bomb car, the construction of the bomb device and the delivery of the warning calls.

The document also contained diagrams of the telephone traffic between Murphy's two phones The last three pages were titled 'General information on Colm Murphy'. This section of the report was a synopsis of Murphy's career in the IRA.

The briefing document ended with the words, 'Due to Colm Murphy's associates and activities he is regarded as a leading member of RSF and Continuity Army Council.'

Fahy and Donnelly had studied the report, the thrust of which highlighted Murphy's commitment to republicanism. This is why the detectives continually returned to politics before asking about the Omagh bombing.

They knew Murphy would engage in any conversation on the Peace Process. Donnelly used the opportunity to develop a stronger relationship, almost appearing sympathetic to the republican. The detectives were playing a long game.

Murphy was subjected to five interviews in total during his first day in custody.

At 1.35 p.m. Kieran King and Tony Reidy interviewed him for two hours. Ten minutes after the second interview ended, two detectives from the National Bureau of Criminal Investigation, Gerard McGrath and Bernie Hanley, began interrogating the republican. They concluded the interview at 5.25 p.m.

Almost two hours later, at 6.50 p.m., Murphy was brought back into the same interview room. This time his adversaries were again Tony Reidy and Kieran King. He was questioned until 8.55 p.m.

At 9.30 p.m. when he thought the detectives on the inquiry had left for the night, Donnelly and Fahy returned. They interviewed him until 11.52 p.m.

Donnelly led the interrogation. It was now time to introduce hard evidence. The detective came straight to the point.

'Can you explain how your phone was in Banbridge on the day of the bomb there?'

Tired and worn out, Murphy was somewhat taken aback by the direct approach. He said he had no idea.

Donnelly asked again.

'Who has access to your phone regularly?' Murphy denied knowing anything. Fahy interjected, putting more pressure on the suspect. He pointed out the obvious.

'It is a clear fact that your phone was in Omagh on 15 August,' he said, not mincing his words. The questions panicked the prisoner.

'I was in the Emerald Bar, like I told you,' said Murphy. The prisoner's body language betrayed him at this point. He looked agitated and nervous. The more questions he was asked, the more fearful he became.

Donnelly asked him one more time.

'Who had your phone?'

'Nobody—I don't know.'

'Did you ring Terence Morgan on Saturday, 15 August 1998 at 12.41 p.m.?'

'I don't recall ringing him—I don't know if I had the phone with me.'

Fahy interjected, 'Then who did you give it to?'

'I didn't give it to anyone.'

'Did you ring Terence Morgan on your mobile at 1.13 p.m.?'

'As I said to you—I don't recall ringing him at all that day.'

'Did you ring Oliver Treanor at 14.10 p.m. on 15 August 1998?'

'I remember talking to Oliver about windows sometime around that time, but I can't remember the exact date.'

'Did you ring Patrick Daly that evening?'

'I don't know Patrick Daly.'

Fahy clarified the ambiguity. 'Who is Séamus Daly's father in Kilmurray*?'

'Pat Daly.'

'Well, did you ever ring Séamus Daly's home number?'

'I did sometimes about work.'

* Small town in north County Monaghan

The questions were asked in fast succession. As a prelude to Murphy's first night in jail, the detectives let the prisoner know that they knew he had played some role in the bombing.

He knew that every question was aimed at making him further implicate himself but he wasn't sure how.

'Was your phone stolen on 14 August 1998 or 15 August 1998?'

'Not to my knowledge,' replied Murphy. Nothing he said made sense given that his phone records showed that he used the phone the following week. To eliminate the ambiguities, Fahy asked if his phone had been missing at the time. Murphy, not knowing what to say, said he hadn't noticed but he was sure it hadn't been stolen.

'I didn't know my phone was gone until you mentioned it.'

'We didn't say it was gone—we said it was in Omagh,' said Fahy.

The truth was that he was on the verge of breaking. He had not planted the bomb and was horrified at the death toll. All he could think of saying was that he wasn't in Omagh on the day of the bombing.

This brought Donnelly back to his original question. 'Who did you give the phone to?'

But Murphy regained his composure. Informing was beyond him. He concealed his emotions as best he could and lied.

'I didn't knowingly give the phone to anyone—normally the phone is always under my control.'

Keen to undermine the alibi, Donnelly pretended to believe him and asked him to explain exactly what may have happened. The prisoner saw the opportunity and launched into a convoluted story about what could have happened. Donnelly listened to his nonsense with great patience. When Murphy had finished, he asked one simple question that clarified his guilt or innocence.

'Can you explain how your phone was in Omagh on Saturday, 15 August 1998?'

Murphy answered in the only way he could.

'I can't explain.'

THE MENTALITY SHARED by the detectives on the inquiry was determination. The massacre at Omagh had made a strong impact on the officers. The tragedy of the bombing was thus raised during the six interviews conducted with Murphy on the second day of his captivity.

The gardaí began questioning him at 8 a.m. Anthony Reidy and Kieran King began the interviews. This time things were different. Murphy refused to answer any questions. He sat with his arms folded and eyes closed until the interrogation concluded at 10 a.m.

At 10.35 a.m. he was taken back to the interview room by Hanley and McGrath. The gardaí noted that Murphy was anxious and worried. He demanded access to his solicitor. All he would say was that he had not been near Omagh on the day of the bombing. Two hours passed and he said nothing.

He returned to the interrogation room at 1.50 p.m. Hanley and McGrath had decided to continue questioning the suspect.

'It has been explained to you that your mobile telephone was used in the North of Ireland and specifically in the Omagh area on the 15 August 1998. You have already said that you had the telephone with you on that day. How do you explain that?'

'Well, what can I tell you? I wasn't in Omagh ever in my life and certainly not on the 15 August 1998. I have told you that I was in my pub in Dundalk on that day.'

'Then can you explain how your mobile was in the North on that day?'

'You can work that out yourselves.'

'Do we take it that somebody had your mobile on that day?'

'Well, I wasn't there.'

At 3.45 p.m. Fahy and Donnelly returned. As the day progressed, he gradually came to accept that there was no use in lying. His bizarre denials in the face of the simple truth made no sense. There is no doubt that the most difficult part of the inquiry was trying to build trust with the dissident. Donnelly and Fahy managed to accomplish this more than the other teams.

In this interview, Murphy admitted to Donnelly that he was scared of reprisal.

'Are you afraid of somebody, or something?'

'What do you think?'

'Are you afraid of people in the Real IRA?'

Murphy was too scared to even answer the question. The same detectives took charge of the following interrogation, which began sitting at 6.45 p.m. It was clear that he vehemently hated the RIRA for the atrocity but he would not allow himself to help the gardaí—even secretly.

Whether he took a change of heart that evening, or whether he believed he couldn't be charged with the Omagh attack, or simply felt compelled to talk, from this point onwards Murphy slowly began to tell the truth.

Sensing a change in his mood, Donnelly asked him out straight who he had given his phones to.

'I can't tell you his name—I only gave him a loan of the phones.'

'Why did you do that?'

'I couldn't refuse him, it was only the loan of phones for a day or so.'

'Why couldn't you refuse?'

'Because of my republican beliefs.'

'What did he want the phones for?'

'I didn't ask—I thought he wanted them to scout a road by a couple of cars—you'd need two phones. Maybe move some gear.'

'What do you mean by gear?'

'Rifles or something like that.'

'Where were the phones collected?'

'At the pub.'

'This guy that collected the phones. Do you know him?'

'Yes—he's one of McKevitt's men.'

'You mean the Real IRA?'

'Yes.'

'Are you in the Real IRA?'

'No, I'm not.'

'When did you get the phones back?'

'I can't remember exactly, Sunday or Monday.'

'Who gave them back, the phones?'

'The same man. I'm not going to name him.'

'What did you say to him?'

'Sure what could I say to him? Nothing—everyone knew that Omagh was a disaster.'

'Did you realise when you got them back what they wanted them for?'

'Yeah.'

THE ADMISSION WAS a massive breakthrough. Foley, who was briefed on an hourly basis by the interview teams, relayed the news to Carty. The statement was in effect the beginning of a confession. Murphy's guarded account of what exactly happened before and after the Omagh bombing was corroborated point by point by the technical evidence supplied by Crime and Security. At that moment, after news of the confession spread, the inquiry team felt elated. For this reason, Foley decided to continue interviewing the prisoner should he have a change of heart. At 10.48 p.m. Hanley and McGrath re-entered the interview room. The decision to keep interviewing the suspect proved to be the most judicious decision made by Foley.

Murphy spoke to his interrogators with a frankness and honesty that none of them expected. He finally admitted he had taken possession of Terence Morgan's mobile phone on 14 August.

'I got that off him on the Friday evening, and gave it to the fellow also, he wanted it to cover moving some gear.'

'When did he give them back to you?'

'Either Sunday or Monday. I'm not too sure.'

'Did he tell you they were used for planting a bomb in Omagh?'

'No, he didn't have to say it. He wouldn't talk about it. It was a disaster, nobody set out to kill anybody in Omagh, it was just a complete mess, a disaster.'

AFTER 24 HOURS in custody, Murphy was talking freely, albeit through the side of his mouth. The detectives, much to the disbelief of the inquiry team, were getting a first hand account of how the bombers reacted in the immediate aftermath of the bombing. There was more to come. As the night wore on, Murphy began talking in loose terms about the CIRA.

Hanley asked if the CIRA had been involved in recent bomb attacks. Murphy answered the question without hesitating.

'Yeah, there was the Markethill one and another one somewhere in Fermanagh.'

'Do the CAC propose to continue bombing?'

'The policy would be to continue but we wouldn't have the support now. A lot of people see the armed strife passed with few exceptions.'

'Had you any operational role in Omagh or Banbridge?'

'Jesus, no way! That's Mickey McKevitt's role.'

'Did McKevitt personally organise these bombs and the others that were intercepted?'

'He probably would. I don't know; it would depend on his position in the Real IRA. There would be different levels.'

The interview concluded shortly before midnight. Murphy was taken back to his holding cell and promptly fell asleep. The detectives were too tired to celebrate. Before they departed, they briefed Foley on the most recent admissions. It was not over yet. They would begin more interviews first thing in the morning.

CARTY AND FOLEY knew they had enough to press conspiracy charges against the prisoner. Murphy's own admissions underpinned the evidence gleaned by Crime and Security. In other words, everything that Murphy said could be corroborated independently by analysis of the phone calls made from his mobile phone. The republican would end up being the prosecution's own witness.

Suffering from elation and exhaustion in equal measure, Fahy and Donnelly arrived for work at 9 a.m. the following morning. They took Murphy from his cell at 10 a.m. and began the final round of interviews. Murphy realised he had said far too much the previous night. Now he was saying nothing.

Hanley and McGrath were more successful.

'From our inquiries, we believe that it was Séamus Daly from Inniskeen who had use of the phones on 15 August,' said Hanley, not really expecting an answer. He was in for a surprise.

'That's the lad I gave them to. You knew all along,' said Murphy.

'Did you give him your phone for the bomb in Banbridge on 1 August?'

'No, not him.'

'You have told us that you gave your phone to Séamus Daly to move gear. You knew it was going to be used in some criminal act.'

'Oh yes I did, but I didn't think he would use it for other phone calls.'

'You know Daly was working with the Real IRA, who were involved in planting bombs in the North. Did you know your phone was going to be used for that, isn't that what you meant by gear?'

'Yes, I knew it would be used for moving bombs. I knew these fellas were involved in moving bombs to Northern Ireland to bomb targets.'

'Did you have any worries about them using your phone for moving explosives to the North?'

'No I didn't. I wouldn't have given it to them otherwise.'

'You have said that you are a member of the Continuity Army Council and there you are helping members of the Real IRA.'

'I am a republican. They knew if they asked me for help, I would give it.'

'There's a link between Banbridge and Omagh with your phone. Did you give it to Séamus Daly that day as well?'

'No, I gave it to Joe Fee. I mean, he took it and used it.'

'Was it Joe Fee who had it in Banbridge that day?'

'I can't say. I don't know. I have fallen out with him. Your people will know we haven't been seen together for months.'

'Was the falling out since the bombing of Banbridge and Omagh?'

'Yes it was.'

'What was it about?'

'Jesus, what do you think? Those fucking disasters—Omagh and Banbridge.'

Colm Murphy was interviewed twice more. At 4.15 p.m. Fahy and Donnelly took a further statement from him. He said little. Three hours later, at 7.30 p.m., he made yet another statement to Hanley and McGrath. This resembled an act of contrition.

Hanley noted for the record that Murphy was deeply distressed about the Omagh massacre. He asked him if he was upset over the loss of lives.

'Jesus, you know I am. I think the loss of innocent lives was a disaster.'

'You must accept some responsibility for the loss of life.'

'I have told you what I know. If I could change things I would. The fact that I am co-operating with you is the sign that I take responsibility for my actions but other people have caused this disaster.'

Those were his last words.

When Foley received the news, he contacted the Director of Public Prosecutions without delay. Copies of all the statements were faxed to Dublin for a legal opinion. Murphy was held in custody.

On the morning of 24 February 1999 he was formally charged with conspiracy to cause an explosion likely to endanger life or cause injury. He was the first person to be charged in connection with the Omagh bombing.

He was driven to the Special Criminal Court in Dublin looking dishevelled and tired that same morning. His appearance lasted no more than five minutes. Foley stood into the witness box to say that when arrested and cautioned, Murphy replied that he had nothing to say. The court refused to grant him bail. He was taken to Portlaoise Prison where he entered the republican wing.

13

ANOTHER INFORMANT

THE REAL IRA Army Council never had any sincere intention of abiding by the ceasefire announced in the wake of the Omagh bombing. The declaration was a tactical move designed to give the Army Council breathing space and time to consider its options. A militant republican organisation to the core, the RIRA used the temporary lull in operations to engage in essential work: arms smuggling.

The arms deal negotiated with the Continuity IRA in the Balkans had come to fruition. However, the Army Council appointed a volunteer from Dundalk to oversee the deal. In typical McKevitt style, details of the venture were withheld from the membership. They knew in general terms what was happening but the Army Council gave them no specifics.

In accordance with the Army Council's instructions, the RIRA man made his way to Croatia in late May 1999 arriving in the coastal town of Split, where he booked into the Hotel Bellevue. He was accompanied by two people from County Armagh.

From Ireland, the group travelled to France where the RIRA man rented a white Citroen van in the northwest. It is not known what route they took to Croatia but the journey probably took around nine days. The operation ran smoothly from beginning to end, but as a precaution, Ante Cubelic, the arms dealer and IRA sympathiser, was instructed to divide the haul. It made good strategic sense to import the weapons in two consignments. If the first was intercepted, there was always the possibility the second would get through, or vice versa.

Cubelic did as instructed. The first shipment was transported overland to Ireland. It was a providential operation for the RIRA; something the security services did not see. With exemplary style and cunning, the new Army Council gave the RIRA rocket launchers, detonators, lunch-box bombs, and enough guns to keep them in the war business for the next ten years.

Crime and Security learned of the operation from an informant weeks after the shipment arrived. Jennings instructed his officials to notify Box at once. The nature of the intelligence he received suggested the weapons would be used against targets in Britain but no one knew when, where, or how.

WORD OF THE arms shipment spread fast among the militant volunteers. The message was clear: the RIRA Army Council had never stopped functioning, even if they had retreated into the shadows because of Omagh. At this time, McKevitt was uncharacteristically happy for news of the arms shipment to be leaked. The acquisition of guns would help counter the negative effects of the Omagh bombing. Public loathing and informants had wreaked havoc on the RIRA, causing widespread resignations.

Even members of the RIRA Army Council had resigned in the wake of the bomb. The most senior officer to resign was the Chief of Staff, 'McGuinness'. His girlfriend had given him an ultimatum that he either leave the IRA, or she would leave him. He chose love above all else. He had also come close to prison. Foley's team found a mortar component in his home and pushed to charge him. He escaped because the same component fitted into a home heating system. The DPP would not run with the charges.

The resignations of people like 'McGuinness' were embarrassing. When he looked back and examined the history of the RIRA, McKevitt concluded it had been a failure in almost every sense.

Privately he admitted that he had made serious mistakes. He now had weapons but no men, no public support and not even the admiration of the republican community. He came to realise that no faction of the IRA could operate without a competent political party willing to disseminate propaganda on its behalf. He concluded that this problem had been an insurmountable stumbling block from the very beginning.

The 32 County Sovereignty Movement had fooled itself when claiming it influenced public or even republican opinion; the truth was that it was a complete failure. Bernadette Sands had made no impact on the consciousness of the Irish public.

Yet he persevered. He would not give up and so brought the remnants of the RIRA together. He demanded proper training, tight security, and secrecy. This was going to be a dangerous and risky undertaking. The emphasis was on building a new IRA with one added ingredient. The inception of this new IRA faction would be dependent on the ability of a political party to advocate its reason for being. He knew he had only one choice—to align himself with Republican Sinn Féin. If he had any wisdom, or even common sense, he would have known that this was not possible.

TWO YEARS EARLIER, the Quartermaster, after serious consultations with 'McGuinness', had ruled out the possibility of the same proposition.

The dissidents had regarded Ó Brádaigh as a dinosaur trapped in the abstention politics of 1986. Abstentionism was the holy grail of RSF. It was the doctrine that the Irish Parliament, the Oireachtas, should not be recognised. When Sinn Féin decided in 1986 to end its policy of abstentionism, Ó Brádaigh and some colleagues walked. Some 12 years later, they were still talking about it.

'They were obsessed by abstentionism. When Ó Brádaigh dies they will all go with him. We felt they were living in a time warp,' said one member of the RIRA Army Council.

Though in the transpiring years, things changed considerably. RSF no longer looked on McKevitt with any degree of respect; they saw him as a liability. The massacre at Omagh had ruled out any formal alliance; it would be political suicide.

RSF had been more than aware of how close they had come to obliteration when some of their members participated in the Omagh bombing. They regarded as a godsend the fact they were not asked to explain the actions of their volunteers.

McKevitt was gaining allies, however. Uncertainty about the Omagh bombing afforded the Quartermaster the chance to attract some recruits. And so for a second time, again without any political organisation in place, but armed with modern weaponry, he began the slow process of building another army.

The genesis for this organisation came from McKevitt himself. Rather than move to take volunteers from the Provisional IRA, he moved to reunite the dissident groups: the CIRA, the INLA and what remained of the RIRA. The unified body would be called Óglaigh na hÉireann, or the IRA once again. They dropped the name 'RIRA' because it was tarnished as a result of the Omagh bombing.

The group met for the first time on a beach on the Inishowen Peninsula in County Donegal in July of the same year, shortly after the Croatian weapons arrived. The group's inception mirrored that of the RIRA. The republicans elected an Army Council and Executive. The membership of the Army Council bore some resemblance to that of the first RIRA leadership, most notably McKevitt retained the position of Quartermaster General.

Séamus McGrane remained Director of Training while Liam Campbell took the title Director of Operations.

At the time, McKevitt, McGrane, and Campbell desperately wanted to align themselves to RSF, so it was only natural that someone from the CIRA was elected. This man was Mickey Donnelly.

He stood six feet tall, possessed a sombre attitude and wore a long beard that made him look like a monk. His comical appearance belied a deep-rooted view of republicanism. As the CIRA's chief activist in County Derry, he made no secret of his absolute hatred for the IRA and Martin McGuinness.

But there was another purpose to his appointment. While McKevitt was using Donnelly to attract members of the CIRA into his ranks, he also wanted him for his American friends. Every move McKevitt made was carefully chosen and had an intended purpose; this was no different. The new IRA needed money. RSF had spent years building up an enviable base of American, cash rich benefactors.

Donnelly had met most of these. McKevitt was aware that there was one man that he had become particularly friendly with. His name was Dave Rupert—a New Yorker with deep pockets and an equally deep commitment to republicanism. The Quartermaster's instincts were seldom wrong but this time the lure of hard cash clouded his judgement. Rupert was a spy.

AT 51 YEARS of age, Rupert was in the throes of middle age when the Federal Bureau of Investigation (FBI) recruited him. Sallow skinned, six feet six inches tall, and very broad, the man who spoke with a deep American drawl was an unlikely informant. However, all the warning signs were there if McKevitt or the RIRA had cared to notice.

The most obvious was that Rupert had no Irish blood. He was of the Protestant faith and born into a devout family in St. Lawrence County in New York. His father was Canadian; his mother came from the backwater town of Madrid in upstate New York. Neither was of Irish descent.

Colourful, entertaining, and bright, he was also a philanderer and con artist. His professional life had been a disaster.

In his formative years in business, Rupert proved himself to be ruthless and capable of anything. He betrayed anyone who trusted him; there was nothing he wouldn't do.

He had an astonishing enthusiasm for building up large companies, which later collapsed because of financial misconduct and deceit on his behalf. At one stage, through a mixture of raw nerve and hoodwinking, he built up a formidable haulage company, owning 39 lorries and 110 trailers.

He gave the impression of a small town boy who had come good, but this was a lie. He was a financial disaster. He owed money to creditors everywhere and he never missed the opportunity to defraud people, even those closest to him.

The end came in 1992 when his trucking business went into receivership after an employee killed three students in a Kentucky road traffic accident. He was sued for $50 million. Rather than challenge a court case he could not win, he liquidated the company and declared himself bankrupt. In the intervening years, he dabbled with the Mafia, engaged in smuggling and showed his willingness to do anything for money.

A combination of love and lust introduced him to Ireland. In the Spring of 1992, he began dating Deborah Murphy. Throughout his life Rupert had shown himself to have no problem in attracting the opposite sex. One night when the two were out drinking, she asked him to go on holiday to Ireland. Intoxicated, Rupert proclaimed, 'Sounds like a good idea to me.'

They later flew into Shannon in County Clare and toured the Ring of Kerry for two weeks. The rugged landscape and the sincere temperament of the Irish struck Rupert; he felt at home. He would later say Ireland made him feel young again; the country revitalised his soul. His relationship with Murphy ended but he returned a year later with another woman, Linda Vaughan. She came from Tallahassee, Florida, and worked as a lobbyist at the State Senate. Vaughan had won a Seán McBride award for her commitment to Irish reunification. She gave Rupert his first introduction to republicanism.

On his second visit to Ireland, the couple toured around the north west. Vaughan's view of the political situation in Ireland was one shared by RSF. Her visit to County Donegal was planned to coincide with a republican commemoration for the IRA hunger strikers in the town of Bundoran. Never an organisation to miss the opportunity to have an influential American lobbyist address their members, Vaughan was invited to the ceremony as a guest of honour by RSF. Rupert accompanied her to the gathering, which was discreetly monitored by Special Branch. The tall American cut a striking figure among the crowds and was quickly noticed by the gardaí. In reality he had little interest in the proceedings but acted in a polite manner to everyone he met.

That afternoon Vaughan introduced him to Joe O'Neill and Vincent Murray. The two men were militant republicans, although this was lost on the American. With that as a starting point, Vaughan was asked back for drinks and food.

Rupert engaged in polite conversation with O'Neill who discussed politics. It didn't occur to him that he was dealing with a faction of the IRA; he knew nothing about Irish politics.

Rupert was not taken by republicanism—but he was mesmerised by Ireland. The beauty of Donegal Bay, the vista of the Blue Stack Mountains and the rugged beauty and mystique of Slieve League, the highest sea cliffs in Europe, captured his senses. He was smitten.

The couple returned to America. In what would soon become standard practice, he parted ways with Vaughan but not his love of Ireland.

He returned to celebrate Christmas 1992. This time he travelled alone arriving at Shannon Airport. The New Yorker hired a car and drove along the west coast through the bleak landscape of the Burren. There was no set plan to the journey. Rupert spent a few days here and there, choosing to stop when something of interest caught his attention. After several days of touring and relaxation, he headed for County Sligo where he looked up his old acquaintances, O'Neill and Murray. He built an immediate rapport with O'Neill on that visit. The two men enjoyed each other's company. They discussed Irish politics, the events of the day, the state of the world and general business well into the early hours. During the day, the two would drive to scenic locations on sight-seeing expeditions. Rupert had more than a pleasant respite from the pace of life in Illinois. The figure of the giant American hadn't gone unnoticed, however.

DETECTIVES ATTACHED TO Special Branch had observed Rupert with O'Neill when the two were driving near Bundoran. The car they travelled in was traced back to Boland's National Car

Rental/Hertz Rental, a reputable firm that operated out of Shannon Airport. In accordance with procedure, the detectives completed a comprehensive intelligence form, which they sent to Crime and Security. Rupert was now a marked man.

Crime and Security began tracking his movements. The report filed by Special Branch in County Sligo was one of the most important ever assessed by Jennings, who was at the time in charge of intelligence. From his own secret sources in the CIRA, the Chief was sure that Rupert wasn't a sworn member or even a supporter, but even with this rationale, it was unclear as to why he was associating with O'Neill, who made no secret of his political beliefs. Jennings had not met Rupert, but realised he could be very useful. Now Jennings took action and contacted his counterparts at the FBI.

He asked them to approach Rupert. In many ways, Rupert was a source of wonderment for Jennings and the other analysts at Crime and Security. Jennings recognised Rupert for what he was. As far as he was concerned, he was a shady American who could be recruited as an informant. The surprise was that the Americans thought this was a good idea.

Patrick Ed Buckley was the FBI Special Agent appointed to make the approach. He knew how to have conversations that never took place. He ran several investigations into IRA operations in America. The relationship between Crime and Security and the FBI was the kind that both valued, though the American's kinship with MI5 was stronger. Later it was decided that recruiting Rupert would serve the interests of both Ireland and the US.

Jennings was an advocate of informants. He believed that a well-tested human source was more important than hundreds of pages of transcripts from eavesdropping devices. Informants tend to participate in the day to day running of organisations, seeking out information, gathering facts and most importantly—they give their opinions. These people were far more vital than any telephone intercept.

Though they dared not admit it, Crime and Security had often found Americans naïve about the IRA, but the agent ordered to oversee the recruitment was different. Tubby, overweight, and rough and ready, Buckley operated out of the Chicago field office and was generally known as a man with no inhibitions. He undertook the secret, covert action at Jennings' request. The most important intelligence task was approaching the informant for the first time.

Buckley went straight for the kill. He called to Rupert's office in South Holland shortly after he returned from one of his trips to Ireland. In the paperwork and intelligence files sent from Dublin to Chicago, Crime and Security had included two photographs: one of Rupert with Joseph O'Neill, and one of Rupert with Vincent Murray.

Buckley planned to produce these on introduction. This would give him impact; let Rupert know that he meant business. Rupert had initially refused to accept Buckley's visit thinking he was investigating him for fraud, however, Buckley persevered, eventually storming into Rupert's office. Tradecraft taught him that first impressions last longest. He immediately produced the photographs and asked how he knew the two republicans.

The physical and psychological effect of this was to stun Rupert. This was risky business. Buckley watched Rupert's every move, scanning his reflexes and body language for any telltale signs of guilt. A mixture of shock and fear was evident on Rupert's face, no matter how hard he tried to conceal it. He was agitated. He became even more agitated when Buckley alluded to the fact that his friends were both IRA men. The revelation took Rupert by surprise. His friends, he said, were both republicans but that was all.

Buckley now made his move. He asked Rupert if he was willing to cooperate with the FBI. Rupert took his card. He knew the meaning of the agent's words; Rupert was no fool.

RUPERT DIDN'T INTIMATE to Buckley if he was interested or not. He did nothing. He continued visiting Ireland under the discreet watch of Special Branch. In the autumn of 1994, this led to fresh inquiries from Crime and Security to establish if he could be recruited or not. Buckley was once again sent to visit Rupert. This time he made sure he was listened to.

There is something in a policeman's character that marks them out as police officers. Buckley walked past Rupert's secretary and straight into his office. He took a seat, folded his arms, crossed his legs, and started making demands. His intentions were obvious, however, Rupert's were not so obvious. He wanted money.

Sensing the opportunity, the first thing Rupert did was to bluff the agent into thinking that he could provide valuable information. In the most sincere way he could, he told Buckley he had no problem helping the police, provided that the FBI paid for the trips he made to Ireland. Rupert indicated he had a lot of information about IRA operations and personnel. This was nonsense; he knew nothing. Thinking he had recruited an IRA insider, Buckley agreed. The truth was that Rupert knew little or nothing. He was playing along for a few dollars.

However, once he agreed to work for the FBI, he took a deep interest in everything O'Neill and Murray had to say. And so another black operation began.

FIRST HE SPREAD the word that he was deeply interested in RSF. Rupert became a spy.

To O'Neill and Murray, Rupert had always given the impression of being an honourable man. They did not suspect a thing.

When he returned to Ireland with his new wife Maureen Brennan two days after Christmas in 1994, he now saw himself as being a central player in an intelligence operation. He showed no hesitation or fear; he was a spy and he loved it. He took notes of everything O'Neill and Murray said and listened attentively to their conversations. He felt nothing: no shame, no remorse, and no fear.

If Buckley was expecting Rupert to deliver grade A intelligence information that could assist the gardaí, he was sorely mistaken. When he returned to Chicago in January 1995, he had little news, though he had obtained a free holiday.

THE BLACK OPERATION proceeded without hindrance. In October 1995, O'Neill flew to Chicago to attend a fundraiser for the Irish Freedom Committee run by Frank O'Neill, an Irish American activist. This was a very important opportunity for Rupert. He had been availing of free holidays and now he needed to prove his worth by showing that his information was accurate and trustworthy. Some of the intelligence analysts did not trust Rupert, believing him to be intellectually unstable. On the other hand, Buckley needed Rupert to work. He had invested funds and time in recruiting him. If he threw in the towel, it would reflect badly on him.

From the moment that O'Neill arrived, he was under surveillance. That evening he was joined by Rupert at the dinner dance. There were about 100 people in attendance. The FBI loved these occasions. As far as the FBI was concerned, it was an opportunity to touch base with the grass roots, to find out what was going on— insiders gossip. In the knowledge that the FBI was watching everything, Rupert went fishing for information, making sure he was introduced to the right people. He was determined to make the right connections. His plan succeeded. Among the list of influential republicans with whom he shook hands was Frank O'Neill himself.

Sitting down to dinner the same evening, Rupert listened attentively to Joe O'Neill, who delivered a charged speech. Much of the address was republican rhetoric, but not all of it. O'Neill had been preparing to make the speech for weeks and had decided to make a direct reference to a CIRA operation. In the crowded room, and surrounded by republicans, he joked about planning a surprise for Charles, the Prince of Wales, if he had visited the west of Ireland during a tour of Ireland several month earlier. A conservationist, environmental campaigner and naturalist, Prince Charles had wanted to travel to Mullaghmore in County Sligo where his uncle, Lord Mountbatten, had perished at the hands of the IRA in 1979. However, the trip was cancelled after a bomb was found in Classybawn Castle where he was due to stay.

Rupert watched the speech from his seat. The joke went down well among the crowd. Rupert wasn't quite sure if O'Neill was serious. He memorised the details as best he could. When the night ended, he reported back to Buckley as to what had happened at this function. He did not know how much money was raised. The entry fee was $100 and raffled tickets were $10 each. There were cash prizes that night, the biggest being $10,000. Rupert's decision to relay the story saved him.

When copies of his intelligence reports were furnished to Crime and Security, the gardaí took notice. Headquarters had received a report from Special Branch concerning an explosive device discovered by the caretaker of Classybawn Estate in Mullaghmore. Suspicions were aroused after the lock on the gates had been cut. When he began checking for signs of a forced entry, the caretaker saw barrels close to the main door of the Castle. The device was crude but deadly.

RUPERT HAD COME good. Ever the ruthless businessman, he saw the opportunity provided by the IRA. He had at the back of his mind that he would like to try his hand at the bar business in Ireland. Certainly, he did have previous experience in the trade in the US.

From Rupert's perspective, everything was about timing and anything was possible. He waited for some time before raising the delicate issue with Buckley. In typical form, when he decided to move he came straight to the point and asked him if the FBI would be interested in helping out with the expenses in return for whatever information he could acquire for him. Buckley made no commitment, but offered to run the idea past his bosses. Incredibly, the answer was yes, conditional on him selling his own trucking business. He sold all his worldly possessions and flew to Ireland with his wife. Ironically, O'Neill made the whole enterprise possible. Rupert had told the republican of his plans and he had taken him to view suitable pubs.

He had found a suitable pub business to lease. It was called the Drowes Bar and was situated in the sleepy village of Tullaghan in County Leitrim.

WHEN HE INITIALLY decided to relocate to Ireland, Rupert was a FBI source. In keeping with protocol, Buckley instructed him to talk frequently with Jennings. One of the garda's greatest talents was his ability to decipher good information from nonsense.

'If you out the nonsense, you get to the truth,' was Jennings' mantra. From his time on the ground in Special Branch, he had learned to spot the liars. He considered Rupert to be an asset, but not a great one. The spy would call Jennings frequently but he never provided a shred of worthwhile intelligence. Jennings saw him for what he was—a con artist way out of his depth.

Rupert's decision to relocate turned into a financial disaster. Old habits die hard. He was incapable of running a solvent business. His accounting methods were questionable. Of course, this was a by-product of the intelligence operation, though this was lost on Rupert. Desperate and broke, he turned to Crime and Security demanding money. He arranged to meet Jennings at a safe location—this time in the back of a van near Mullingar, County Westmeath.

Rupert was told the harsh reality of his situation. Virtually every scrap of information he provided was gossip, much of which was already known. Convinced of his own self-importance, Rupert made a last push for money. It was no good. From the beginning, Jennings knew that Rupert was a weak resource. He had spearheaded the drive to recruit him and pushed the project from the sidelines. He wanted as many human resources in the IRA as could be recruited. As far as he was concerned, Rupert was simply another agent. Not bad, not good either.

He was an American who had a jaundiced view of the world. He knew nothing about the IRA, and most importantly he didn't understand the mindset of the republican movement. It was beyond him.

Rupert didn't like a word of it. He expected financial aid. When it wasn't forthcoming, he called his lawyer and instructed him to contact Jennings at once. Rather than trying to protect the informant's identity, the lawyer said Rupert would go public with his story if he weren't paid cash immediately. Jennings answered the threat the only way he knew how.

If Rupert wished to say he gave the gardaí information on the IRA, that was his business, however, he thought it prudent to give some advice. If Rupert went public, Rupert would be murdered. The sound of his voice convinced Rupert's attorney of his seriousness.

Having failed to extort any money from Crime and Security, Rupert decided to return to the US. He raised the issue of financial support with Buckley and the FBI. According to his reports of the time, he saw the FBI as his only support. He didn't want to work with the gardaí. With the Provisionals on ceasefire and fully committed to constitutional politics, the idea very much appealed to the Americans. Rather than abandoning him, they created a special category for him. He was offered a contract to map the dissident republican movement in America and Ireland.

IN THE MIDST of his shady work, Rupert was summonsed to a meeting with Buckley. The two met at a field office in Chicago where Buckley came straight to the point: he asked Rupert if he would spy for MI5.

MI5 were deeply interested in the CIRA. Not that Rupert knew much about them. The assessment by MI5 was the CIRA was becoming a serious threat to British interests. Rupert signalled he would. He would raise the issue of payment at a future date. It was an unwritten rule that the Garda would be left out of the picture.

Relations between MI5 and Crime and Security were constructive but nothing compared to the allegiance sworn to the Americans by the British. It was an oath that the two agencies took seriously. MI5 didn't want Crime and Security to know they were now involved with Rupert. This was partly for professional concerns but equally for reasons of jealousy. MI5 had top grade intelligence on the internal structures and rivalries in the IRA; they just couldn't analyse or interpret the information; Crime and Security could.

The fact that MI5 could not accurately predict opinion in the IRA almost drove a minority element within T-branch to distraction. That this was well known to the British government and the Northern Ireland Office did not help relations.

Recruiting Rupert would provide MI5 with some independent information on the dissidents. In essence they would have their own spy in place, which made perfect sense and good planning.

RUPERT STRUCK A deal and reached an agreement that would see him earning $1.25 million. From now on, every time he visited Ireland, he would first stop off in London to meet MI5. To keep MI5 and the FBI fully informed, he agreed to e-mail what he learned in each visit. To ensure the operation could not be compromised, he would encrypt the e-mails. This way, they couldn't be read by anyone else.

Rupert was an avid spy. He almost saw himself as a FBI agent assigned to a dangerous task. The deception worked because no one wanted to believe they were being duped, or were complicit in the spying operation. All the warning signs were ignored. Rupert managed a small business. Even if the company was thriving, it could not have sustained his lifestyle, or travelling arrangements.

FROM THE VERY beginning of the spying operation, Rupert never dared engage in any terrorism. He didn't join the IRA for military reasons; armed insurgency was not his scene. He was terrified of the IRA. He was a spy, not an undercover operative. More importantly he was not guaranteed immunity if he was caught. In other words, he didn't want to get his hands dirty, although he was participating in a dirty operation.

The spy's entire experience of militant republicanism was one of talk. The possibility of something dramatic happening never crossed his mind. When the RIRA bombed Omagh, he flew home immediately but returned to Ireland shortly afterwards.

At a RSF Ard Fheis, Rupert was introduced to Mickey Donnelly. He would provide the spy with a suitable introduction to McKevitt. The black operation involving Rupert could have easily fallen apart at this point. Donnelly was an obsessive republican. In his own mind, Rupert thought Donnelly was unstable; a hard-line advocate of violence. To his MI5 handlers, he described Donnelly as one of the most dangerous people he had ever met in Ireland. What further perturbed him was that Donnelly made no secret of ongoing talks with the RIRA. Rupert knew Donnelly was talking about McKevitt and the RIRA.

MI5 AND THE FBI zeroed in on the news. Rupert was now earning his money. The Irish desk at MI5 were more than keen to keep him in place. He met senior figures in the CIRA. He was introduced to John Joe McCusker, the second in command to Des Long, the O/C of the CIRA. Rupert met McCusker at O'Neill's home in Bundoran. Geraldine Taylor, the O/C of the CIRA's Belfast Brigade was also in attendance.

Rupert said McCusker asked him to get six single CB radios to be used for communication and possibly detonation equipment. He never explained to him how these things were meant to work and Rupert didn't ask. He was too scared. Rupert was now in the heart of dissident republicanism.

It was at this point that Donnelly spoke about ongoing meetings he was having with McKevitt. And this provided the golden opportunity for MI5 to insert an agent in the heart of the RIRA.

14

INSIDE THE SECRET ARMY

ON 29 AUGUST 1999, Rupert met with Donnelly and Philip Kent, a CIRA dissident, at Cullen's Bed & Breakfast in Bundoran. Donnelly was eager to get moving. They had to attend an important meeting at the Slieve Russell Hotel in County Cavan scheduled for that afternoon. Rupert's MI5 handlers had expressed grave concerns about this particular meeting. Once he attended, there would be no turning back. They were off to meet McKevitt.

Donnelly was trying to make an impression on McKevitt and the new improved version of the Real IRA. Donnelly figured his allegiance with Rupert was the sole reason for his nomination to the new Army Council. His analysis was on target. It was not like Donnelly to miss an opportunity to impress the leadership by introducing a prominent American fundraiser in person. This was somewhat of a coup from Donnelly's view of the prevailing situation.

The truth was that McKevitt wasn't interested in meeting anyone least of all Donnelly whom he could just about tolerate. He regarded Donnelly as an inward looking man who didn't know his own limitations, nor was he a good judge of people.

When Donnelly, Kent, and Rupert arrived at the hotel, McKevitt was nowhere to be seen. They waited for a long time. Clearly

McKevitt didn't want to attend the meeting. Donnelly was embarrassed. Kent and Rupert felt a little awkward.

Rather than leave empty handed, Donnelly asked Rupert could he borrow his mobile phone. He made a few calls eventually making contact with Séamus McGrane. Rupert listened into the conversation. Donnelly changed the meeting venue to the Four Seasons Hotel in County Monaghan, a drive of little under an hour.

Rupert did not like a word of it. The dread that he was walking into a trap was at the forefront of his mind. What if he had made a mistake? What if they knew he was a MI5 spy?

His fears were quickly proved groundless. When his party arrived at the hotel, there sitting in the lounge was McKevitt with McGrane.

The atmosphere was cordial. Rupert was introduced to the RIRA delegation. He said little, he was too scared to talk. It was apparent to him immediately that McKevitt was in charge even though he said nothing. Donnelly did the talking.

Although Rupert would later claim McKevitt talked about the RIRA, this was a lie. He never said a word of admission. Donnelly did the talking, proclaiming the new improved IRA had absorbed 98 per cent of CIRA military.

McKevitt remained stone-faced while Donnelly explained the group's new command structure, which included a 12 person Executive and an Army Council, of which no more than two delegates could be politicians.

Rupert stayed silent. He listened attentively. He didn't interject in Donnelly's speech. He wanted to give the impression that he shared an equal dislike of the Derry republican.

MI5 had profiled McKevitt many times. The best intelligence agents had briefed Rupert on what to say, which was nothing. He duly obliged.

McKevitt had an almost telepathic sense, which made him wary of strangers. The only thing McKevitt wanted from Rupert was for him to use whatever influence he possessed to coerce the CIRA into the project, and if possible to use his influence with Joe O'Neill to bring RSF on board as a political front for his new military grouping. This was a tall order.

Rupert had been well advised by his handlers. MI5 knew there were deep divisions between the Quartermaster and Ó Brádaigh. During the 1981 Hunger Strike, McKevitt had wanted to kidnap four British Lords and their sons and hold them on forced starvation as long as the Hunger Strike continued. Ó Brádaigh had blocked the plan.

McGrane made some contributions to the discussion which Rupert noted. Ever the naïve American, when Rupert heard Donnelly introduce him as Shay, he took it as short for Che Guvara.

FOR MORE THAN five years Rupert had worked as a spy against the CIRA. Now was the time to make an introductory speech aimed at arousing McKevitt's interest. He had everything prepared, the whole story and what he thought would interest the Quartermaster.

The American began by speaking about his background in computers, his relationship with the CIRA and RSF, and the republican community in the US.

McKevitt was impassive. Ice cold to the core, when Rupert finished talking, McKevitt said nothing, not even asking questions. To do so would have betrayed his nature and personality. This left Rupert in a position where he had to keep talking.

McKevitt knew the American was trying to impress him. MI5 had positioned the spy to have the broadest possible appeal to the RIRA. Although he knew nothing of any significance, Rupert was trained to say the right thing; he left the meeting promising he would endeavour to get RSF on board. There was no point in him saying anything else. And so the meeting broke up.

Rupert returned to Bundoran that evening and went back to America on 31 August. For more than 20 years, MI5 had wanted to place a spy near to McKevitt, the mastermind Quartermaster. Now the game was on.

The focus of the secret FBI and MI5 black operation now switched. Rupert was told to do everything McKevitt wanted. On his return to America, he visited Boston and New York where he spoke with Joe Dillon and John McDonagh, two members of the Irish Freedom Committee. Although McKevitt wanted RSF to act as a political front, American cash was to the forefront of his mind.

Through Rupert, MI5 moved to amalgamate the RIRA and CIRA to thwart the entire dissident movement. The operation began with baby steps. The first thing Rupert attempted was to ask the republicans who funded *Cabhair*, a support group for CIRA prisoners, to switch their allegiances to the Irish Republican Prisoners' Welfare Association, an offshoot of the 32 County Sovereignty Movement.

Besotted by a need to make an impact, Rupert became openly confrontational and hostile towards the conservative elements of American republicanism who supported Ó Brádaigh, particularly John McDonagh.

'When the Real IRA started up, he tried shift the focus over to them from Republican Sinn Féin and the Continuity. He started, using the language of the Provisionals and Sinn Féin, saying the CIRA were geriatrics; that the Real IRA was a more serious organisation,' McDonagh said later.

No one thought he was a spy. In fighting was not a new element in republicanism. McDonagh simply assumed Rupert wanted to take control of the group and its finances. The reality was that Rupert was participating in a cleverly planned and executed intelligence operation.

He tried to influence policies and shift support from the CIRA to McKevitt.

'When you join the Irish Freedom Committee, you know it supports the Continuity IRA. NORAID supported the Provisionals. He wanted to shift the focus.'

The spy's efforts in New York were fruitless but he succeeded in challenging the status quo in Boston and Chicago. In September 1999, the Chicago branch of Irish Freedom Committee held its annual fundraising function. Rupert made sure Martin Galvin was invited as a guest speaker. The event raised between $14,000 and $15,000 showing McKevitt what he could do. According to

McDonagh, the amount of cash raised gave Rupert the credibility he badly needed.

'In getting Chicago and Boston to break away, he probably got credibility, he was able to say this is how dedicated he is to the organisation.'

Rupert's modus operandi was typical of a scheme incepted by T-branch at MI5 headquarters. His arguments were clever, and ironically supported by the successes of Special Branch and Crime and Security. 'He kept on saying look at all these prisoners, but you're only supporting a few, while the Real IRA has loads. Which is a pretty good argument,' McDonagh has said. The security services also used the operation to plant devices in homes. Rupert gave out computers and software to important American republicans which transmitted e-mails to MI5.

However, the majority of the Irish Freedom Committee took an immediate dislike to the New Yorker. He pushed too hard for too much, too fast. And he was resisted at every possible turn. The spy's initial moves were to set the tone for the entire operation. Anything was possible as long as it got the end result; McKevitt's head on a plate.

THE IRISH INTELLIGENCE services monitored the dramatic reorganisation of the RIRA from afar. Only this time, all the human intelligence indicated McKevitt had more volunteers and access to arms. The information was more specific—McKevitt knew another Omagh would wipe him out for good and thus wanted to attack Britain.

Jennings more than anyone else knew Campbell was running a misinformation campaign to throw the spies. To mount a counteroffensive against him to combat what could turn out to be transparently false intelligence would be foolhardy. Crime and Security found themselves in a compromised situation. This was a guessing game because there were no specifics. They could only act on facts, and only when there was evidence to support them.

There was one other problem. The Irish government had played down the significance of the RIRA after the Omagh bombing. The drumbeat of consciousness had stopped. Government spokesmen proclaimed, without a shred of irony, that the RIRA was over and this was reported verbatim in the national press. Of course, this was all nonsense.

Not alone was McKevitt in the full throes of rebuilding his army, Garda Headquarters were also reading secret briefing reports on McKevitt's arms acquisitions. The reports compiled from human and technical surveillance painted a bleak picture for the Department of Justice and the Taoiseach's officials. Nothing was simple, there was no success story and there was a deep reluctance to acknowledge the error.

The only people not unduly concerned by the flurry of interest in Óglaigh na hÉireann were McKevitt and Bernadette Sands. While the RIRA established a new set of rules and procedures, they married at a small ceremony at Dundalk Registry Office on 9 September 1999. The couple organised a small reception in County Monaghan for that evening. The American lawyer Martin Galvin attended the wedding but afterwards took the opportunity, while addressing a republican meeting, to issue his own warning. 'Dissident republicans,' he said without hesitation, 'are getting stronger.'

His comment was proverbial. Although McKevitt was still trying to entice RSF to formally join forces with the RIRA, he did not discount the 32 County Sovereignty Movement.

The group's credibility was not at the high level of its noticeable successes but rather at the dead bottom of its political ineptitude. But this was a game of illusion. In the same month, the movement opened a branch in County Derry. This was squarely aimed at annoying Sinn Féin and the IRA, whose foothold in the city was beyond repute. There was more to come. That same day, at a separate meeting in the city, messages were read out from republican prisoners in Britain and Ireland. The statement came in two parts. The student bombers—Hyland, Grogan, and Mulholland—drafted the first. The second came from a number of RIRA volunteers jailed in Northern Ireland awaiting trial. The two groups announced they both wished to be known as Irish

Republican Army prisoners and voiced support for Óglaigh na hÉireann. But it was the students who delivered the call to arms. 'Unity is the key to the survival of our movement,' they proclaimed.

CRIME AND SECURITY deployed every available resource to deal with the resurgence of the RIRA. Through covert pressure and overt force, the spying department designed a plan to deny McKevitt of his chief lieutenants. Jennings was unaware that Rupert was working for MI5, or even had dealings with McKevitt. MI5 specifically warned the informant against telling the Garda anything. Box did not want Crime and Security knowing anything.

The strategy of the time was to deny McKevitt of his best lieutenants. Special Branch and Crime and Security took the view that McKevitt's closest confidante, McGrane, was instrumental to the RIRA, perhaps more than anyone thought.

McGrane was a fanatical republican. From Dromiskin in County Louth, he not only oversaw training the volunteers in guns and weapons but he operated as McKevitt's personal security advisor. Rather rotund, rugged, and committed to IRA insurgency, he was the one man the Quartermaster trusted.

He was well known to Crime and Security. He had been on the Army Executive of the IRA, one of the philosophical republicans who opposed Adams' plan on principle. His brotherly-like friendship with the Quartermaster made him a prime target. Exerting pressure on McKevitt was the name of the game.

An informant who answered to Special Branch had reported that McGrane was currently overseeing all training courses for new IRA volunteers. The intelligence suggested that McGrane trained new members at a firing range somewhere near the village of Stamullen in County Meath.

Jennings, working in conjunction with the National Bureau of Criminal Investigation and Special Branch, deployed the NSU. McGrane's phone was monitored. Security reports were sought on anyone he called.

McGrane was skilled in the art of anti-surveillance. When driving, he never took the same route twice. He constantly monitored the movements of cars behind him. It took weeks for a detailed picture of his modus operandi to emerge.

The information given to Crime and Security suggested McGrane would personally train a group of new recruits on the evening of 20 October 1999. The venue would be in the grounds of Herbertstown House in Stamullen.

Now it was a matter of waiting. A separate team of undercover officers had monitored McGrane from early that morning in the expectation that he would arrange security and transport to the firing range.

At 7.45 p.m. four vehicles were seen arriving at a farm and people got out. McGrane was there along with Séamus McGreevey, a farmer from Stamullen, Martin Conlon, a volunteer from Armagh city, Damien Lawless, and two brothers from Grange Abbey Drive in Donaghmede in Dublin, Anthony and Alan Ryan. There were also two school boys with the gang. One was 15 years old.

The gardaí watched them get into a horse box pulled by a jeep. Minutes later, it took off in the direction of Stamullen tailed by the NSU. In keeping with a commitment to tight security, McGrane didn't want any of the trainees to know the location of the firing range.

The party arrived at the firing range 30 minutes later. From the undergrowth, the detectives watched as the volunteers stepped from the box and were directed towards a mound of earth, the entrance to a disused wine cellar. McGrane and McGreevey went to a hide nearby and removed a piece of piping. This contained the training weapons.

One man was seen carrying a rifle and sitting guard at the entrance to the cellar. Once McGrane had taken possession of a weapon, it was time for the ERU to move. Armed officers ran towards them and shouted, 'Armed gardaí on duty!'

Seeing the commotion, McGrane and McGreevey, who had two-way radios, ran for cover but were arrested. John McDonagh was the third man in their company. He was arrested at the cellar.

Gardaí called on the others to come out and they emerged one by one and were arrested.

When they were all accounted for, the detectives walked into the firing range where they found an assault rifle, a sub-machine gun, a semi-automatic pistol and a rocket launder. The weapons, magazines and ammunition had been laid out on sheets. The cellar even had a lighting system powered by a generator.

The real surprise was the RPG 18 rocket launcher. This was the proof that an arms shipment had arrived from the Balkans. The real tragedy was that McKevitt narrowly avoided being arrested—he was in a pub situated nearby, and had planned to participate in the training session. The Quartermaster had escaped once again.

RUPERT RETURNED TO Ireland on 4 November 1999. By this time Donnelly had been sidelined. At the beginning of the trip, he went to Bundoran and spoke to Joe O'Neill at his home about the possibility of supporting an amalgamation of RSF and the RIRA. O'Neill was straight in his answer to the proposition. He said, 'Over my dead body.'

The two men, who had been friends for years spoke for a little while longer before Rupert left for County Louth. Ruthless to the core, Rupert felt nothing. He terminated the friendship there and then.

This allowed him to get on with the business of infiltrating the RIRA. MI5 prepared extensive profiles on McKevitt, which Rupert consumed. On that trip, he stayed at the Carrickdale Hotel in County Louth. Everything worked according to plan. For some unfathomable reason, McKevitt took Rupert into his confidence.

He began meeting him and introduced him to Campbell and Frank O'Neill, the fundraiser from Chicago.

In the first meeting they discussed McGrane's arrest at the training camp. McKevitt was anxious about what had happened, perhaps a little guilty. He referred to McGrane as his right hand man in charge of training. However, he was adamant that everything would be okay. The Quartermaster said the arrest, although a set back, was only a bruise to the activities of Óglaigh na hÉireann because he had prepared for such an event.

No one knows why McKevitt trusted Rupert. The most likely explanation is that Rupert had a detailed profile of McKevitt supplied by MI5, which permitted him to ingratiate himself in a way like never before. Either way, McKevitt went on to tell the spy about the Libyan arms deal, and his resignation from the Provisional IRA.

According to Rupert, McKevitt said he had full control over all the IRA arms dumps and that the IRA leadership at the time did not know where they were. The Quartermaster also explained his philosophy on arms acquisition, saying he purchased the least expensive, disposable, and destructive arms.

Rupert spent some time in McKevitt's company. They spoke about politics and the future of republicanism. Money was all-important. To continue raising money, McKevitt wanted more transparency. He wanted to appoint a liaison person between the RIRA Army Council and US-based republican support groups to inform the fundraising leaders on how their money was being spent.

That trip was important to the black operation. Within days of his arrival in Dundalk, Rupert was asked to attend a meeting at a housing estate on the west side of Dundalk called by McKevitt. Rupert delved further into the organisation.

At the meeting Rupert was introduced to two members of McKevitt's engineering cell. The first man was an educated electronics technician; the second was a bomb-maker. Rupert told McKevitt he knew a lot about computers. The impression given was that he would acquire materials for weaponry. In truth, MI5 were guiding him into the RIRA's Engineering Division. If he joined the department at some point in the future, he could bug detonators or TPUs. The sky was the limit as far as the security services were concerned.

The talk that night was of detonating techniques. Rupert would later say the engineers were probing his knowledge of components and electronics. As a result of this meeting he was given a list of things to get.

First on the list was two clean laptop computers to be used with public phones, hook-ups for remote detonation and coded warnings, digital radios with US frequencies and parking meter timers. They also wanted black powder for barrack busters, marine magnets strong enough to hold 8lbs, voice synthesizers, encryption software, giant size flashbulbs, catalogues from spy supply stores, and electronics houses.

Rupert was now at the heart of the RIRA. He was a confidante of McKevitts. The Quartermaster spoke about targeting preference. Things had changed since Omagh. Attacks on targets outside Ireland were to the forefront of McKevitt's mind. His second strategy was to target people who took seats in Stormont; the third priority was British army bases in Northern Ireland. Murdering members of the RUC was fourth on the agenda.

Rupert's ruse of pretending to dislike Donnelly worked. During the trip, McKevitt admitted that Donnelly had been appointed to the Army Council on a temporary basis in order to facilitate the introduction of the CIRA members.

Donnelly, he said, was more trouble than he was worth. He had wanted to kick off the military campaign by shooting an RUC officer in Derry city.

MCKEVITT WOULD MEET Rupert every few days. The talk was always the same. He would say there was no room for politics in his military organisation. In one of his first meetings, he mentioned that he had two operators in Massachusetts.

One of these men was a trusted gunman who had worked on a South African arms deal. This man was a former member of the French Foreign Legion. McKevitt called him James Smith.

McKevitt had said if one was thinking of assassinating someone like the British Prime Minister, Tony Blair, he would use Smith to do the job. Rupert knew nothing of Smith but McKevitt said he would put the two men in touch.

Smith was not his real name. This man was a trained soldier. He had entered the US in August 1996 under the visa waiver programme using his own personal passport issued in London in 1987. He was authorised to stay until October 1996, however, he obtained a separate passport in the name of James Patrick Smith by an elaborate fraud. The real James Smith was an innocent party.

In July 1997, a man wandered into Store Street Garda Station in Dublin and asked Sergeant Anthony Twomey to sign his passport application form. He said his name was James Patrick Smith and he lived in Dublin city centre. This man sent off his passport application and two weeks later received a passport.

McKevitt gave Rupert the soldiers contact details and told him to work Smith towards weapon procurement. During the same conversation, McKevitt mentioned another volunteer who he had sent over to Boston. This man was Dáithí McLoughlin, a volunteer from County Monaghan. He had caused a lot of trouble, eventually being thrown out of a safe house for disciplinary reasons. Although he was a married man, he also had a girlfriend who he called from the house, thus exposing himself to arrest.

In the intervening days, McKevitt let his guard down even further. He continued to break every rule in the book.

The one thing that Rupert came to realise was that McKevitt desperately wanted to organise an attack to overshadow Omagh. Rupert took this to mean whatever he was planning would muster confidence in his group. Obsessed and determined, McKevitt would discuss the topic for hours with the New Yorker.

He gave examples of what his first target might be—a major attack against British troops or against London city.

The spy gained an insight into the mind of the republican. A Quartermaster to the core, McKevitt spoke about modern warfare, saying large military weapons were no longer of any use. When he resigned from the Provisional IRA, he said he took handguns and some small automatic weapons, such as Uzi sub-machine guns. All the military guns were left behind.

THAT PERIOD WAS crucial to the black operation. Fully aware that Rupert embellished everything he said because he was being paid, MI5 and the FBI had still pulled off an intelligence coup. And they didn't make one mistake. Rupert provided top grade intelligence.

Above: The funeral of James Barker, one of the children murdered by the Real IRA in the Omagh bombing.
© *Photocall Ireland*

Left: James Barker, whose father Victor, petitioned the Real IRA to renounce it's campaign of violence.

Left: The Omagh relatives calling for action against the Real IRA. From left: Kevin Skelton, Michael Gallagher and Victor Barker.
© *Author's Private Collection*

Above: Detective Superintendent Tadgh Foley, the garda who ran the Omagh investigation at Monaghan Garda Station.
© *Author's Private Collection*

Left: Assistant Commissioner Kevin Carty, who oversaw the garda investigation into the bombing.
© *Photocall Ireland*

Above: Colm Murphy, the first man to be convicted for the Omagh bombing. Murphy was a seasoned republican who vehemently opposed the Good Friday Agreement.
© *Photocall Ireland*

Right: Lawrence Rush, whose wife Elizabeth was murdered at Omagh. Rush became a tireless campaigner against the Real IRA.
© Photocall Ireland

Left: Séamus McKenna, one of five people being sued by relatives of those killed in the Omagh massacre.
© Garda Intelligence

Right: Séamus Daly, who is being sued by the relatives of those murdered in the Omagh bombing.
© Garda Intelligence

Above: Surveillance photograph of
Michael McKevitt.
© *Garda Intelligence*

Right: FBI and MI5 spy Dave Rupert
who recieved $1.25million to
infiltrate the Real IRA. Rupert
testified against McKevitt in the
Special Criminal Court.
© *Kelvin Boyes*

Below: A rocket launcher seized by
gardaí at a Real IRA training camp at
Stamullen in County Meath.
© *Photocall Ireland*

Above: A colour party stand guard over the body of Joe O'Connor, the Real IRA's leader in Belfast. O'Connor was shot dead by the Provisional IRA near his home in Ballymurphy.
© *Kelvin Boyes*

Left: Joe O'Connor with his young son shortly before his assassination.
© *Courtesy of Nicola O'Connor*

Above and left: Liam Campbell's secret bunker that lay beneath his house. Detectives from Special Branch found CB radios and other materials used for terrorism when they raided his home.
© *Garda Intelligence*

Above and left: The Real IRA mounts a foot patrol on the streets of Stranbane in County Tyrone. The Real IRA uses such oportunities to recruit new members and attract support.
© *Joe Poland*

Below: Michael McDonald, Declan Rafferty, and Fintan O'Farrell who were lured to Slovakia by undercover MI5 officers posing as Iraqi intelligence agents. All three are serving life sentences in Britain.
© *Garda Intelligence*

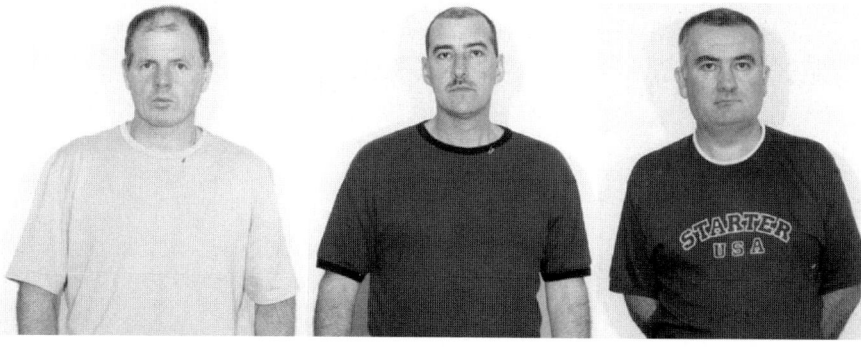

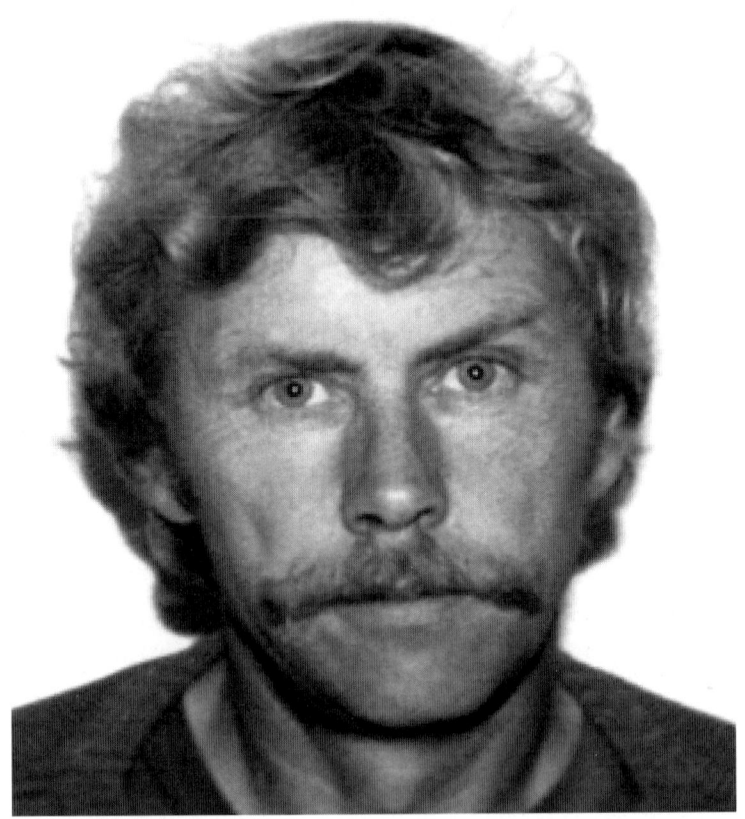

Above: Real IRA victim David Caldwell, who was murdered when he picked up a lunch box containing a small bomb at a building site where he worked.
© *Courtsey of the Caldwell family*

Left: John Paul Hannan, who was 16 years old when he agreed to help the Real IRA bomb targets in central London. Hannan was not a member of the Real IRA but was introduced to republicanism through smuggling and racketeering.
© *Garda Intelligence*

Left: A British pound coin stamped with the letters RIRA. The coins were circulated in the immediate aftermath of the Omagh bombing.
© *Author's Private Collection*

During that visit, they were joined by Frank O'Neill. McKevitt had made him temporary liaison officer for the RIRA Army Council in America. The appointment was designed to encourage the Irish Freedom Committee to start supporting Óglaigh na hÉireann. In the meetings, which were always held close to Dundalk, McKevitt outlined the chain of command in the new IRA. He said he was the boss, Liam Campbell was second while Bernadette Sands McKevitt was third.

Every word McKevitt said was noted and sent to MI5 through encrypted e-mails. Rupert returned to America on 24 November 1999. He had told McKevitt he would take the list of materials his engineering unit requested to see if he could obtain the necessary equipment. His true intention was to bring the list to the FBI and MI5 to see what could be done.

THE SPY DIXON had rebuilt his life in the months following the conclusion of the black operation. Dixon used the money he earned through espionage to his long-term advantage. He extended his minibus business. The tax free cash injection allowed him to broaden his horizons and reshape his life. His business went from strength to strength and he distanced himself from crime.

He no longer associated with 'Jones', or passed information to the gardaí, though he retained the right to phone Crime and Security if he was ever in trouble, or suspected that his cover was blown.

The black operation had been run like a military operation. There had been no careless oversights by the gardaí. There were no clues left behind which could have given the game away. No one ever managed to identify the spy. The finger of suspicion was left pointing at 'Jones' which in turn created a moral dilemma for the RIRA. The republicans could not decide whether 'Jones' was the agent or not.

Dixon had run the gauntlet and lived to tell the tale. Single-handedly, he had changed the fortunes of the RIRA. Jennings had also cut him free. He didn't owe anyone anything. The operation had been an overwhelming success. Then, the unthinkable happened.

KEVIN CARTY WAS the police commander in charge of the north-west division of An Garda Síochána. In this capacity, he was responsible for law enforcement operations in the region and intelligence gathering. In the autumn of that year, Carty was told that serious allegations had been made against a number of gardaí stationed in County Donegal. The allegations had been discounted by senior officers in the division but Carty would not accept their assurances.

Anyone who knew Carty knew he was a man who trusted no one. Working in absolute secret, he began making his own discreet inquiries. His decision proved to be a proverbial one.

In the months that followed, Carty uncovered a web of corruption and garda malpractice that rocked the very foundations of the police force. The people of County Donegal knew for a long time that elements of the gardaí engaged in extortion, fraud and fitted up innocent suspects. But there was little anyone could do. The corruption was endemic. The list of officers that fell under suspicion was startling; Carty knew some of them personally.

The sheer scale of the corruption in County Donegal—which extended to Dublin city—shocked Garda Headquarters and the Department of Justice. The list of allegations seemed endless. Detectives stood accused of framing innocent people, perverting the course of justice and even manufacturing explosives which they later seized as IRA arms. But there was one problem that no one dared mention; John White was among the accused.†

White was accused of planting a shotgun at a travellers' camp near the village of Burnfoot in County Donegal in May 1998. At the time, White had been investigating the murder of a County Mayo pensioner called Edward Fitzmaurice, who died after thieves broke into his home in Charlestown, beat him up and tied him to a chair.

Carty was privately aware that White had at the same time played a defining role in combating the RIRA but this was now irrelevant. One of White's colleagues, Thomas Kilcoyne, told detectives assigned to the anti-corruption investigation that White had planted the gun.† The officer was later arrested and questioned about the Burnfoot incident. The interview was conducted by Nacy Rice, a Chief Superintendent, and Tadgh Foley, the head of the Omagh bomb inquiry.

During the long hours that he was in custody, Kilcoyne outlined a number of serious allegations against White. He claimed to have seen White plant a sawn-off shotgun in a caravan at the halting site. Kilcoyne's statement was straightforward. He spoke about White's investigation skills, his knowledge of the underworld and the scant details that White told him about the secret operations mounted by Crime and Security against the RIRA.

Rice and Foley were legally obliged to take notes of everything the officer said. There could be no exceptions. Kilcoyne did not understand the sensitivities surrounding White's work and talked freely about one Paddy Dixon. He said White had told him about the informant.

The cat was already out of the bag when Dixon's name was mentioned by Kilcoyne. Irish newspapers had already published a series of articles about White's secret work against the RIRA and the fact that he handled an important informant. Dixon had read the articles with disbelief and slowly began to get nervous. The net effect of the disclosures compromised Crime and Security and the black operation.

Matters came to a head when White was arrested and charged with a firearm offence by members of Carty's anti-corruption team. White emphatically denied the charge and pledged to clear his name. He was suspended from duty albeit on full pay. The more publicity that White's arrest generated the more vulnerable Dixon became. Crime and Security were forced to act.

The New Year passed and more information entered the public domain. In January 2000, Dixon was driving his minibus through the village of Ashbourne in County Meath when he saw gardaí standing on the road ahead of him. Thinking he was passing through a road traffic checkpoint, he stopped the vehicle and stepped out. The two gardaí asked him if his name was Patrick Dixon. He confirmed that it was and one of the detectives introduced himself as being from Special Branch. Dixon was told that his life was in grave danger and he was being taken into protective custody. Dixon was spirited away to a safe house in County Wicklow never to been seen again.

THE PASSING OF the millennium heralded a new coming for McKevitt. Although the intelligence community knew about the RIRA, after some debate and discussion, the new Army Council decided to reveal itself by issuing a public statement. On 20 January, in a telephone call to the media, Óglaigh na hÉireann condemned the new Northern Ireland Executive and pledged to continue to struggle for republican goals.

'Once again, Britain has refused to accept the will of the Irish people and has chosen deception, manipulation, and coercion to engineer a fraudulent pact to maintain its presence in Ireland. Once again, Óglaigh na hÉireann declares the right of the Irish people to the ownership of Ireland. We call on all volunteers loyal to the Irish Republic to unite to uphold the Republic and establish a permanent national parliament representative of all the people.'

The statement was a call to arms. In some respects, the RIRA Army Council was wasting its time; the republican movement was not listening. McKevitt's endeavours to amalgamate the CIRA into Óglaigh na hÉireann had failed.

The CIRA flexed their muscle on 6 February when Mahon's Hotel on Mill Street in the backwater town of Irvinestown in County Fermanagh was blown up. Warnings were given to local radio stations 35 minutes earlier. Although no one was injured, the attack sent a clear message to not only the British government, but also to McKevitt: the CIRA was still in business. They operated independently of the RIRA.

Three weeks later, on Friday, 25 February, Óglaigh na hÉireann nearly killed dozens of British soldiers. Volunteers in County Derry constructed a large bomb, consisting of a Mark-19 timer unit and three gas cylinders, each packed with HME. The device was hidden inside a stolen van, which was driven into Shackleton Camp at Ballykelly.

The bomb was parked beside the accommodation block used by the First Battalion of the Royal Welsh Fusiliers. The timer exploded just after 3 a.m. and the blast was heard over a wide area, however, no one was killed. The message was clear. Óglaigh na hÉireann was also back in business.

JENNINGS HAD TRAINED in the FBI Academy in Quantico. In the intelligence community, there is an unwritten rule that each country pays its own informants. Through his own spies, he found out that MI5 was paying Rupert. He brought the matter to a head. Red-faced, Box admitted it was also running Rupert. The official explanation was that they were afraid the operation wouldn't work. No one believed them. T-branch down-played what had happened but both MI5 and Garda Headquarters now knew where they stood with each other. Elements of T-branch had taken a chance and got caught. But Jennings, however, saw the chance to get McKevitt. Now the operation changed from being intelligence driven to a prosecution. At this point, Crime and Security stood back and passed the inquiry to Martin Callinan of NBCI and Diarmuid O'Sullivan of Special Branch. They would oversee the case. MI5 were not happy about this. From now on, everything would have to be sanctioned by Garda Headquarters. T-branch did not want the details of their spying activities exposed but were powerless to say no.

Rupert returned to Ireland at the beginning of February. Jennings was aware of this and consequently the NSU was watching his every move. He brought $9,900, four personal organisers, and video conferencing equipment sought by the engineering unit. MI5 had authorised him to spend some of the money he raised for the IRA to purchase the organisers because they believed there was no danger to life. The RIRA had never used such items in the construction of a bomb.

This time, Rupert was more than confident in his dealings with McKevitt. The mystery had gone; McKevitt was not invincible, nor was he particularly security conscious. An easy conjecture is to say that he was desperately under pressure. In fact, he wasn't. He simply ignored his own rules. If he had conducted the most cursory security checks on Rupert, he would have realised that something was wrong. But he didn't and that's where he went wrong. The spy attended four meetings with McKevitt on this trip.

The NSU monitored McKevitt's clandestine terrorist business discreetly. This was all about building a prosecution case against McKevitt. There would be no mistakes.

The first meeting took place at a house in Oakland Park in Dundalk. Mounting surveillance on the location was difficult. The house was situated in a cul-de-sac.

Detective Sergeant Thomas Healy of NSU was tasked with spying on the meeting. His secret operation started at 7 p.m. Trying not to draw attention to himself, through the corner of his eye he observed a silver Alfa Romeo T-Spark. The briefing reports prepared by Crime and Security had noted that McKevitt's son Stephen owned this car. The intelligence was correct.

The detective saw there were two people in the car. The driver was Stephen McKevitt. In the passenger seat was David Rupert, who was dropped off. At 7.30 p.m. a green Renault Megane van pulled up. This time McKevitt himself was the passenger. When the car stopped, he took a brief look around, stepped from the car and walked through the door.

INSIDE THE HOUSE, the Quartermaster revealed the most intricate workings of the RIRA to Rupert. He first started talking about guns. He said he had posted three handguns from America to Ireland, though he confessed they had not arrived.

As for the growth of Óglaigh na hÉireann, it was getting stronger. Recruitment was underway in Dundalk, Counties Louth, Tyrone, and Armagh.

He told Rupert that he wanted to take the war to the heartland of London to exact a huge financial toll. He told him he was waiting for Gerry Adams to declare decommissioning before he started to wage a campaign. This was all propaganda. McKevitt insisted the RIRA was getting stronger. Rupert saw this as false advertising.

That meeting lasted over an hour. It ended at 8.55 p.m. When they emerged, the gardaí were still watching outside. Rupert delayed leaving, wanting to make sure he was being viewed. He stood in the front garden of the house for a few minutes, casually talking to McKevitt. At 9 p.m. a blue coloured Ford Fiesta entered the cul-de-sac. Rupert and one of the engineers left in this car. McKevitt was collected by his son minutes later.

The second meeting took place at Greenore and involved the RIRA Army Council. Those present included McKevitt, Campbell, Kieran McLaughlin, Maurice Healy from Belfast and Rupert. McLaughlin and Healy were new members of the Army Council.

McKevitt produced the $9,900 Rupert had given him previously and officially handed it over to McLaughlin, who was the new Director of Finance. The talk that night was of the embarrassment the IRA had faced when a gunrunning racket they organised from Florida was exposed. The RIRA had benefited because they were running the same system. McKevitt actually thought it funny that the heat had been taken off them because the PIRA was blamed for the operation.

He mentioned the arrest of Thomas Redmond in Wexford, the die-hard supporter of the RIRA.

Although Redmond had been arrested and charged, all was not lost. In yet another enormous breach of security, McKevitt said he had been tipped off about a Garda raid on a workshop used by Redmond.

McGrane was a notable absentee from the meetings. This didn't perturb McKevitt much. According to Rupert, when Stamullen was raided, he ordered six new training camps to be set up to maintain confidence in the recruits.

The next meeting took place at the Carrickdale Hotel where Rupert was staying. At this meeting McKevitt came straight to the point. He wanted money and guns. Sitting in the hotel lobby, he asked Rupert to get two .25 caliber lathes, parts for pistols emphasising that he needed these urgently for high security operations.

By this stage, McKevitt appeared to have placed all his trust in Rupert. He talked freely to the spy. He mused over political developments and showed a vulnerability that few people would have believed possible. McKevitt, though, had good reason to believe that Rupert could get weapons. In America, Rupert had bought guns. The infoRmAtion collected through the black operation by MI5 and the FBI was never intended to be produced in court. The agencies permitted the spy to get weapons for the IRA and Rupert obliged. He also planted bugs in people's homes.

'He bought guns and ammo across the States for the RIRA, that's why McKevitt trusted him. He had broken the law. As far as McKevitt was concerned, he had a proven track record of gunrunning,' said a CIRA source.

Rupert was tolerated because he could get guns and money, but money was never far off the agenda. Specifically McKevitt asked Rupert to accumulate over £10,000. This was a tall order that McKevitt appeared to have no compunction in asking.

A Quartermaster to the bone, the acquisition of arms was always on McKevitt's mind. Since their initial meeting, McKevitt had asked the spy to meet his sleeper in Massachusetts. Rupert was given James Smith's name. He was to work with him to create an arms procurement network in the United States.

It was clear to MI5 and Crime and Security that McKevitt now placed his absolute trust in Rupert. Not only did he expose himself but he endangered the entire organisation. The fourth meeting Rupert attended was in the presence of the RIRA's engineering unit. In attendance was McKevitt, Rupert, the bomb engineer, and the electronic engineer.

It was at this meeting that Rupert began to worry. The electronic engineer said the four organisers he had sent from the US would be used as long delay timing mechanisms for explosive devices. Rupert panicked because it never dawned on him or his handlers that they could be used for such a purpose. He simply thought the RIRA wanted the devices for recording purposes. During this meeting, the engineers told him they had perfected the use of cellular phones as a trigger to detonate an explosive device. When the news was relayed to Crime and Security and MI5 it caused pandemonium. The RIRA was becoming an even bigger threat.

THE BUSINESS OF the RIRA was never far off the agenda. In Rupert's company, McKevitt talked about the daily running of his army. At that last meeting, he complained bitterly about stupidity among the volunteers. In a recent robbery, one volunteer had used firearms that were more valuable than the proceeds of the robbery. If they had been caught, he pontificated, they would have lost the weapons. On the matter of guns, he admitted he had purchased a lot of weapons in Eastern Europe, but he needed to get his hands on US dollars to pay for them.

The entire Balkans operation had been fraught with risk. Ironically, he said he was worried about being discovered because he hadn't enough money to pay the smugglers. The first shipments of guns were smuggled from the continent in lorries. More than anything else, he was afraid that some of the drivers involved might be tempted to import drugs. If this were to become public knowledge, that would be a disaster for the organisation.

When he finished complaining, he asked the spy to obtain some items he needed. MI5 had prepped Rupert to ask if he could take notes. These would be useful when the operation concluded and the Garda wanted to press charges. The notes could be admitted as evidence.

Therefore, Rupert asked if he could note the details. No problem, said the Quartermaster, warning the spy to be careful. McKevitt outlined a shopping list. He wanted remote control model helicopters, parking timers, marine magnets, infra red detonators, mercury switches, laser fibre optic cable, and handguns.

The fifth meeting was held with Campbell and two men Rupert didn't recognise. They met on the west side of Dundalk. McKevitt arranged the meeting, the sole purpose of which was to introduce Rupert to Noel Abernathy, a volunteer. He was going to be in the US at Easter time to answer any questions there might be concerning army operations. The meeting lasted no more than a few minutes. The spy returned to the US on 28 February 2000. He was alive and had pulled off another intelligence coup.

THE BLACK OPERATION slowly gathered evidence to secure a charge against McKevitt. But that wasn't enough to stop the RIRA. The organisation resumed a potent bombing campaign. Weeks after Rupert returned home, the RUC seized 500lbs of explosives after stopping two cars travelling on the A1 in the direction of Hillsborough.

The HME was being transported to Belfast to be made into a bomb. The attacks continued and increased in frequency.

On 6 April, the Derry Brigade tried to bomb Ebrington Army Barracks. The local IRA men had shown themselves to be ingenious in their willingness to design and build new types of bombs. This time, the device consisted of 5lbs of home-made explosive and was lowered by rope over the perimeter fence.

15

BACK IN ARMS

MI5 AND CRIME and Security were deeply anxious about Rupert. Jennings had grave reservations. He didn't like the spy one bit. He believed him to be untrustworthy and a liar. Jennings was right. Rupert embellished everything to please the intelligence services. But MI5 now needed Rupert, and he knew it. Crime and Security knew some of the things that Rupert said were lies, but it was crucial that the operation continued.

On 22 April 2000 Rupert met Abernathy off his flight from Dublin to Chicago and took him to a local meeting of the Irish Freedom Committee. There Rupert held a question and answer session about the army and outlined the chain of command in Ireland. Rupert, speaking like the accomplished performer he was, reiterated the policy of no claim, no blame. He spoke about the necessity of punishment attacks and told everybody that Mickey Donnelly was no longer in Óglaigh na hÉireann. The relationship between the Provisional IRA and Óglaigh na hÉireann was on the verge of all out war, he warned. A leading volunteer from County Tyrone called Paddy Fox had been kidnapped. He gave a lengthy dissertation on the abduction.

Rupert and Abernathy went their separate ways after the function.

MI5 and the FBI monitored everything from a distance. At the FBI, Buckley saw the covert war as increasingly important. Rupert was to obey McKevitt's every word, he told him. On 24 April, he flew to Worchester in Massachusetts where he met with the mercenary Smith. The two met in a hotel. The FBI watched everything, recording the conversations with hidden microphones and cameras. Smith was a rough and abrasive Dundalk man. Because McKevitt had ordered him to work with Rupert, he assumed that the necessary security checks had been carried out. But he was wrong and he revealed more inside information to the spy.

The conversation went one way. Smith did the talking. He told the spy that he had shipped some shorts* to Ireland. He said he met with a man called John Hurley in Boston who was a fundraiser. According to Smith, Hurley said he would help with the prisoners' fund, but needed something in writing. Smith suggested that they get an accommodation address from McKevitt to ship timers and Glock pistols to Ireland. He had a catalogue that contained military equipment and he asked Rupert to bring it to McKevitt for him to choose what he wanted.

In their conversation, Rupert was the one who asked questions. And Smith answered. He told Rupert of his association with McKevitt and his South African days of procuring arms. They joked before departing. The two men made arrangements to meet soon.

BACK IN IRELAND, the RIRA Army Council had decided to unleash a new campaign on Britain. No one would sanction a full-scale assault on targets in Northern Ireland. The possibility of a civilian being murdered was too frightening to even contemplate. The logical alternative was to bomb London. The make up of the Army Council had changed drastically by this time, although Campbell remained in command of the war machine.

After months of planning and backed up by the Croatian weapons, he deployed three ASUs into Britain. The ASUs were made up of young teenagers and more experienced republicans. Their instructions were to choose strategic targets. Through bombing and

---

* Republican slang for pistols

attacking specific locations, Óglaigh na hÉireann planned to make its presence felt at the heart of the British establishment. The RIRA also felt a successful bombing operation in Britain would attract disenchanted IRA volunteers into the ranks. Not since the beginning of its war in late 1997 had the Army Council sanctioned such an audacious move.

THE CAMPAIGN WAS launched in the early hours of 1 June 2000 when Londoners heard a loud bang on the south side of the River Thames. It was 4.30 a.m. Adrian Larkman, who lives near the bridge, was wakened by the noise.

'I work nights and I was cooking when there was a loud bang. The windows of my house shook. I dialled 999 and I was apparently the first person to call. I put my boots on and went outside five minutes later and there were already policemen there.'

A bomb had exploded under Hammersmith Bridge causing severe damage. The bomb had been placed at the end of a cross beam, which directly supported the carriageway.

The effect of the blast was to punch a hole through the web of the crossbeam, the hole being about 50cm long by 30cm high. It didn't collapse the bridge but did force the police to divert traffic. After the explosion, the area near the busy junction of the A4 was sealed off, severely disrupting traffic. The RIRA had finally struck. The Army council was delighted.

The decision to mount attacks in Britain panicked MI5. The Hammersmith bomb was an embarrassment. T-branch was furious. There was some intelligence that the RIRA were preparing an attack, but questions were being asked nonetheless. There was no excuse for letting the bombers slip through the net. The Security Service knew full well that the bombing would act as a magnet for disaffected republicans. This was confirmed when Rupert met with Smith a week later in America. Smith was very excited. The attack had given him a new lease of life. He wanted to get weapons back to Ireland, as quickly as possible. There was one problem, however. He believed the American security services were monitoring all mail. It was, said Smith, too hot to ship weapons. However, he told Rupert that he needed $5,000-$10,000 to buy weapons. Rupert promised him that he would do his best.

The success of the Hammersmith attack encouraged the Army Council to mount more attacks into Northern Ireland. These attacks were strategic in their approach and were designed to annoy and provoke the British. On 20 June, the Belfast Brigade managed to place a small bomb at the official residence of Peter Mandelson, the Northern Secretary. The device was found in a bag in the grounds of Hillsborough Castle. This was a spectacular attack. No lives were lost but the RIRA got publicity. Ten days later, Campbell's unit blew up the Dublin to Belfast railway line. The purpose of the bomb was to monitor the reaction of the security forces and how they dealt with the situation. Campbell himself later admitted that he had used a small device and had even informed the neighbours that this was going to happen so they would not be frightened.

THE SPY RETURNED to Ireland on 19 June to attend an Ard Fheis of the 32 County Sovereignty Movement at the Carrickdale Hotel in County Louth. He brought with him $9,300 and two laptop computers. The $9,300 was a gift from the Irish Freedom Committee for prisoners' welfare. Rupert had reluctantly brought the laptops after consultations with the FBI and MI5 who did not believe they could be used for detonation purposes. He was wary after the incidents with the electronic organisers.

McKevitt was glad to see the American. He discussed how the Hammersmith bombing was carried out. In typical McKevitt style, he said other people had set up traffic problems when the bomb went off to create further confusion and his technicians had created a new style of detonating switch.

A week later, on 26 June, Rupert was invited to attend a meeting of the Army Council at a house on the Greenore Road. In attendance was Kieran McLaughlin, Campbell, and McKevitt. There was also a man called Dominic from Letterkenny in County Donegal present but he was unknown to Rupert. McKevitt took control of the meeting from the start. He said that he was now in a position to replicate the attack on Hammersmith Bridge.

Then, almost as if his speech was rehearsed, he said he was in need of more money, detonator cord and ammunition for .41 calibre weapons and a particular type of lightweight sniper rifle. Of course, Rupert knew this was for his benefit.

The meeting was not an Army Council gathering as such. But it was a place where sensitive information was exchanged. The engineers had been due to arrive but they did not show. Rupert asked Campbell for the accommodation address requested by Smith. The Director of Operations gave him the name of a company in County Kildare.

McKevitt constantly raised the issue of money. He began exerting pressure on Rupert to deliver.

At that meeting, Rupert gave the republicans the military catalogue that Smith had given him in the United States. McKevitt would sometimes try and show an affable side to his character. At this meeting he described how he and Smith had bonded in South Africa after the Good Friday Agreement when they were trying to procure arms in a deal that was two years in the making.

Much of the meetings would be consumed by Army business. Campbell wanted to talk about Donnelly, who had been thrown out of the RIRA but was still causing trouble. He proposed kidnapping him in an effort to get him to behave. If this didn't work they would kill him. Again McKevitt was against this: it would be bad PR to kill him. Donnelly had a wife and children.

Among the other issues discussed was the 32 County Sovereignty Movement's Annual General Meeting. McKevitt believed the turnout proved they had overcome the Omagh bomb disaster. Security issues were also discussed. McKevitt said he had a source in the Irish postal service who informed him the mail was being watched very closely and that he should not use it.

At the time, there was room on the Army Council for more personnel. This issue was raised by Campbell who said that two of the engineers were suitable material, but they had to be kept clean, in other words, their identities secret.

Rupert's visits exposed the unorthodox running of the RIRA. There was no set structures to the secret army. The Army Council would meet and chat about bombings. Politics were not discussed. Rupert had a further meeting with Campbell, along with two electrical engineers, in the same house that the Army Council meeting was held in on the Greenore Road. Campbell chaired this meeting.

It proved to be a valuable source of intelligence for Rupert and the security services. He learned details about two other RIRA units, apart from the engineering department. There was one labelled 'General Operations', headed up by Campbell. The other was the robbery division, tasked with organising raids on banks and post offices. Before that meeting closed, Campbell and the two engineers reviewed the list previously compiled by McKevitt. They revamped it and numbered it. The list now consisted of mercury switches; electronic matches; flashbulbs; electronic light timers; radar guns; a software package called Apogee Rock Sim 4; a scanning device and an infrared device. Campbell remarked that if they had used scanners before, McGrane would not have got caught at the training camp at Stamullen. He also wanted a white noise generator with digital voice changer and a collection of stun guns.

Rupert's presence hadn't gone unnoticed, however. On the Sunday after the 32 County Sovereignty Movement's AGM, he saw a front page article in *The Sunday Times* entitled 'Real IRA Picket Jack Straw's home.' His name was mentioned in the piece. He was described as a millionaire businessman who had made a major personal contribution to McKevitt and the RIRA and for that he was put in charge of fundraising for the organisation in the US.

Rupert panicked when he read the newspaper. He was torn between being worried by the publicity and pleased that he had made it into the papers.

LIFE FOR MCKEVITT was now beginning to take a new direction. The RIRA was functioning properly: the bombs were exploding and no civilians were being killed. McKevitt relaxed somewhat. This was his biggest mistake. MI5 and Crime and Security were playing a long game. The strategy was to destroy the RIRA. If it had to permit some acts of terrorism until it could achieve this aim, then that was necessary as long as the prime target was still in its sight.

McKevitt, however, made a serious mistake. He told Rupert at one of the meetings that he was going to the continent later that month. He was even more specific. He said he would be concealed in the floor of a lorry. Wary of Campbell's tendency to engage in dangerous operations, he said he had left orders to the Army not to exploit the marching season in Northern Ireland. The security services placed him under 24-hour watch. It proved a worthwhile exercise.

ON THE MORNING of 13 July, Croatian TV broadcast an unusual story when it reported that police had intercepted an arms shipment in the south of the country. The weapons had been seized 60 kilometres east of the city of Split, in the mountainous region called Cista Provo. The town where the guns were found was Dobranje, a small farming community close to the border with Bosnia. The village had been surrounded by special police units working on intelligence supplied by the Croat Secret Service.

The information available to the police was deadly accurate. On the previous evening, a commando team of police headed straight for a bar at the bottom of the village—within hours a number of arrests had been made. At the same time, officers started mounting searches of farms and buildings in the area. Ranko Ostojic, the Chief of Police in Split, oversaw the operation. Hidden in the middle of a hay shed, officers found a huge military arsenal.

Forensic officers began cataloguing the find. There were 7 RPG18 Rocket launchers, one of which had a closely matching serial number to the one found in Stamullen. There were TNT packs of explosives which also bore remarkable similarities to the packages found in Stamullen.

There were 20kgs of the Bosnian explosive TM500, half of which had been strapped together by one inch Sellotape, bearing the batch number 8303. The gardaí had discovered six and a half kilos of TM500, packed in exactly the same way and bearing exactly the same batch number at the Stamullen training camp. There were more similarities The Croatian find also yielded an RPG 18, identical to the one found at Stamullen.

The shed where the weapons were found was owned by the Cubelic family, a family so prominent in Dobranje that part of the area has been named after them. Tomaslav Cubelic was arrested in the village, along with an older brother. Their cousin Ante Cubelic, who had since moved to the Croatian capital of Zagreb, was arrested a few days later as he came out of a lock up garage.

He was nailed. The police mounted further investigations into Cubelic. He had worked for an international aid agency called Caritas Italiana where he had come into contact with 'Bob'. This information was passed to Crime and Security, who later arrested the CIRA operator. But there was not enough proof to press charges against him. McKevitt had been tailed The security services had monitored his every move but had decided not to arrest him. Instead, they cut one of his Balkans supply route.

MEANWHILE THE RIRA offensive in Britain continued. On 19 July, the ASU working in London planted a small bomb on a railway line near Ealing Broadway tube station. The ASU phoned in several bomb warnings including a claim that a bomb was about to explode near the scene of a birthday pageant for the Queen Mother in Whitehall.

The London Metropolitan Police were forced to shut down all tube lines, causing severe travel disruption to the underground services. The package left at Whitehall was later discovered to be someone's bag—but there was no bomb.

The threats had the desired effect. Passengers travelling on the London-bound Great Western services were forced to take South-West Trains Services from Reading into London's Waterloo station. Heathrow Express services were suspended. The Army Council was delighted. The RIRA had spoiled the Queen Mother's birthday celebrations. In what would become policy, attacks on London were followed by an operation in Northern Ireland.

On 11 August, the RUC intercepted two milk churn bombs in Derry city. More than 15,000 members of the loyalist Apprentice

Boys were due to hold a parade in the city that day. It was a lucky interception. A white Astra van had crashed through a police checkpoint in the dead of night. The RUC gave chase. The van headed for the border.

The bombers escaped across the border. The gardaí later found the van abandoned in County Donegal at Imlick near Carrigans village. It contained 500lbs of explosives.

Their next attack was even more audacious. On 13 September, two bombs were placed at a British Army training base in Derry city. The first bomb contained 80lbs of explosives and was planted inside a wooden hut at Magilligan Army Camp. The device partially exploded when a soldier opened the door of a wooden hut. During a follow-up search, a second bomb was found. Magilligan covered 2,200 acres and was not only used by soldiers but by young cadets, the Territorial Army, civilian rifle clubs and local farmers whose livestock grazed on selected areas. Any one of them could have been killed or maimed.

The bomb attacks were the work of the Derry Brigade, which showed itself to be more than willing to take risks.

DESPITE, OR PERHAPS because of, the success of the English campaign, the Army Council decided to organise a spectacular attack in Britain. The RIRA came up with the ideal target; the offices of MI6.

In all the years of the troubles, the offices of Britain's two intelligence agencies—MI6, which covers foreign spying and MI5, which deals with Britain and Ireland—had never been attacked by republicans. It was a prestige target; if successful it would show the world that the RIRA had not been defeated.

At 9.40 p.m. on the night of 20 September 2000, a member of the London ASU drove through south London on a motorbike, weaving his way through traffic to the Vauxhall area in the south of the city. He headed straight for a small public park just south of 85 Vauxhall Cross, the imposing £240 million building, which is now home to MI6. He pulled up at Spring Gardens. There was no one about; the park was deserted. The biker stopped in the middle of the park. The massive MI6 building was literally in his sights.

He calmly produced a Russian RPG 22 anti-tank rocket launcher, which he carried in a holdall. The republican had rehearsed the routine on numerous occasions, and within seconds, was looking through the eyesight and pointing the war head. Without hesitation, he raised the launcher to his shoulder, took aim and fired. He was 200 yards away from MI6.

The missile exploded just below a window on the eighth floor where Sir Richard Dearlove, the Director General of the Secret Intelligence Service, works. As soon as the projectile hit the target, the volunteer grabbed the holdall, ran back to his motorbike, dumping the launcher cylinder en route, and sped off.

The grenade slammed into the building with a loud bang. The rocket is designed to destroy tanks and other armoured vehicles. It is also able to slice its way through one metre of concrete, but the MI6 building had been reinforced. The rocket caused only light damage to the building.

Although no one was killed, or even seriously wounded, the attack was a stunning success for the RIRA. It generated headlines around the world. The RIRA had not only struck in Britain, but at the heart of the British establishment.

The MI6 attack emboldened Campbell. It was audacious, daring and shocked the British public to the core. The Army Council now pushed for similar attacks in the North.

Six days later, train services between Belfast and Lisburn were suspended while soldiers defused a bomb planted on the railway line. The police were forced to evacuate a nearby shopping centre following a telephone warning. As a result of the find, the Black Road's slip road onto the M1 motorway was also closed. The RIRA couldn't be stopped.

PETER MAGUIRE HELD the position of Director of Operations at Garda Special Branch. Maguire knew the workings of the IRA better than most. He had been recruited into Special Branch after he joined the force and spent his entire career spearheading operations to counter the Provisional IRA. His real talent, though, was a razor sharp eye for legal detail and developing case law.

Maguire was a qualified barrister who looked at the RIRA not only as a splinter group, but as part of a historical movement. Experience had taught him that the successes of the various incarnations of the IRA was dependent on their formative years; if they failed to generate support and attract recruits in their infancy, the factions usually disappeared.

When the RIRA regrouped after the Omagh bombing, Maguire interpreted the move as a dangerous warning sign. If McKevitt managed to overcome the enormity of the Omagh bombing, then anything was possible. This was Maguire's considered opinion.

More than anything else, Maguire believed the authorities desperately needed to break the RIRA. The intelligence files that landed on his desk each day suggested an upsurge in recruitment. If the RIRA continued to grow, the Government could find itself facing another 30 years of bloodshed. To counter the RIRA and the CIRA, the state needed to be pro-active.

The Special Branch officer was a firm advocate of pursuing republicans through the legal process and developing case law. His commitment to this strategy had a proven track record. However, Maguire had begun considering new ways of prosecuting the dissidents.

The most inventive solution he devised was simple in its ingenuity. He pushed the Director of Public Prosecutions to charge republicans with being members of the IRA. Laws prohibiting IRA membership already existed on the statute books but the legislation was rarely used for historical and legal reasons.

Maguire thought the time had now come for rank and file IRA men to know the Garda meant business; that extreme republicanism would not be tolerated. He pushed the DPP to act. He began by preparing a report, which was forensic in content on how republicans could be charged with IRA membership on the word of a Chief Superintendent.

After months of secret communications between his office and the DPP, the two sides agreed to send Maguire's report to George

Birmingham, an eminent prosecutor. Birmingham spent some time examining Maguire's submission. He concluded that Maguire had constructed a watertight argument that few people could disagree with. It was legally sound. The DPP gave the go ahead for Special Branch to begin making arrests.

16

THE CAMPAIGN

THE ATTACK ON MI6 sent a shockwave through the British security services. It bore all the hallmarks of a Campbell operation. Back in Dublin, Crime and Security watched almost helpless as the Real IRA spun out of their control. Reading the reports submitted by informants, which stated that Campbell wanted to mount a string of similar attacks, Crime and Security made a decision to take him out. The Peace Process depended on it.

While the success of the RIRA was attributed to McKevitt, Campbell was an important, and even defining, influence. Crime and Security knew full well the important role that he played on the Army Council; he was the one person who advocated war at every opportunity.

For some time, Maguire had been at pains to charge Campbell with membership of the RIRA. Intelligence gathered by Crime and Security suggested that Campbell—who was a smuggler by trade— had some type of secret room in his home at Upper Faughart, several miles north of Dundalk and a stone's throw from the border. His house had been searched by Special Branch at least eight times in recent years in an attempt to establish if the information was correct. However, each search yielded nothing. All that was about to change.

On the morning of 3 October 2000, Maguire's team gathered at Dundalk Garda Station in County Louth. Detective Sergeant Jim Sheridan and Detective Inspector Diarmuid O'Sullivan, Maguire's second in command, were both present. O'Sullivan briefed the team on how he wanted the house searched. On approaching Campbell's home, gardaí would take up positions at every window on the ground floor. They were told not to move and to watch Campbell's every move. If he walked into the kitchen before opening the door, the search would concentrate on the kitchen. It was simple logic: the officers believed that if there was a secret hide in the house, Campbell would run to it when he knew the gardaí were at the door.

The gardaí arrived at Campbell's home at 6.20 a.m. When the premises were secured, Detective Sergeant William Hanrahan, who had physical possession of the search warrant, slowly approached the front door of the house. Hanrahan knocked on the door. He asked Campbell to open up but there was no response.

O'Sullivan was also standing at the door when he noticed the outline of a person making hurried movements along the hallway, going in the direction of what he thought was the kitchen. Members of the search team kept watching through the windows while Hanrahan shouted at the figure to stop. O'Sullivan, who had never moved from his allotted position, saw the same person come back from the kitchen area and return upstairs. A few minutes later, the same person, who was unrecognisable through the frosted glass, returned downstairs. After a few more warnings from the gardaí, the shadowy figure decided to open the door. It was Liam Campbell.

Hanrahan pulled him to one side and informed him the officers had a warrant to search his house. A die-hard republican to the core, Campbell tried to push the gardaí out the door, even throwing a few punches in the process.

Hanrahan moved to restrain the republican, telling him as he did that he was now being arrested under Section 30 of the Offences Against the State Act, on suspicion of being a member of an unlawful organisation. Campbell was handcuffed and placed in a waiting patrol car. O'Sullivan then introduced himself to Campbell's wife, Bernadette. The officers began a detailed search of the house. The first pieces of evidence they found were three plastic bags hidden in the back of a reclining armchair in the kitchen cum living room area. The bags contained two two-way radios marked number one and number two. A second bag contained a Motorola GP340 hand held radio and six aerials. The third bag contained £2,000 sterling. A Panasonic mobile phone was also hidden in the side of this armchair.

In the meantime, gardaí searched other parts of the house. They found an Ericsson mobile phone, documents for a motor car, appointments diary, white cotton gloves, walkie talkies, another diary and two cash boxes.

The search continued for an hour until a detective on the team opened a press in the hallway. O'Sullivan had seen the frosted image of Campbell making his way to the press earlier that morning. When the garda took a closer look, he noticed a tiny gap around the base of the press. After tugging at this for a few moments, he then lifted the bottom to find it concealed an entrance. He called O'Sullivan and Sergeant Vincent Jackson at once. Peering into the hole, the gardaí could see a steel ladder, which led down to a bunker.

O'Sullivan sent a man down into the hole. Moments later, the officer found an electric light and switched it on. The light allowed the three officers to have a good look at Campbell's bunker. It wasn't a myth, it did exist after all. The bunker was 9 feet long, 6 feet wide and 5 feet 6 inches in height. The base was covered with sheets of aeroboard, which were in turn laid on top of sheets of chipboard. There was an unconnected radiator lying against the wall. The construction was similar to many such underground bunkers discovered by the gardaí over the years in the fight against the IRA. Such bunkers were used by paramilitary organisations both for safe storage of munitions and hiding volunteers on the run.

O'Sullivan immediately called Maguire on his mobile phone and asked him to send a team from the Garda Technical Bureau in Dublin. The bureau would examine the bunker. They arrived at 1 p.m.

Having completed the search of the house, the garda team began searching a garage, shed, and the surrounding lands. Inside the garage was Campbell's Audi car along with the usual paraphernalia to be found in any garage. But there was more. The search team found two packets of cotton gloves, two disposable body suits and £660 in cash.

The team also found a roll of plastic tubing, a roll of black insulating tape, a pair of rubber gloves and a rucksack in the garage. While the items may appear to be everyday, innocuous purchases, when all are combined, they painted a far more sinister picture. The detectives believed, that combined, they were strong evidence of paramilitary activity. O'Sullivan meticulously collected all the evidence. The gardaí seized everything, saying the items were possible evidence of bomb making. There were also 15 cases of champagne found in this shed. Everything was transported to Dundalk Garda Station.

The search concluded at 2 p.m. O'Sullivan and the others travelled to Kells Garda Station in County Meath, where Campbell had been taken. Teams of gardaí interviewed him at length. He never said a word, refusing to answer even the most basic questions. He was caught and he knew it.

Maguire oversaw the operation and the interrogation from behind the scenes. He knew he had enough evidence to press charges. He had been in consultations with the DPP, briefing legal officer Niall Lombard on the day's events.

The blue plastic containers found in the search had been encountered previously in terrorist incidents, according to Maguire. They are used to store arms because they are waterproof and can be stored underground. Similar barrels had been used to store HME.

There was other evidence found at the house and its grounds. The plastic tubing seized was of the type used to make improvised detonating cord. The tubing is used to house PETN and RDX explosives, both commonly used by republican paramilitaries. As for the disposable body suits and gloves, they have been frequently used in an effort to thwart forensic detection.

Special Branch had a rock solid case. At 4.30 p.m. the DPP instructed Maguire to have Campbell brought before the Special

Criminal Court in Dublin to be charged with membership of an unlawful organisation. At 5 p.m. the suspect was released from custody under Section 30 of the Offences Against the State Act and re-arrested by Hanrahan outside Kells Garda Station under section 4, Criminal Law Act, 1997. This was in accordance with procedure.

At 6.05 p.m. he was taken to the Special Criminal Court by Special Branch. At 7.30 p.m. he was charged with membership of an unlawful organisation. Within the space of 48 hours, Campbell had been arrested and charged. It was a body blow to the RIRA.

THERE WAS ANOTHER body blow coming. On 10 October, the BBC programme *Panorama* broadcast the names of five men allegedly connected with the Omagh bombing. The corporation had earlier fought off legal attempts to injunct the broadcast. Among those named were Campbell, Colm Murphy, Séamus McKenna and Séamus Daly. Although Murphy had yet to stand trial, the documentary revealed the contents of his interviews in garda custody. This had the net effect of causing a flurry of legal activity in the courts. Murphy's lawyers demanded a mistrial.

Three days after the *Panorama* programme, things got even more serious for the RIRA. Ever since its formation in late 1997, there had been a torrent of media speculation about the possibility of a feud erupting between the Provos and the RIRA. The IRA dismissed the RIRA as nothing more than a joke organisation. They had christened them the 'Coca-Colas'—because they were the 'Real Thing'. But, under the surface, there were increasing tensions as the RIRA slowly began to make an impression in Belfast and other parts of Northern Ireland.

That tension exploded on 13 October when the Provisional IRA assassinated Joe O'Connor, the Officer Commanding of the West Belfast Brigade of the RIRA. O'Connor was 26-years-old and a married father of three. He had just left his mother's house on Whitecliffe Parade in Ballymurphy and was getting into a car when the gunmen approached. The masked men shot him at point blank range. He died within seconds.

Although no one admitted responsibility, it was clear within hours that it was the IRA. What was not so clear, however, was the reason why he was killed. O'Connor had verbally abused the IRA's Adjutant Officer, who was a leading member of Sinn Féin. The IRA also feared O'Connor and viewed him as a threat.

Either way, the entire republican movement was shocked by the killing. People feared that the RIRA would seek immediate revenge. That fear appeared to be borne out when the RIRA issued a statement shortly after his murder.

'Our volunteers will be protected, and at a time and place of our choosing, those guilty of this offence will be dealt with accordingly. This is not an idle threat and should not be treated as such. Nor should it be interpreted as a signal for all-out indiscriminate attacks on innocent republicans loyal to the Provo leadership.'

The truth was that the RIRA Army Council didn't care. O'Connor was a thug and a criminal. So far, the RIRA have not exacted that revenge.

RUPERT RETURNED TO Ireland on 17 October, four days after O'Connor's killing. He booked into the Carrickdale Hotel again, where he held several meetings with McKevitt. This time money was thin on the ground. He brought $6,300 from the Irish Freedom Committee and a computer he had bought in the name of Anthony Blair for Bernadette Sands McKevitt.

When he arrived, he called McKevitt on his mobile to make arrangements to meet him. Once more McKevitt let his guard down. At the first meeting, he spoke about a RIRA car bomb attack on Stewartstown in County Tyrone that July. Rupert was curious. And so were MI5.

The spy asked McKevitt why the bomb had been set when he had earlier said he didn't want more car bombs in the wake of Omagh, except in central London or beside military bases. McKevitt was apologetic. He said it had actually started out as a planned attack on a British Army movement but when the troops did not show up, the Active Service Unit decided to transport the bomb into the town where they detonated it. McKevitt said that he had disciplined the volunteers for doing so.

Rupert could see McKevitt was in high spirits. The Quartermaster said he wanted four MI6-type attacks per year, attacks in which the security forces came under direct machine gun fire.

He also said he wanted those attacks backed up by at least one explosive device per month placed on the British Rail system. They, in turn, would be backed up by about two warnings per week in the form of bogus calls. This was sure to cause maximum disruption and publicity.

He told Rupert that he had several teams operating in Britain, which he used on a rotating basis for attacks, always holding the team going to do the next job in a form of quarantine. The other teams were continuously carrying out reconnaissance of possible targets.

The conversations inevitably returned to money. McKevitt constantly stressed the need for funding and directed Rupert to start a smuggling operation in the US to finance the RIRA activities in Ireland. He knew Rupert was a smuggler and wanted to avail of his skills.

WITH MCKEVITT'S DECISION to revamp the RIRA came a change in the leadership of the Dublin Brigade. The mole hunts in the capital had caused friction among the brigade. When the hunt to identify Dixon failed to locate the guilty party, the Army Council stood down the entire brigade. However, the crackdown didn't last long.

It was inconceivable that Dublin should have no brigade. When the Army Council reconstituted the unit it appointed Declan Carroll, a 24 year old volunteer from Edenmore Crescent in Raheny as an important leader. From the moment of his appointment, he was targeted by Special Branch. The Garda wanted the RIRA leadership to know they still knew everything.

Carroll made no secret of his republican credentials and wore his republican beliefs on his sleeve. His first public appearance of sorts had occurred the previous August when he carried the coffin of

Robbie Doolin, an acclaimed actor who had joined the RIRA after the Omagh bombing.

The RIRA attracted recruits from all walks of society, however, Doolin was an exception to the rule. He was a screen actor and was on the verge of greater things. His career was cut short when he died from a heart problem brought on by a combination of cocaine and physical restraint following an altercation.

Doolin was overtly republican though few realised how deeply his sympathies ran. He was known throughout Ireland for playing Willie in the RTE comedy *Upwardly Mobile*, however, his acting career stretched through stage, television, and film as well as in directing and producing. His first major break in television came in 1991 when he played the real-life role of Kenneth Best, the Corkman who had been brain-damaged by the Wellcome three-in-one vaccine. He made international headlines in the drama documentary series *Against The Odds* for the BBC. He had also starred in the films *The Commitments* and *The Snapper* and also in the series *The Family* for BBC. Carroll had worn military-type clothing at Doolin's funeral. He went out of his way to be noticed.

On 29 November 2000, Special Branch raided his home. The search concentrated on his bedroom and proved good. Detectives found a forensic document on how to make explosives, a mobile phone document, and a document on how to avoid giving information during police interrogations. He was charged with IRA membership but released on bail.

MCKEVITT WANTED TO make it big. He wanted to form alliances with other terrorist groups and rogue governments that shared his hatred of the British. He told Rupert he was looking for some kind of state sponsorship and asked him to keep his ear to the ground. He was hoping someone would contact them and offer the RIRA guns, bombs, and cash.

McKevitt's desire to become a client of a foreign state was too good an opportunity for MI5 to ignore. That same desire led to a sting operation by MI5, which deprived McKevitt of three senior volunteers.

The security services decided to try and trap McKevitt. They used Saddam Hussein as the bait. They created a plan—code-named Operation Samnite—that would see its officers posing as Iraqi intelligence agents, offering the RIRA cash and weapons to help fund a war against the British.

The first contact was made through a north County Dublin republican in late 2000, just weeks after McKevitt told Rupert he was looking for an ally abroad. MI5 sent a letter to a RIRA supporter in north Dublin. The authors said they were Middle Eastern journalists and wanted to research a series of articles on the RIRA, the organisation that had been so audacious as to attack the HQ of MI6. Later they 'admitted' they were representatives of Iraqi intelligence in a series of telephone calls and claimed they wanted to help the RIRA. The Army Council took the bait.

On 19 January 2001, the agents were told to ring a mobile phone number in Ireland. Their call was answered by McKevitt himself. Five more calls followed and, on 7 February, the first meeting was held at a location in Eastern Europe. It was attended by two key lieutenants of McKevitt, Declan Rafferty from Dundalk and Fintan O'Farrell from Monaghan. They met a British agent who they believed was an Iraqi official called Samir. At that first meeting, the two men admitted the RIRA's involvement in the MI6 attack. They promised they could be even more successful, if they had the right equipment. The two sides met again in April, this time in Slovakia. Another republican was part of the delegation: Mickey McDonald, a RIRA hardman from County Louth. McDonald was a drug dealer and thug. The two sides settled down to dinner. At the table, McDonald wrote out a shopping list on a piece of tissue paper. The wish list contained 5,000kgs of plastic explosives, 2,000 detonators, 200 rocket-propelled grenades and 500 handguns. He was unhappy at the prospect of the 'Iraqis' keeping the written shopping list: he knew it was evidence against him. But one of the 'Iraqis' reached over, blew his nose with the tissue and put it in his pocket.

MI5 WERE NOT the only security agency running a clandestine operation against the RIRA. Crime and Security and Special

Branch were engaged in the darkest of subterfuge. Forensic analysis of bombs constructed by the RIRA showed the same engineers constructed the detonating mechanisms used in scores of attacks. Crime and Security continued to run a number of high level informants in the RIRA and these identified the engineers as twin brothers from Finglas in north Dublin.

Kenneth Patterson was 31 years old and a separated father of three. He had served in the Irish Army from 1990 until August 2000. When he left the Defence Forces, he started working in the private sector as a general worker in a plastics moulding plant. Only those close to him and his twin brother, Alan, knew they were militant republicans.

Every shred of intelligence gathered by Special Branch suggested the brothers were running a state of the art bomb making factory. Similar TPUs had been found on 41 occasions since they were first used in a bomb found at Hackballscross, near the border, in the spring of 1998. The British police had found similar timing mechanisms in the devices used to bomb London.

Special Branch trailed the twins everywhere. There was a lot of accurate intelligence on the brothers which suggested the bomb factory was located somewhere in Dundalk town centre.

The surveillance operation came to fruition on 9 June 2001 when the brothers were arrested near Dundalk Train Station. One of the brothers carried a Nike sports bag. When the twins sat into a waiting car, a Special Branch car pulled up behind and sounded its siren. When the vehicle was stopped and searched, gardaí found incriminating evidence. The Pattersons were caught carrying a TPU and two balaclavas. The timing unit in their possession had two time settings, one for 60 and one for 120 minutes.

The arrests sparked off a series of house searches in Dublin and Dundalk. The intelligence on the bomb factory had been accurate. It was located at a workshop at McEntee Avenue.

Three quarters of a kilo of Semtex explosive, an air pistol and a quantity of ammunition were later located at an apartment in Dublin. There was enough Semtex to make two under car booby trap bombs or a booster for a larger bomb.

An apartment at Marmion Court in Dublin city resulted in significant arms seizures. Gardaí found Mark 19 time-and-power units—an updated and improved version of previous units.

The Pattersons were caught red handed. The two later pleaded guilty to the unlawful possession of explosive substances. Alan Patterson pleaded guilty to additional charges of unlawful possession of three-quarters of a kilo of Semtex explosive, an air pistol and a quantity of ammunition at Marmion Court. The Garda had struck another blow against the RIRA. MI5, though, were about to pull off another one.

IN JULY, THERE was a third and final meeting of the Iraqi and RIRA operation, this time in Slovakia. The two sides again discussed the RIRA's arms needs and the Irish delegation said they wanted sniper rifles and missiles. MI5 were bugging the meeting. They had also flown a team of lawyers to the Balkans. These advised the agents on how to proceed. The lawyers listened to the talks as they happened. When their lawyers heard the RIRA ask for weapons, they knew they had the evidence they needed. As the meal was going on, the British authorities applied for an international arrest warrant to the Slovakian authorities. When the Irishmen left the restaurant, they were quickly arrested by Slovakian police.

The trio were later extradited to Britain where they pleaded guilty to conspiring to cause an explosion. The arms smugglers were jailed for 30 years each. It was a bitter blow to the Army Council and McKevitt. In McDonald, he had lost one of his key allies. But he had others.

JAMES SMITH WAS McKevitt's man on the ground in America. Rupert was only a liaison officer; his role was to pass messages between the two men. Rupert, though, would also keep McKevitt informed about Smith's personal life. During a previous trip, Rupert told McKevitt that Smith had a new girlfriend—she had a military background and was helping RIRA efforts in the US. This was a cause of concern to McKevitt. 'Nobody is in unless I say they are in,' he shouted. McKevitt told Rupert to get Smith to move away from

Massachusetts and sanctioned him to use $2,000 of the Irish Freedom Committee money to this end.

When he returned to America, Rupert relayed the order. Smith was a soldier and obeyed, though all he did was move across town. McKevitt was very annoyed over this because one of his operators had disobeyed a direct order.

During this trip, McKevitt told Rupert he had taken personal control of the investigation into Joe O'Connor's murder as Campbell had been arrested and had not got bail. He told him there was a safe house north of the border and he brought down the new O/C of the Belfast Brigade to interview about the killing. The other person in the car at the time O'Connor was shot was also brought down from Belfast. McKevitt said he told this person that if he told lies during the investigation he would be shot.

The volunteers gave the names of the people who did the shooting and also gave the name of another witness. McKevitt then ordered that this independent witness be invited to come down and give evidence. The witness apparently corroborated the volunteer's evidence when questioned. This was all normal business as far as McKevitt was concerned.

Rupert had in the meantime brought over the Apogee Rock Sim 4.0 software McKevitt's engineers had earlier ordered. The engineers hoped to use the software for terrorism. When Rupert met McKevitt, he told him that it was there for him in the hotel room at the Carrickdale. McKevitt said he would get someone to pick it up. When Rupert arrived back at the hotel, he was met by a courier who said, 'Do you have a package for Stephen?' Rupert handed the software to him.

In the course of the black operation, McKevitt and Rupert became closer than close. Rupert's ingenuity at gaining McKevitt's trust was stunning. He was a super spy. He obtained intelligence and information every time the two men spoke. One day, they were out for a drive and McKevitt said he had sent representatives to a conference on human rights. He had wanted the delegation to make contact with states that might be interested in sponsoring the RIRA, but they came home empty handed.

On the same car journey, McKevitt asked Rupert about his thoughts on attacking the British Naval vessel that patrolled Carlingford Lough, the water border between Northern Ireland and the Republic. He wanted to attack the ship in the same way the USS Cole had been destroyed in Yemen by the extremist Islamic organisation, Al Qaeda. The only problem was, unlike Al Qaeda, the RIRA had no suicide bombers.

The conversations rarely veered from the issue of arms procurement. McKevitt asked Rupert to set up an arms dump in the US for all the items they had bought. His instructions were clear. He told Rupert to collect whatever arms Smith had bought and to put them in an arms dump. The two also discussed very important Army Council business. McKevitt revealed that Campbell was to be replaced on the Army Council if he was not released by the upcoming Friday, as per the rules of the army. The truth was that McKevitt and Campbell were not seeing eye to eye. McKevitt was moving to take control of everything. He told Rupert that, because of Campbell's arrest, he now had to take a more hands on approach to the day-to-day operations of the RIRA. He was now having to give orders directly to people. Campbell, however, got bail.

Rupert spent that afternoon at McKevitt's house installing a computer for Bernadette. When he was there he noticed one of the bookshelves contained a pocket guide for hotels in Yugoslavia and a French road map. He took notes of the same. Little passed him. He returned to Chicago on 22 October 2001.

ALTHOUGH THE RIRA never attained the same level of support achieved by the Provisionals, McKevitt's organisation did launch an effective bombing campaign that autumn. Bomb-makers graduated from the training department and produced a steady stream of explosive devices capable of outwitting the British Army's jamming signals and counter-terrorism devices. The war effort, though, continued to be hampered by informants and surveillance.

On 26 October 2001, four days after Rupert flew back to America, the RUC intercepted a partially-made 600lbs bomb during searches of Hannahstown, which is on the outskirts of west Belfast. It was

destined for the show jumping championships at Olympia in
London. The bomb was due to be transported by ferry from Larne
in County Antrim to Stranraer in Scotland then south to London.
The route was the one chosen by the IRA to transport the 1,000lbs
dockland's bomb, which ended its 18 month ceasefire in February
1996.

An informant had betrayed the operation. The Army Council was
undeterred, however. To streamline efficiency and deter the
security services they shifted operational control back to the border
from Belfast, where informants were less easily recruited.

The next attack came on 11 November but, again, was foiled by
the RUC and British Army. Officers stopped a van containing the
device at Teemore crossroads near Derrylin on the main
Enniskillen to Dublin road. Two scout cars accompanying the bomb
car were also stopped during the operation. The ASU managed to
escape in the incident in which RUC officers fired two shots.

JAMES SMITH WAS now a key figure in the RIRA, albeit from afar.
When he was back in Chicago, Rupert maintained an e-mail
correspondence with the soldier about the instructions handed out
by McKevitt. The Quartermaster had told Smith to transfer his
dump to Rupert. This was an ideal chance for the FBI to intercept
any weapons Smith wanted to send to McKevitt. Once the
whereabouts of the weapons was confirmed, their specialist units
could affix small transmitters to the weapons. This would allow
them to be followed and intercepted.

Rupert eventually met Smith on 20 December at the Holiday Inn
in Worchester in the state of Massachusetts. The FBI had bugged
the room and hired an adjacent room to mount the security
operation. Like a spider waiting for a fly to enter its web, Rupert sat
on the bed and waited.

When he appeared, Smith was carrying a shoulder bag full of
various bomb-making equipment and guns. The entire meeting was
filmed and recorded by the FBI. The deal took less than 30 minutes.
Smith completely incriminated himself. When he was finished,
Smith said goodbye. The FBI let him go. He wasn't arrested even

though they had proof of his involvement. If he had been stopped, Rupert's cover would have been blown.

Smith was deported to Ireland weeks later. News was relayed to Crime and Security, however, they did not tell Special Branch. Smith wasn't arrested. He re-entered Ireland and resumed his life.

Crime and Security now realised they had an opportunity to jail McKevitt for once and for all. Discussions began with Rupert, the British and the FBI, in late 2000 and the following January the spy eventually agreed to testify against McKevitt. This, of course, was for money. He had cut a deal. The dramatic development remained a closely guarded secret.

IN THE MEANTIME, McKevitt continued to command the RIRA Crime and Security maintained their vigilance. The coming of 2001 brought more attacks. The bombs were now getting bigger. On 16 January, the RUC intercepted a 1,100lbs bomb at Brootally Cross on the Monaghan Road in County Armagh. It was primed and ready for use. The police believed it was to be used to attack a passing RUC patrol.

Days earlier, the RIRA had mounted another unsuccessful attack, this time in Cookstown in County Tyrone. A device was thrown at a passing police car, but it failed to explode.

The RIRA was never a group to let personal feelings rule its decision making process. But that January, the Army Council decided to revenge the embarrassment it suffered at the hands of the BBC *Panorama* programme. The Army Council was deeply angry at the BBC naming Campbell.

The attack took place on 4 January. The ASU phoned in two warnings. The first was received by a London hospital and the second by a charitable trust at around 11.30 p.m. It was a Saturday night. One of the three ASUs operating in Britain abandoned a black taxi laden with a bomb outside the corporation's news centre in the Wood Lane area of Shepherd's Bush. The warning was deliberately false and the device went off as bomb squad officers tried to carry out a controlled explosion. Television staff had already been evacuated but one London Underground worker suffered deep cuts to his eye from flying glass. Heavy damage was also caused to the front of the building.

MI5 had been waiting for the attack to happen. They were also keeping an open mind about possible links between the blast and the explosion at a nearby Territorial Army barracks in February, which blinded a 14-year-old cadet. Stephen Menary had his left hand blown off by a bomb packed inside a torch at the TA centre in South Africa Road, Shepherd's Bush. Although Campbell was on bail facing membership charges, he was still very active. He wanted the BBC and MI5 to know this.

On 13 February, gardaí in County Monaghan located a mark-15 type mortar near Newtowncunningham during a planned search of an area several miles from the border. An informant had betrayed the operation. The device did not contain any explosives but was similar to the mortar fired at the Ebrington army base in Derry city.

THEN, ON 15 March, something that no one expected happened. The families of the 29 bomb victims murdered in the Omagh bombing launched an appeal to raise £2m to fund a civil suit against the RIRA and five individuals. The families planned to sue the RIRA. The action was the brainchild of Victor Barker, whose son James died in the blast, and caught the public's imagination. From the moment it began, it received high profile support. Former Northern Ireland secretaries Peter Mandelson, Tom King, Peter Brooke, Lord Hurd, Lord Prior and Lord Merlyn-Rees signed in support of the Omagh Victims' Legal Fund.

The legal action began with a civil writ issued at Belfast's high court naming five men. Those named were Séamus McKenna, Michael McKevitt, Liam Campbell, Colm Murphy, and Séamus Daly. The RIRA was also named as a defendant but there was no mention of the CIRA. McKenna was a bricklayer from Dundalk. He had worked for Colm Murphy. Daly came from Culloville. He also worked as a labourer for Colm Murphy. The civil action stunned the RIRA.

However, McKevitt would soon have more serious problems to face than a civil case for compensation. His career as a republican was about to end.

17

THE NEXT VICTIM

FOR 30 YEARS McKevitt had proved to be an elusive and dangerous quarry for the gardaí. He engaged in terrorism in the name of Ireland, imported enough weapons to equip an army, yet had never been caught. That was all about to change.

In late February 2002, Rupert sat down with Martin Callinan and Diarmuid O'Sullivan and made a full, detailed statement about his involvement in the republican movement. Callinan and O'Sullivan had overseen the black operation on behalf of Garda HQ. When he was interviewed, he related how he came to Ireland in the early 1990s; how he fell in with the Republican Sinn Féin supporters; how he was introduced to McKevitt; how McKevitt asked him to purchase items for the RIRA in America and how McKevitt talked of his plans for various operations. He left nothing out. He even put in small vignettes that he believed would help corroborate his claims when he took the stand. For example, he specifically mentioned his visit to McKevitt's house to install the computer software. On that visit he deliberately looked at a bookshelf, where he saw a guide to Yugoslavian hotels and a French road map. Both would later be found at McKevitt's home—proving that he had actually been there.

Rupert was also secreted into Ireland. The ERU brought him to Counties Donegal and Louth. He identified the houses and locations where he met McKevitt and Campbell. The gardaí took further statements from him about this. The prosecutions case had to be watertight.

The statement he made was sent to the DPP. When the Irish authorities read it, they knew immediately that McKevitt was finished. Not only did they have enough to search McKevitt's house, they knew they had enough to see McKevitt convicted—and jailed for a long time. They believed he could not only be charged with membership of the RIRA, but also the newly created offence of directing terrorism. That offence was introduced to the Irish statute book just weeks after the Omagh bomb. It carried a maximum penalty of life in prison.

It was time to bring him in.

McKEVITT'S DAY OF reckoning came early on 29 March 2001. The time was 6.45 a.m. Diarmuid O'Sullivan and William Hanrahan led the search on his home at Beechpark in Blackrock in County Louth. The gardaí were met with no animosity when they knocked on the door. McKevitt opened the door and allowed the gardaí into his home. It was early in the morning and present were McKevitt, his wife Bernadette and their three children.

At 7 a.m. O'Sullivan arrested McKevitt under the terms of the Offences Against the State on suspicion of being a member of an unlawful organisation. He was formally cautioned but made no reply.

He was then driven to Balbriggan Garda Station in north County Dublin, where his details were recorded in the custody record by Garda Joe Kilcoyne. Once in custody, he asked to make a phone call to his solicitor James McGuill, who was based in Dundalk town.

BACK AT BLACKROCK, the gardaí began the slow process of sifting for evidence that they hoped would back up the evidence that Rupert was likely to give in court. They seized a large volume of documents, together with the Compaq computer Rupert had bought in America and a Lacie hard drive. They also found the road map of France and a booklet of Yugoslavian hotels that Rupert had mentioned in his statement. They found another Packard Bell desktop PC. All were seized.

In anticipation of his arrest, Peter Maguire and his team had spent three days drafting a set of 750 questions which the interrogators would put to McKevitt. Maguire had spent some time examining Rupert's statement and drafted questions material to membership of the RIRA and directing terrorism. The questions were crafted with the sole intention of securing charges against the republican. McKevitt would have no way out.

At 4.40 p.m. that day, gardaí began interviewing him. McKevitt was repeatedly asked if he was a member of an illegal organisation —he repeatedly denied any involvement in any illegal organisation. Officers then turned their attention to his relationship with David Rupert. One of the interrogators came to the point.

He said, 'Michael, do you know David Rupert from the USA?' McKevitt replied, 'I don't know him by name.'

The Quartermaster was then asked, 'Do you know a person by the name of David Rupert and he is about 6 feet 7 inches in height and he is from the USA?'

'I know nobody of that name.'

In a later interview the next day, starting at 2.33 p.m., McKevitt was again asked, 'Do you know David Rupert?'

He replied, 'I don't know a David Rupert.'

He repeated mantra replies to whether he knew Rupert.

'I can't recall any meeting with David Rupert,' he would say, and 'I am not a member of an illegal organisation.'

Laterally, he decided to make 'No reply' comments to questions asked of him by interviewing members.

During the second day, McKevitt began to panic. His ice cool exterior began to melt away. He couldn't understand how the gardaí had pieces of paper which he had scribbled on months previously. The receipt which he gave to Rupert with the words 'Received from IFC the sum of $6,500' and signed Pat O'Hagan was there. Special

Branch also had another piece of paper which he gave to Rupert. This was the name and address of James Smith.

The interrogation teams put other evidence to him. He knew his career in the RIRA was over. He was going to jail. The gardaí were simply going through the motions before they went to court. He was right. Later that night, McKevitt was rushed to the Special Criminal Court and charged with directing terrorism and membership of the IRA. He was shocked. The RIRA began to fall apart.

DERMOT JENNINGS WAS promoted to the rank of Assistant Garda Commissioner for his services to the State shortly after McKevitt's arrest. His replacement was Martin Callinan who took over as Chief Superintendent at Crime and Security. He and O'Sullivan flew to Chicago to meet Rupert on 18 April 2001. The purpose of the visit was to take a further statement from the spy to clarify some legal matters. Callinan was already in possession of the e-mails Rupert had sent to the FBI and MI5. This meeting was important.

At the meeting Callinan produced 12 photographs and asked Rupert if he recognised anyone. He did. Number two was the owner of the house he pointed out to gardaí in Jenkinstown where the Army Council meeting had taken place. Number three was Joe O'Neill, number four was Michael McKevitt, number five was Bernadette McKevitt, number six was Séamus McGrane, number seven was Liam Campbell, number eight was Des Long, number nine was Ruairí Óg Ó Brádaigh, number 10 was John Joe McCusker but he didn't recognise numbers one, 11 and 12.

Rupert was also shown photos found by gardaí during the raid on the McKevitt home. Two of the photos were taken at the 32 County Sovereignty Movement meeting at the Carrickdale Hotel. The subject of each photo was the same but he didn't know the identity of the person. But he did recognise himself in the background of each of the pictures. Another picture was of Marion Price —again Rupert was visible in the background. The fourth photo was from the same meeting and showed Bernadette McKevitt walking towards Rupert.

CAMPBELL SHOULD HAVE been dismissed from the Army Council once he had been arrested, however, the rule was ignored. Campbell was out on bail and still had plenty to offer the RIRA. He assumed control of the RIRA and decided to step up the English campaign. On 14 April, the London ASU attacked a post office sorting centre at Edgeware Road. This time no warning was given.

The bomb was planted outside the sorting office in a bricked-up former doorway and was a replica of the device used to attack Hammersmith Bridge. It contained between half and one pound of high explosives. The building was a small delivery office dealing with mail for the NW9 area, and one of 100 similar-sized buildings in London.

The Army Council continued the campaign at home but not with the same success. The British Army and PSNI, as the RUC was now known, intercepted a fully armed 'barrack buster' mortar bomb packed with 90kgs of high explosives in County Tyrone. It was found inside an abandoned van near Altmore Forest, between Dungannon and Carrickmore. A man living in the area received an anonymous phone call to his home and found it himself before alerting the authorities. A hole had been cut in the roof of the van for the bomb to be fired towards its target. Meanwhile, the London ASU started to get cocky. On 6 May, they returned to the Edgeware Road and left another half-pound device in exactly the same spot as before.

CAMPBELL WAS WITHOUT question the most senior figure in the RIRA to face membership charges so far. However, he was not the first to be convicted. That distinction was given to Dermot Gannon, a CIRA member from Mulhuddart in west Dublin. He was convicted for IRA membership on 1 June 2001.

Gannon had been arrested the previous October during an operation against the CIRA mounted by Special Branch. His accomplices were two Dubliners: Gabriel Donohue, from Alpine Heights in Clondalkin, and his older brother Anthony, a taxi-driver from Palmerstown.

Anthony Donoghue was a CIRA supporter and acted as a quartermaster of sorts for the Dublin region. He used his brother to store weapons though he wasn't a militant republican. The two men pleaded guilty to the charges and both received suspended prison sentences.

Anthony Donoghue was given a five-year sentence suspended for five years and was fined £3,000. His brother, Gabriel, was given a two-year sentence suspended for two years. The Special Criminal Court realised that he had been pressurised into helping the CIRA.

Gannon, however, decided to fight his case. He was a militant republican. When his home was raided by Special Branch, the search team had found an Army uniform, a forged driving licence and four CB radios, but there were no guns or ammunition. Gannon was arrested and taken into custody. He expected to be freed within hours but he was charged with membership of an illegal organisation under the 1998 Offences Against the State (Amendment) Act.

This was the legislation introduced in the wake of the Omagh bombing. Under the Act, a person's refusal to answer garda questions during interrogation can be used as evidence in court. Gannon ignored this fact. His trial before the Special Criminal Court lasted three days and broke new ground. Special Branch alleged that Gannon was the leader of a weapons-gathering unit of the CIRA and had control over the weapons seized from the Donoghue brothers.

The evidence against him consisted of the CB radios and a uniform found in a press under the stairs in his house. Among the other items uncovered were two black berets, one of which was Irish Army issue. A driving licence had also been found in a kitchen press but Gannon did not drive.

The real evidence came from Gannon himself. Gannon had refused to co-operate with the gardaí from the beginning. He refused to answer any questions despite being warned that such action could be used as collaborating evidence against him. His refusal to answer any questions helped the gardaí build a case against him. The testimony of a Chief Superintendent was enough to secure a conviction for IRA membership.

When Basil Walsh, who was the Chief Superintendent in charge of Special Branch, testified that Gannon was a member of the IRA, the Special Criminal Court accepted his word. Gannon himself could certainly have weakened the effect of such evidence by giving evidence in court, but he declined the opportunity. Gannon was a CIRA operator and would not recognise the court.

When he was found guilty and sentenced to five years, he stood up, gave a clenched-fist salute, and shouted, "Up Óglaigh na hÉireann, you wankers!" as he was led from the dock. His exit from court may have been entertaining but it had deadly serious repercussions for the RIRA and CIRA. A legal precedent had been established.

CRIME AND SECURITY working hand in hand with Special Branch continued to run agents inside the RIRA. These provided grade A information which permitted the gardaí to strike with surgical-like precision against specific targets. Operations were planned and executed with specific targets in mind. The strategy had a powerful impact on the RIRA. It collapsed morale. No one knew who to trust or where the gardaí would strike next. It was clear to all sides that Crime and Security and Special Branch knew everything that happened inside the secret army. The truth was that many arrests were the result of intrusive surveillance operations. Other arrests were the results of black operations. Informants would give precise details to their handlers which would allow Special Branch to strike with deadly precision. Special Branch brought dozens of suspects before the Special Criminal Court on membership charges.

One black operation mounted that summer secured the conviction of two important RIRA volunteers from the midlands region. Richard Whyte was a trained sniper with the Defence Forces. He was 31-years-old and came from the village of Kildangan in County Kildare. Although a member of the Defence Forces, Whyte was a militant republican.

The second target was John Maloney of the neighbouring village of Athy. Maloney was a republican who had been involved in an 'extremist nationalist organisations for some time.' He had threatened to leave the RIRA in the wake of the Omagh atrocity saying no true republican could ever condone such a calamitous massacre. However, he remained a member.

He knew he was under surveillance for some time. Strange cars and vans cruised by his home round the clock. One day he noticed a dog barking at what he thought were rabbits in a hedge only to discover a detective wearing combat fatigues lying in the undergrowth. Maloney told the officer not to waste his time and go home. Maloney and Whyte were old fashioned republicans who didn't engage in smuggling or crime. They were loyal to the cause. That's what made them prime targets.

On 7 July the two were arrested after Special Branch found a RIRA training camp in dense woodland in Kilart Bog. Detectives had found an assortment of guns, ammunition and documents at the camp, which Whyte managed. Forensic examinations on a balaclava found at the camp revealed a microscopic flake of dandruff. A DNA sample extracted from the evidence had linked Whyte to the training camp. The two were subsequently jailed for their role in running the camp, which had trained over 50 volunteers. Whyte caused a few chuckles when he was sentenced. As he was led from the dock, he shouted 'Subservient imperialists!' at his trial judges.

THE SPECIAL BRANCH offensive did not terminate with the arrests of Maloney and Whyte. On 29 July, Campbell, Declan Carroll, the young Dublin commander, Seán Mulligan, a seasoned operator from Carnalughoge in County Louth, and Robert Brennan, a volunteer from Dublin, were all arrested.

The four were attending a secret meeting of the RIRA at the Neptune Hotel in Bettystown in County Meath. An informant had alerted Special Branch to the meeting. Plain-clothes detectives were already in place before the RIRA delegation even arrived.

Brennan was monitored entering the hotel carrying a holdall bag. He was discreetly tailed to a room where Campbell and Mulligan were waiting. They had just got down to business when the door came crashing in. Inside the holdall carried by Brennan was a stun-gun. Carroll arrived while gardaí searched the room.

All four were charged but only three sought bail. Campbell made no application although Carroll did. This was vigorously opposed by the gardaí who noted that he was already on bail facing charges. This time, bail was refused.

Brennan was subsequently found guilty of IRA membership. He was jailed for four years. Mulligan was also found guilty of IRA membership and jailed for five years.

Mulligan was a committed RIRA volunteer from County Louth. He had four previous convictions including one for the attempted murder of a garda. The convictions, dating back to 1977, included unlawful possession of firearms with intent to endanger life and assault with intent to rob.

He had it coming to him. His trial judges heard that items found during a previous search of his home included documents with the specific reference: 'The war is nearly over and some volunteers wanted to get something for themselves.' Carroll was also convicted and jailed. Campbell is still facing charges in relation to this offence.

OMAGH CONTINUED TO haunt the conscience of Ireland. The bereaved families never stopped in their campaign to bring the bombers to justice. When the relatives of those murdered at Omagh engaged on the path to find out what happened, they uncovered a conspiracy of silence in the RUC/PSNI. The police had received warnings prior to Omagh and failed to act. The families could trust no one. They heard varying accounts of what happened. One version came from a former Provo called Kevin Fulton. He went public that July.

Fulton was a double agent who recounted sensational allegations about Omagh. He was a former British soldier turned RUC and Customs agent from Newry, County Down. He claimed to have given the RUC advance warnings that the RIRA were planning an attack. His story was as follows: He said he had been speaking to a well known dissident republican in the south Armagh border area who told him the RIRA were planning to move explosives into Northern Ireland 'over the next few days'. He also said the dissident he named as 'Mooch' had dust on his clothes consistent with grinding down fertilizers used in explosives. Fulton named several dissidents in a call to the RUC. However, he did not name Omagh as the target. The RUC chief constable Sir Ronnie Flanagan dismissed the allegations as 'an outrageous untruth'.

Victor Barker was also unimpressed by Fulton's claims. Fulton went to see Barker in his home shortly after the allegations first appeared.

'Fulton alleges that the bomber was an undercover agent who is being protected by MI5, which is why they are doing nothing to get the bombers. I rang Sir Ronnie Flanagan to ask him about this. Flanagan said to me, "This is categorical rubbish."'

Barker chose his words carefully in describing Fulton. He said he believed the spy was not a totally reliable witness.

'Everyone has an agenda. I took the view that Fulton had an agenda too and his agenda was getting paid.'

However, the allegations stuck. There was worse to come for the RUC. Following Fulton's claims, the Northern Ireland Police Ombudswoman Nuala O'Loan, decided to carry out a full investigation.

The probe uncovered details of an anonymous phone call made to Enniskillen RUC station on 4 August, 11 days before the bombing. The caller said two AK47 rifles and a grenade launcher were to be used against the RUC in or around Omagh. Police sources say that in response to this, the local commander directed that most of his officers be dispersed to provide a security cordon and to try and intercept any planned attack. This caused further controversy.

WHILE THE POLICE were preoccupied with the past sins of the RIRA, the Army Council was looking to the future. The Army Council was now controlled by smugglers loyal to Campbell. They had no interest in republican politics. They just wanted to continue the war. On 1 August, 20kgs of HME was found in a car at the long stay car park at Belfast International Airport. The warning was vague and an initial search proved fruitless. A second warning phoned to a Catholic priest pinpointed the vehicle; the device was hidden in a silver Volvo that was stolen in east Belfast on 21 June. The device was successfully defused.

London was next. Just one day after the Belfast attack, a car bomb exploded in Ealing Broadway, an area busy with pub and restaurant goers. A warning was received but a number of people were injured. The London ASU had struck again. In what was now normal procedure, a bomb would explode in London and be quickly followed up with another bomb in Northern Ireland. Within days of the Ealing attack, a primed bomb, containing 350lbs of HME in a creamery can, was discovered in a stone shed connected to a house in Glenaness Road near Sixmilecross in County Tyrone. The shed had been used as a workshop with drilling and light engineering equipment.

CAMPBELL'S TRIAL ON IRA membership came to court that same October. Remarkably he decided to recognise the Special Criminal Court and give evidence. IRA suspects rarely, if ever, offer to give evidence. Campbell decided otherwise when his three trial judges rejected submissions by his lawyer Michael O'Higgins that he had no case to answer. When this happened, Campbell threw caution to the wind. He took the stand and condemned the RIRA without a shred of irony.

'I don't agree with violence,' he said.

To the amazement and shock of those who witnessed his performance, Campbell portrayed himself as a struggling farmer who farmed five acres and rented another 12 near the border.

Under cross-examination, he told his defence counsel that he was not a member of the 'Real IRA' or the IRA for that matter. He went further, at one point, proclaiming that he did not support the aims of the 'Real IRA'. When asked if he condemned RIRA actions, he simply replied, 'I don't agree with violence.'

Of course, this was all nonsense. The more he said, the more he incriminated himself. The judges saw through his lies and sentenced him to five years in Portlaoise Prison.

The Director of Operations, the man who commanded the RIRA, was finally put behind bars. His conviction signalled another investigation. By this time the Criminal Assets Bureau had begun investigating his wealth. The bureau would later register a judgement for €820,000 against him.

ON 30 OCTOBER, the Belfast Brigade upped the pace and detonated a bomb on a hijacked bus outside a west Belfast police station. The device exploded on a bus on the Stewartstown Road near the gates of the Woodbourne base, as army experts tried to defuse it. Two armed and masked men had ordered the sole passenger off the bus and placed the device, carried in a holdall, three seats behind the driver and ordered him to drive to the police station. On arrival the men fled and the driver raised the alarm.

An army bomb disposal team carried out a number of controlled explosions on the device to try to defuse it, but during the operation it exploded.

Houses on the Stewartstown Road were evacuated and many elderly residents were forced out of their homes that night. The local police divisional commander said it was a 'reckless terrorist act in which people could have died or been injured'.

'The bus driver was forced to drive a bus containing a bomb along a busy route past housing and other traffic to the police station. This not only endangered the bus driver, but other road users and people living opposite the police station.

'No one was killed or seriously injured because the bomb exploded downwards.'

THE ASU IN London never stopped their attacks. On 3 November, the bombers planted a car bomb in Birmingham city centre. But this was to be the last attack. The ASU were arrested during an undercover Customs and Excise investigation into a fuel tax scam when equipment for a car bomb was found in a remote Yorkshire farmhouse. At least, that was the official story.

The five were Aiden Hulme, 26, his brother Robert, 23, and Noel Maguire, 34, James McCormack, 31, and John Paul Hannan, 19.

Hannan and McCormack admitted their part in the attacks when interrogated. The others fought and lost their cases. None had previous convictions for the RIRA. Their arrests were hailed as a major breakthrough in the fight against the RIRA but they were the scapegoats. None had built the bombs used in the offensive. The real bombers and engineers had escaped. Few believed that British Customs and Excise had stumbled upon the youths. The consensus was they were set up by an informant, perhaps one of the bombers.

The RIRA were convinced that someone at the highest levels worked for the security services. The CIRA got involved in trying to identify the mole and pointed the finger of blame at a smuggler who worked with Campbell. The truth was that no one knew. McKevitt had also asked himself the same question but couldn't find an answer.

THE CAMPAIGN IN the North continued. On 5 December, the British Army defused a bomb containing 35kgs of home-made explosive found under a railway line at Killeen Bridge in County Armagh. Two weeks later, on 19 December, the CIRA said it was responsible for detonating a device at the customs office on the Killyhevlin Industrial Estate in Enniskillen, County Fermanagh.

The New Year brought even more attacks. On 4 January 2002, there was a pipe bomb attack on a police officer's home in Annalong in County Down. It was the second time the officer's home had been attacked. The crude bomb was left under a shovel in a shed at the back of his house. On 3 March, a small explosion injured two boys in County Armagh. The boys, aged 15 and 16, suffered slight shrapnel wounds and burns when a bomb was planted in a police cone at Farmacaffley point-to-point races in County Armagh.

With McKevitt and Campbell behind bars, the RIRA became factionalised. The new Army Council mounted bomb attacks without having any political agenda or strategy. The stream of attacks indicated that the Army Council had lost control. RIRA Units now operated independent of each other.

JOHN WHITE HAD maintained his innocence from the day of his arrest. The detective sergeant claimed he was the victim of a conspiracy to silence him. He claimed to have told Jennings that Dixon had been asked to steal a car for a bombing days before the Omagh massacre. The information, White said, was tantamount to an advance warning. He gave precise details—times, dates, and locations. He went further. He said Crime and Security had allowed the RIRA to bomb Northern Ireland to protect informants and had missed opportunities to intercept stolen cars through ineptitude. He was specific in his details.

His story focused on three separate incidents. The first concerned the Mazda 626 which 'Jones' ordered from Dixon in February 1998. White said Crime and Security had missed the opportunity to attach a beacon to the vehicle when it was first stolen. The car was subsequently used in a mortar attack against a RUC Station in Moira that same March.

He made severe criticisms of Jennings. The most serious concerned the Omagh bombing. White suggested that Jennings knew the RIRA was planning a major bomb attack in the days before the massacre but failed to alert the RUC. His story concerned the car that Vinny and McNamara had been ordered to steal days before the attack.

The media was wary of the story for various reasons. For a start, White was facing serious corruption charges. It was also the case that his allegations were not supported by any evidence apart from his own word.

However, his story circulated like wildfire. White himself maintained secret contact with Dixon, who by this stage didn't know who to trust. The two had met each other after Dixon was taken into protective custody. Dixon gave Special Branch the slip on more than one occasion to meet White. On these occasions, White recorded his conversations with Dixon to prove his allegations. He needed some form of corroborative proof because he wasn't going to let the matter rest. And he didn't.

White was determined to bring the matter into the public domain. In January 2002, he made an audacious move and contacted

Michael Gallagher, the spokesman for the Omagh Relatives Support Group. He introduced himself as someone Gallagher should meet. The Omagh campaigner agreed to listen to White's story. Gallagher was struck and dumbfounded by the detective's apparent sincerity. White claimed in no uncertain terms that he was being set up but no one would listen to him.

Gallagher believed his story without question and offered to contact Martin Bridger, an investigator from the Police Ombudsman's Office in Northern Ireland. Bridger received the call at his office and listened to Gallagher. He explained that he had no authority to investigate members of the Garda; the position was clear. Gallagher, speaking with a grave sense of urgency, insisted that he should meet White. Bridger eventually agreed.

The meeting took place on 21 January that year at the Silver Birch Hotel in Omagh town. Gallagher accompanied White to the hotel where he introduced him to Bridger, and two other investigators, Stephen Hill and Irene Menzies. Once the formal introductions were over, Gallagher departed. White proceeded to outline his story and the secret work and methods used by Crime and Security. The conversation was brief but had the desired effect. The British investigators were interested and arranged to meet for a more formal debriefing session.

The second meeting took place two weeks later on 13 February at the Fir Trees Hotel in Strabane, County Tyrone. This time Bridger was accompanied soley by Menzies. White outlined his story yet again. The two investigators noted that White had a remarkable ability to recall details without having to read or refer to his own reports.

At this meeting, White passed over documentation which he claimed corroborated his story. Among the items he gave the Ombudsman team were a video cassette of news bulletins, a conversation he recorded with Dixon when he escaped from protective custody, and a computer disc which contained two reports. The first was a statement he made on the Omagh bombing and a second statement on the Burnfoot incident. There was also a report of a conversation he had with Chief Superintendent Nacy

Rice of the Donegal division about his personal security and welfare. The two sides met in late February when White gave a more detailed picture of the events surrounding the Omagh bombing.

The clandestine meetings coincided with Colm Murphy's trial which began in early February and lasted 25 days. The trial was filled with allegation and counter allegation against the gardaí. During the course of the trial, the court ruled that two detectives had fabricated evidence against Murphy by adding details to a statement and making alterations. However, a defence application to have the case thrown out was correctly rejected and Murphy was found guilty. It was a landmark decision.

Before sentencing, Murphy's lawyer said his client had 'no hand, act or part in the outrage at Omagh.'

'There were', said the barrister, 'degrees of concentric circles.' Murphy, he said, was a 'long, long way from the centre of the conspiracy. He was not a bomb-maker, he wasn't a member of the Real IRA, but was someone who could be relied upon to be a sympathiser.'

THERE IS NO doubt that the Police Ombudsman's Office took White's story seriously. When the investigators had completed their inquiries, Nuala O'Loan, the Police Ombudsman, drafted a detailed report for the Irish government. The report was 12 pages long and was called 'Report Raising Concerns of the activity of An Garda Síochána during 1998'. The report was a written account of White's story although he wasn't named. The author gave him the codename Bush, Dixon was called Budget, and 'Jones' was called Jones, though Jennings and Carty were named.

The document—marked secret—was formally presented to the Irish government when O'Loan met the Minister for Foreign Affairs Brian Cowen at unrelated talks in Dublin in late March. The report was then sent by Cowen to the Department of Justice, which had responsibility for the Garda. The Government managed to keep the report's existence secret for about a week before the news broke.

When the report was leaked to the press, O'Loan's Office was forced to issue a public statement which read:

'The office of the Police Ombudsman was introduced by some of those bereaved by the Omagh bomb, to a Garda officer who claimed to have new information about events leading up to, and after the atrocity.

'We examined the information made available to us and satisfied ourselves that it did not contain matters to suggest alleged misconduct by the PSNI/RUC officers. We will not, therefore, be launching any investigation as a result of the information.

'As the material related to matters in the Republic of Ireland, the Police Ombudsman's Office has now passed the information to the Department of Foreign Affairs in Dublin. It has also provided a copy of the material to the Police Service of Northern Ireland.'

Garda Headquarters reacted with a mixture of disbelief, shock, and rage. White was a member of the Garda suspended on corruption charges.

THE GARDA COMMISSIONER Pat Byrne issued a full denial of the allegations but the Government decided to play it safe. The Minister for Justice, John O'Donoghue, hastily organised an independent investigation into the allegations. In a public address, O'Donoghue said he was assured by Byrne that the allegations were false.

'While the serving officer of the Garda Síochána was not named in the Ombudsman's report, there have since been media reports to the effect that the serving officer of the Garda Síochána behind the allegations is, in fact, a suspended officer of the Garda Síochána facing criminal charges in relation to unrelated matters.

'It is also the case that the behaviour of the officer concerned will be the subject of scrutiny at the Tribunal of Inquiry which the Oireachtas has established in relation to matters concerning policing in Donegal.

'Notwithstanding the source of the allegations and the circumstances surrounding the manner in which very sensitive information impinging on issues of national security was made available to an agency outside the jurisdiction, the Minister, after careful consideration and consultation—including consultation with the Garda Commissioner—decided that the allegations contained in the report should be examined independently by persons with relevant experience and qualifications to look into sensitive security matters.

'The Garda Commissioner has assured the Minister that there is no basis for any suggestion that there was information available to the Garda Síochána which could have enabled them to prevent the Omagh atrocity.'

The team appointed by O'Donoghue to investigate White's allegations were Dermot Nally, the former Secretary to the Government, Eamon Barnes, a former Director of Public Prosecutions, and Joe Brosnan, a former Secretary of the Department of Justice.

Crime and Security reacted with disbelief to the contents of O'Loan's report, which effectively accused them of allowing the RIRA to bomb Northern Ireland. The Government was more pragmatic. The Taoiseach's trusted advisors agreed that O'Loan's Office simply referred the controversy to the Irish government because they didn't know what else to do.

THE POLICE SERVICE of Northern Ireland watched the dramatic events unfold from a distance. The Omagh inquiry team was now headed by new personnel. Eric Anderson had retired and was replaced by Norman Baxter, a detective superintendent. Another senior police officer was seconded from the Merseyside Police to conduct a review of the Omagh inquiry. His name was Phil Jones.

The new PSNI investigation team were intrigued by White's story. In the darkest of subterfuge, detectives assigned to the PSNI arranged to meet White to access his information for themselves. This was an unorthodox move. The PSNI flew White to a secret location in Britain where he was debriefed for three days. The operation was conducted on a need to know basis. Garda Headquarters were not to find out. The PSNI provided White with accommodation in a hotel where he was questioned at length about the black operations mounted by Crime and Security. Elements of the PSNI concluded that White was lying while others believed his story.

Through their mammoth intelligence gathering apparatus, Crime and Security learned that White had been formally interviewed by the PSNI within days of his return. The immediate effect of the news was to collapse the good relationship that existed between the two police forces. The detective branch at Monaghan Garda Station politely declined to entertain their counterparts from Omagh Station. The decision by the PSNI to question a serving member of the Garda, who was suspended for corruption, proved too much. Elements of the PSNI were now treated with contempt. The garda detectives who investigated the Omagh bombing had also investigated White. There would be no sharing of intelligence or pooling of information.

ON 29 MARCH, a booby trap bomb was discovered under a car at Sion Mills in County Tyrone. It was fitted with a mercury tilt switch. The man targeted by the bombers was a former member of the Royal Irish Regiment. The attack signalled an upsurge in RIRA operations across Northern Ireland. The new Army Council wanted to flex its muscles.

Two weeks later, on 13 April, there were two bomb attacks on police stations in County Down. Six days later, on 19 April, the CIRA carried out a bomb attack on a police training college in Belfast. The bomb damaged gates and fencing at the Garnerville complex in the east of the city.

Less than a week later, on 26 April, the RIRA attempted to drive a large firebomb into the centre of Belfast. The device was left abandoned after the ASU involved panicked.

Three days later, on 29 April, a 150lbs home-made device partially exploded at the main gate of Maghaberry Prison in County Antrim. The device was left in a white vehicle which pulled up outside the perimeter gate to the prison. No-one was injured.

There was another brief lull. But then, on 17 July, the RIRA fired a device at a police car in County Down. The officers escaped injury after the projectile bounced off their car without exploding on the Killough Road near Downpatrick. Given the upsurge in activity, it was inevitable that someone would be killed. It was only a question of who, when, and where.

ON 1 AUGUST in Derry city, the local ASU left a booby trap at a Territorial Army base on the Limavady Road in the city. Earlier that morning, at 7 a.m., David Caldwell was preparing to go to work at his home just outside the city. He called up the stairs to his partner Mavis McFaul, who was still in bed. He told her he was heading off and said he would see her later that evening. A few minutes later he called up again, this time to tell her that her tea was ready.

'I said, "If you don't get out that door I'll kill you."'

David went out the door laughing. It was a domestic scene that was being replicated all over Ireland and Britain.

At 7.40 a.m. Mavis heard someone knocking on her door. It was the police. David had been injured. They didn't tell her how or where. They urged her to get to the city's Altnagelvin Hospital as soon as possible. A million thoughts and fears rushed through her head.

'I thought he went out without his glasses. I thought maybe he must have hit a woman or something or a car down the road.'

The one fear that didn't assail her was the suspicion that he had been attacked by republican bombers.

Accompanied by her eldest daughter Leslie, Mavis arrived at Altnagelvin less than 20 minutes later. Even though there were police officers in the hospital waiting for her, she didn't think that her partner had been seriously injured.

'I said, "Jesus, what damage has he done with this tractor?"'

A policewoman followed her into the hospital. Mavis wanted to know how badly injured he was.

'She said Davy was hurt to the face and hand. I asked what happened and she said she didn't know yet. But she did. She came back out, the girl was all choked up because it was a nightmare what she had seen. She came back in and told me Davy was involved in an explosion.'

Even then, terrorism was the furthest thing from her mind.

'I said to Leslie that a gas cylinder had blown up. I saw them running back and forward and I thought they were getting him ready for the theatre. The policewoman came in at 8.50 a.m. and said Davy was in an IRA bomb. My whole world swirled. I said it couldn't be, there's peace. I asked how bad and she said just a wee bit burned.'

Mavis glanced up at the clock on the wall. It said 9.20 a.m., the moment her life changed for ever.

David Caldwell was a 51-year-old civilian contractor. He was working at a building site at the base when he noticed a discarded lunchbox. It was sitting on a table in a hut used by the workmen. Caldwell prided himself on his cleanliness and regularly tided the hut after his colleagues had used it. When he picked up the lunchbox, the bomb hidden inside exploded. The blast blew off his hand. Colleagues heard the explosion and ran to his aid. He was still conscious when the ambulance came for him. He shouted for Mavis while he was being carried into the ambulance. He knew he was going to die.

CALDWELL HAD SUFFERED severe injuries. A doctor gently broke the news of his death to Mavis.

'The surgeon came in and asked me to sit down. He told me he was the doctor. He said, "If I told you I did everything in my power for Davy, would you believe me?"

'I said, "Yes, is he going to theatre now?" He said Davy passed away. The doctor said that when Davy heard I was in the hospital, he smiled and said, "She's on time."'

Mavis McFaul's world collapsed.

'Everything went haywire. I said, "It couldn't be." The doctor told me then, "He was calling out for you." The policewoman said he was calling for me in the ambulance and he said he was afraid.'

Mavis and her two children went back to the sanctuary of their home, but the respite was short lived. Already, the family had become the focus of attention for the media. She was only in the door a few seconds when she realised she had to go back to the hospital. She had to see Davy.

'I just walked in and then I said, "This isn't right, we never saw Davy".

'One of my brothers came with me and he asked me if he could go in and see him first.'

Her brother walked into the room and viewed the body. It was a horrific experience. He wouldn't allow her to see the body.

'I have never before seen a fella turn green. Water just came out his mouth and he said to the doctor under no circumstances was I to see the body.'

The victim had lost a hand and had also sustained head injuries and shrapnel wounds to the chest and stomach. He was the first victim to die at the hands of the RIRA since Omagh. Caldwell left behind his partner Mavis and three daughters; the youngest, Gillian, was only 14-years-old.

The RIRA Army Council were quick to claim responsibility. Their victim had been a member of the UDR though he had left 18 years previously. He had been a private and a dog handler. He liked to work with dogs. He had left the security forces because it was too dangerous.

'He used to say that when they were out in the bad weather and lying in the hedges that it wasn't worth it. You are risking your life, he said, for what? He said nobody gave a damn, you were just a number. He said if anything happened to him, he might be remembered a year down the line, but after that, you're just another name added to the list. He loved the UDR and he loved some of the people he worked with, but I could see he was just getting fed up with it.'

Caldwell was an innocent victim. The bomb could have killed anyone.

HOWEVER, THE RIRA was about to mutate. Caldwell's killing happened at a time of deep rivalry in the RIRA. A feud had begun. Campbell and McKevitt, who had been comrades, stopped talking to each other. Another split was looming.

The feud began in Portlaoise Prison. On 20 October, a number of RIRA prisoners in Portlaoise Prison said they wanted the RIRA leadership to disband. They accused the RIRA Army Council of descending into common criminality, of making huge profits by smuggling contraband across the border. They went further and issued a public statement.

'We will not demean our struggle or provide succour to our enemies by revealing the comprehensive catalogue of evidence which has exposed this leadership,' the statement read.

'However, we do feel duty-bound to state that this Army leadership's financial motivations far outweigh their political commitment to our struggle at this time. IRA prisoners find this morally and politically unacceptable. We believe that the current Army leadership has forfeited all moral authority to lead the IRA. We are left with no option but to withdraw our allegiance from this Army leadership.' The statement was signed 'IRA unit, Portlaoise.'

McKevitt was a signatory.

Only a small number of the prisoners in Portlaoise demurred from the statement. These included Liam Campbell, who was moved from the RIRA wing of the prison to another part of the complex after tensions heightened between the two groups. There is no doubt that McKevitt was behind the statement. He knew the evidence against him was beyond question. He now abandoned his militant republican beliefs in the hope that the Government was listening. The majority of prisoners supported him because they wanted to get out of prison. The real surprise was that McKevitt expected the statement to be taken seriously. Campbell and the new Army Council had always been smugglers. McKevitt knew Campbell had been expelled from the Provisionals for smuggling.

Campbell was adamantly opposed to any disbandment because the Army Council were his men. The RIRA divided in two. McKevitt headed one side: Campbell the other, which had taken control.

The statement was unprecedented in the history of republicanism. Prisoners, of whatever hue, had never before issued such a startling ultimatum to their comrades on the outside.

The 32 County Sovereignty Movement found itself caught in the middle. They chose to remain silent and refused to take a position, though some couldn't contain their contempt.

'The prisoners had no right to say those things,' said one republican.

'When you go to jail, you lose all status and all ranks within the organisation. I can never recall prisoners ever making any demand like this before.'

The new Army Council was made up of smugglers. They were making a fortune for themselves in the lucrative world of criminality. This was true, but the statement was a ploy by the RIRA prisoners—including McKevitt. The analysis by Crime and Security was that he hoped the Government would go soft on him if he seemed to be backing a sort of Peace Process. The Government ignored the statement.

THE NEW RIRA Army Council quickly gave their response to the demand.

On the same day the statement was released, an ASU mounted a failed bomb attack on the police station in Castlederg in County Tyrone. A coffee jar containing explosives and nails was thrown over the wall of the station, but failed to explode. No one was injured. The following day, RIRA units also caused havoc in Belfast and the surrounding areas by calling in several hoax bomb alerts. The leadership of the organisation then made its first public statement in response to the prisoners calling on them to disband. In their statement, the leadership chose to simply ignore their jailed former comrades.

The statement said, 'We warn all civilians to stay away from military installations and Crown Force personnel. A number of recent attacks have had to be aborted due to the presence of civilians in the vicinity. Anyone entering military installations does so at their own risk.' The message was simple: the RIRA are continuing the war but they were not the only ones.

THE NALLY INVESTIGATION was granted unrestricted access to the State's most sensitive files held at Crime and Security. The files were the most classified held by the Garda. The investigators examined the reports concerning the clandestine operations that involved Dixon. The investigation was not limited to an examination of paperwork; the gardaí who participated in the operations were interviewed. Carty and Jennings were questioned about their dealings with White, who was also questioned at length.

The inquiry team did not, however, interview Dixon. The spy had moved to Britain as part of his membership of the Witness Protection Programme. Dixon categorically refused to return to Ireland to face any questions. As far as he was concerned, he had suffered enough.

It didn't take long for the inquiry team to conclude there was no truth to the allegation that Crime and Security could have prevented the Omagh bombing. White's assertions that gardaí had permitted the RIRA to engage in acts of terrorism as part of some conspiracy were also disproven.

However, this was lost on elements of the PSNI who organised a smear campaign to damage the gardaí. Some PSNI officers went to enormous lengths to damage Crime and Security. They invented stories and circulated them in the hope that they would appear in the media. The same falsehoods were told to relatives of those killed in the Omagh bombing.

The stories were spurious. At one point, some PSNI officers claimed the NSU had provided the vehicle used to scout the route used by the Omagh bombers. The campaign of black propaganda focused on individual gardaí who they falsely claimed were complicit in terrorism.

A minority in the PSNI even claimed that one of the Omagh bombers worked for Crime and Security, and had informed his handlers of the bomb's production and delivery. Of course, this was black propaganda. Their motive was simple. Some of those involved believed Crime and Security controlled the RIRA through informants. Other officers had a dislike of the gardaí. Some possessed a sectarian attitude towards their colleagues south of the border. The members of the PSNI Omagh inquiry were embarrassed by their colleagues but were powerless to stop them.

But there were other influencing factors at play. MI5 did not want McKevitt's trial to proceed. The British Security Service had no interest in pursuing criminal charges against members of the RIRA. MI5 operated in the shadows as a secret intelligence agency. The agency conducted intrusive surveillance on specific targets to protect the police from allegations of illegality. Box was not constituted to gather evidence for use in criminal trials. The agency excelled at long-range surveillance but knew nothing of preparing evidence for criminal prosecutions in Irish courts.

It was only when McKevitt was charged that officials at T-branch in London realised they would have to have to reveal their spying activities in public. Worse again, agents would be exposed to cross-examination by lawyers acting for McKevitt. Never before had the agency faced the possibility of such public scrutiny.

Management at MI5 were also embarrassed about the contents of Rupert's e-mails and intelligence files they held in their headquarters. Agents had warned Rupert not to consult Crime and Security on the covert operation. The American was certainly not to mention their involvement in the operation.

In one e-mail, an agent had instructed Rupert not to talk to Crime and Security at the initial stages of the project When the material was eventually disclosed to McKevitt's defence team, it was embarrassing for the Security Service. It looked unprofessional and did nothing to enhance the already strained relationship between Garda Headquarters and the British Security Service.

18

FACE TO FACE

TO THE OUTSIDE world, the Omagh families appeared to have come to terms with their terrible grief. The truth was that the bombing haunted their every waking moment. The months and years passed but the terrible grief inflicted on the families would not go away.

Parents who lost children in the explosion found it almost impossible to forget the horror they endured that summer. They were overcome with grief on birthdays and at Christmas time. Everything seemed lost. Little by little, they stopped talking about Omagh and retreated into normality. There was no consolation to be had because nothing that anyone could do would ever bring the dead back to life. Some suffered in secret; they never spoke about their grief, they maintained a silent dignity and consoled themselves in the knowledge that some of the bombing team were now behind bars.

The less fortunate had nervous breakdowns, developed psychological problems and became prone to panic attacks. Their personal lives and marriages were adversely affected, and in some cases destroyed; the gruesome drama that unfolded in Omagh town refused to subside.

The murder of young children, particularly the careless and gruesome way it happened, gave rise to the inevitable question of what to do next.

Victor Barker was one of the few people in the relatives' campaign who was most clear-sighted about the situation. When his wife Donna Maria was asked to identify their son's shattered body hours after his brutal murder, her life changed forever. No matter how hard she tried, she could not pick up the pieces. The loss of James was a heart-rending and unforgettable human experience, which drained every piece of confidence and faith she possessed. She came to hate republicans with a vengeance; she hated the hypocrisy of the RIRA, and focused all her energies on making someone accountable for her son's death.

James was the Barker's eldest son. The family had moved to the seaside town of Buncrana in County Donegal with the intention of raising their four children in rural Ireland.

Victor had continued to work as a solicitor in London and commuted between the city and Buncrana while Donna Maria raised the children. Life was good to the family. They lived for weekends when they got together to enjoy life and go on family outings.

When James died, their lives fell apart. The image of James lying dead on a mortuary slab haunted the couple. There was no consolation to be had because the fate of their family had been irrevocably altered by the RIRA.

Victor and Donna Maria found their shattered life in Ireland too much to bear; their grief was incomprehensible.

They cursed the RIRA. Donna Maria never thought such tragedy would befall her. She came from a nationalist background and had sung at the funerals of the 13 Catholics murdered by the British Army on Bloody Sunday when she was a girl. Now she cursed the notion of a united Ireland.

The Barker's ordeal intensified in the months following the bombing. Victor dedicated his energies to combating the RIRA in every conceivable way. He protested at their meetings, petitioned government ministers to persecute them, and openly confronted the dissidents through a barrage of media interviews.

His despair gave him no peace. The couple suffered in secret for two years before they decided to return to England. The home they had built in County Donegal was filled with too many memories.

When they finally decided they could no longer fight the demons, they returned to Surrey. In what was the hardest decision he ever made, Victor arranged to have his son's body exhumed and re-buried near their new home in the south of England.

Life changed somewhat when the Barkers returned to Britain but their shared grief was as raw as it ever was. The nightmares subsided but only for a time.

Anger still consumed Victor. He continued to write to government ministers and even sent the photographs taken of James' body lying still on a mortuary table to the British Prime Minister Tony Blair.

He gave those in authority no peace and excused himself from the normal protocols of diplomatic correspondence. He rightly demanded that Sinn Féin urge all republicans to help the PSNI and Garda to hunt his son's killers; his plea fell on deaf ears but that never stopped him.

He knew the criminality and stupidity of the RIRA had caused the death of his son and had dreamed up the concept of suing the bombers.

He had done everything, and more, in his power to make the RIRA accountable, but often wondered what the dissident movement thought of him. As the years passed, he gradually came to the conclusion that he needed to do something drastic and brave.

Once he realised that he would never have a moment's peace unless he did the unthinkable, he made arrangements to return to Ireland, find the RIRA, and talk to them face to face.

THE PROBLEM HE faced was contacting the RIRA at a time when McKevitt and Campbell were behind bars and the organisation was bitterly divided. He knew he could never bring about a genuine ceasefire but he believed that no man could argue with the grief of a heartbroken father.

No other virtue could have served him better. By this time he was beyond seeking retribution; he simply wanted to prevent more bloodshed. And so began a secret and personal journey into the very heart of the RIRA.

He began by asking some associates if a meeting would be possible. He never expected the RIRA to accede to his request, which was delivered by word of mouth through an intermediary in November 2002. Because the organisation had broken into warring factions, he asked if he could talk to republicans who had maintained a neutral position. He had no wish to talk with any one faction to the detriment of the other.

At the time, the RIRA had become a group of free wheeling mercenaries and smugglers answerable only to themselves. They lacked a command structure and political ideology other than to intermittently attack the British security forces in Northern Ireland and bomb London.

Barker was unaware of the underlying problems he faced and proceeded to send and receive messages to influential republicans over a two week period. These were exploratory moves.

He told no one of his efforts, which he conducted in strict secrecy.

The fact that not one of his representations appeared in the press encouraged the republican protagonists to respond. In the first week of December, he received the news that would thrust him into the centre of face to face talks.

In that spirit he was asked to make arrangements to fly to Dublin. An intermediary would escort him to a meeting. Security and discretion were of the utmost importance; neither side wanted to attract the attention of Crime and Security, the PSNI or MI5.

By a stroke of good fortune and coincidence, Barker had arranged to meet the Taoiseach Bertie Ahern at government buildings on 4 December. He asked if it would be possible for the meeting to happen on the same day.

The RIRA had no problem with this but stressed the need for security. Barker gave his word.

He flew into Dublin arriving minutes after 11 a.m. where he was met at the airport's arrivals lounge by the senior investigating officer from the PSNI Omagh inquiry, Norman Baxter.

The policeman knew Barker was meeting Ahern but had no idea of the pending confrontation with the RIRA. The purpose of Baxter's meeting was John White, the allegations concerning the black operations mounted by Crime and Security, and the need for further legislation to combat terrorism.

Barker listened attentively but had more pressing issues on his mind; this meeting lasted no more than 30 minutes.

Barker's intermediary had watched Baxter from a safe distance and collected him the minute the PSNI officer left the airport.

THE LOCATION FOR the meeting between Barker and the RIRA was the Hawthorn Hotel, a small hostelry in the village of Swords in north Dublin. The intermediary had arranged a secure room there where the two sides could talk without interruption.

The drive from Dublin Airport took longer than normal. Traffic was heavy. Barker was also anxious.

Apart from the intermediary, no one knew the true purpose of his clandestine visit.

They were running late and by the time they arrived in Swords village, they were 20 minutes behind time. When Barker and the intermediary walked into the hotel, Francie Mackey of the 32 County Sovereignty Movement and two IRA men known to the intermediary were waiting in the lobby.

The first had been a member of the Army Council elected at Oldcastle and had held the position of Director of Publicity.

The second man came from County Kilkenny. He was an aging republican whose views were respected by the RIRA.

Aware that Crime and Security would mount surveillance on the location if given the opportunity, the actual location for the discussions was changed at the last minute. The intermediary brought the republicans to another room and then returned with Barker whose emotional senses were now at their height; he felt an inner rage that made him want to scream, mixed with a deep sense of clarity and purpose.

He stopped momentarily before he walked into the meeting room, took a deep breath, held his head high and said, 'I'm going to be okay.'

The councillor Mackey was already on his feet when he walked through the door.

'Mr. Barker,' he said, 'on behalf of the 32 County Sovereignty Movement, I would like to offer our deepest condolences to your family on the loss of your son.'

Barker took his hand, thanked him for the gesture, and asked them all to sit down. And the dialogue began.

BARKER TRIED TO show he was a sincere man. He talked about the loss of his son, how it affected his family and the heartache inflicted on the Omagh families.

'I have come here as a heartbroken father and nothing else. I have no agenda and there are no cameras from Sky News waiting outside. I just want to talk about the continuing violence to see if I can do something to stop the bloodshed,' he said.

'Too many people have died. I'm not here seeking revenge,' he insisted.

'I don't want any family to suffer. The Real IRA must stop it's campaign of violence. That's all I want.'

Mackey interjected at once to say he was there on behalf of the Sovereignty Movement and no one else. These words caused Barker to raise his voice slightly and ask, 'Surely you don't expect me to believe that?'

Mackey reaffirmed his position once more. The other two men in the room remained silent. In contrast to his own expectations, he had begun delivering the most judicious speech of his life.

'James,' he said, 'was a bright 12-year-old boy when he died. He wasn't an enemy of the IRA. He wasn't a British soldier or a spy. He was a schoolboy out with a group of friends for goodness sake.'

He refused to allow his emotions to take control and made a conscious effort not to get upset or visibly angry.

'I am an Englishman and I understand why Irish republicans want to reunite their country. But can you tell me why my 12-year-old boy was murdered? What good came from his killing and how could any organisation justify murdering innocent men, women, and children? I'm trying to understand you. I need to know why this happened.'

Mackey was about to answer when the former Army Council member interrupted and asked, 'How many Irish mothers have cried the same tears having watched their children being murdered by the British Army?

'I am not going to say I don't support the IRA, or speak to you with a forked tongue. I'll talk straight to you. I'm an IRA man and have been all my life.

'The fact of the matter is that there is a war being fought in the Six Counties and innocent civilians get killed. I'm sorry that your son was killed but the British forces of occupation have killed thousands of Irish people through the centuries. They are the problem. If you want to stop the IRA, ask your own Government to leave our country.'

The statement was republican rhetoric but honest and candid. Barker did not appreciate the message but was struck by the republican's honesty.

'I accept your honesty but if that is the case, what had my 12-year-old son got to do with your cause? He was a schoolboy on a day trip for goodness sake. He wasn't a soldier; he wasn't threatening anyone.

'Have you ever lost a child? I raised James since he was a little baby, we nourished him, we cared for him; we stayed awake at night when he was sick; who had the right to take his life? He was just a young boy. Do you understand that?'

His words were spoken with such honesty that none of the delegation dared respond. Barker spoke with elegance and for the sake of innocent lives.

'You have to stop this campaign of violence. It's pointless and futile. I am an Englishman and I believe there will be a united Ireland sooner or later. There is no need for more people to die.

The people of Ireland have voted for the Good Friday Agreement. No one wants more bloodshed.'

Barker spoke with energy and precision, and with the hope of making the republican delegation think. There is no doubt that they were struck by his absolute sincerity because Barker professed that Britain had committed human rights abuses in Northern Ireland, which were inexcusable. But he suggested that this did not give any group the right to murder the innocent. They all agreed. The most intriguing part of the conversation concerned Ireland's shared history with Britain.

Barker was proud to be British. He spoke about how the British had fought the Germans in World War Two. He was proud of his military background. This granted him a certain prestige with the IRA delegation who proclaimed without a shred of irony that British soldiers had done the world a service by gunning the Nazis out of the skies.

'Those who fought the Germans were brave men and deserve the respect of all,' said the Army Council member.

The conversation developed further. Mackey and the two RIRA officers listened with great attention. At times, there were curt exchanges between the two sides. The perceived failings of the Good Friday Agreement were debated and discussed. Barker quickly realised he was wasting his time trying to convince his adversaries of the positive aspects of the Agreement. But instead of feeling demoralised by the reaction his speech provoked, he asked how something positive could be achieved. In plain language; he wanted to know if the RIRA was still committed to violence.

The elder of the two RIRA delegates had listened to the sharp exchanges but had said nothing. Now he looked Barker straight in the eye and said, 'Mr. Barker, there is a feeling among some sections of Óglaigh na hÉireann that armed insurgency is now counter-productive. But you have to understand that we find ourselves in a sensitive position. Nothing is simple.'

The sentence was brief but said everything. Barker understood the true meaning of the words. It was a reference to the ongoing feud among the republican prisoners in Portlaoise Prison and the absolute failure of the RIRA's military campaign.

Barker interpreted the statement as a positive development because he had anticipated some sort of confrontation. The meeting broke up with each side promising to contact the other. The conversation had lasted more than three hours. When he left the hotel, Barker walked out into a bustling evening. The discussion gave him a sense of purpose that remained with him for a long time to come. In a sense the two sides accepted each other's position.

However, his day was not over yet. Hours behind time, he was driven at speed into Dublin city to meet the Taoiseach. The traffic hadn't subsided which forced Barker to call ahead on his mobile phone to say he was running late. When he arrived at government buildings, he was ushered into Ahern's private office.

The Taoiseach was himself delayed, arriving five minutes late.

When he did make an entrance; he was accompanied by two advisors who noted every word he said. Ahern was warm and friendly, and spoke to Barker as if he was a long lost friend.

The official reason for the meeting concerned the civil action taken by the Omagh families against the bombers but the subject quickly turned to the RIRA and the possibility of a true ceasefire.

Barker introduced the topic of acting as an intermediary much to Ahern's surprise.

'I have been trying to talk to the Real IRA and I think there is a possibility they will meet me. Do you think that would be worthwhile Taoiseach?'

Ahern eased back into his seat and considered his words carefully. One of his advisors took the opportunity to interrupt the conversation. He read from an official report, drafted by Crime and Security.

'Our information would suggest that the people now in charge of the Real IRA are wedded to violence. The organisation has divided. You would be better waiting a few months to see what happens, perhaps next April.'

This, of course, was an oblique reference to the predicted end of McKevitt's trial. Ahern had kept silent but now chose to speak.

'I don't want you to waste your time, Victor. I don't believe the Real IRA wants a ceasefire, we have tried and we failed, but you know Victor, I remember when our old friend senator Gordon Wilson began talking to the Provisional IRA and asking them to stop.

'Well everyone gave out about him, and said it was a waste of time. But you know what, in some ways, Wilson did help because it put the notion of politics in their head. He told them there was another way forward.

'We did try talk to the Real IRA through Fr. Alec Reid but they had a problem with him. And it came to nothing,' mused Ahern.

'What I'm saying to you Victor, is that if you think something good can be achieved, then work away. You certainly won't be doing any harm and you may get through to someone.'

'I don't want you to waste your time but I don't want to stop you from achieving something good. You won't do any harm.'

The meeting ended on that note.

19

THE TRIAL

MCKEVITT'S TRIAL BEGAN hearing evidence on the morning of 10 June 2003 having been stalled several times through failed legal challenges. Instead of feeling hopeful about the chances of acquittal, his spirit was broken. He hated prison and could not adjust to the solitude of life in a cell. He felt claustrophobic, he missed his wife Bernadette and the affection of his children.

Inside his prison cell, he found himself drained of all optimism and what little mental strength he possessed. He was consumed by despair.

The book of evidence compiled by the prosecution made frightening reading. He could see that Rupert had embellished some parts of the story but the central axes of his claims were true. The spy had fooled him and he had no credible defence.

Crime and Security, working hand in hand with MI5 and the FBI, had got close. There was no solution to his predicament; the inescapable fact was that he was guilty. He knew it; his family knew it and anyone familiar with his story knew it. In the end, when he had lost all hope, he realised he had two options; he could plead guilty, or fight his case. He chose to fight because he couldn't bear the indignity of pleading guilty.

Once he decided to fight, his strategy became clear. He needed to destroy Rupert's credibility, question the American's motivation for testifying, and above all else, prove that he was a compromised witness. This was a high-risk strategy burdened with contradictions.

The main problem McKevitt faced was that he couldn't afford to cross-examine Rupert about his knowledge of the RIRA. That would do more damage to his defence than good. Instead, he chose to question the spy about his past life and business dealings. This destined the strategy to failure from the minute of its inception.

THE OPENING OF McKevitt's trial was no anti-climax. The operation to deliver the RIRA's founder to the Special Criminal Court began at 8 a.m. that morning when he was handcuffed to two prison guards in the confines of Portlaoise Prison. Minutes later he was seated into a mini-bus with blacked out windows and driven to Dublin city. The journey took over an hour. Unmarked garda cars and three military jeeps carrying armed soldiers flanked the minibus. When the convoy reached the Special Criminal Court, the soldiers alighted and sealed the road adjacent to the court while McKevitt was ushered inside.

The gardaí took no chances with security inside the court, which was packed to capacity. Armed detectives maintained a watchful eye on the public gallery, which was filled with journalists, writers, and interested members of the public. McKevitt himself was brought into the court through a tunnel that led from an underground holding cell to the dock. As he appeared from the tunnel, he gestured to his wife, then turned to face the judges. He was visibly shaken when he saw the number of people that turned out to witness his demise.

He recognised Lawrence Rush at once but wouldn't look at him directly. Rush felt consumed by rage when he saw McKevitt. He wanted to strike him.

The joy of seeing McKevitt in court for the litany of crimes he had committed was ruined by the hurtful memories of the Omagh bombing. Every one of the Omagh relatives seated in the public gallery that day felt similar sensations. In this whirlwind of contradictory emotions, the families remained composed. McKevitt himself was deeply nervous and like a true coward, refused to look in their direction. He had dressed formally for court. He wore a navy jacket, white shirt and tie, and a pair of slacks. Rush thought to himself that the accused looked more like a schoolteacher than a gunrunner, and he mused aloud that appearances can be deceptive.

The dock in the Special Criminal Court is raised about five feet above the ground. From this position, McKevitt had a bird's eye view of the court. He was seated on the same level as his three trial judges: Justice Johnson, Justice Reilly, and Justice O'Hagan.

Seated below him in the court's well were the opposing legal teams. To his right sat the prosecution team led by George Birmingham and Brendan Grehan, two senior counsel. His own defence team sat to his left. The defence comprised two senior counsel, Hugh Hartnett and Philip Magee. Hartnett was a giant of a man whose physical presence filled the court. He possessed a razor sharp wit that at times could be brutally comical. McKevitt's solicitor James McGuill completed the line up. He sat behind the barristers. A bell sounded minutes after 11 a.m. which signalled the arrival of the three judges. And so began the trial of Michael McKevitt.

THE PROCEDURE IN such trials begins with an address by the chief prosecutor. In accordance with this long established procedure, Birmingham began addressing the court only to be interrupted by Hartnett. McKevitt wanted permission to sit with his legal team for the duration of the trial. The submission marked the beginning of what would become a highly adversarial trial. The three judges were slightly bemused at McKevitt's strange request. However, they acceded to his request. With that McKevitt stood up, brushed past the prison officers and gardaí seated around him and made his way towards the solicitor's bench. The path took him within feet of Rush who continued to restrain himself from striking out.

Birmingham quickly made up for lost time. He delivered a powerful synopsis of the prosecution's case, outlining Rupert's incredible story of drama, espionage, and terrorism. The speech encapsulated the black operation that had caught McKevitt unaware. The barrister had spoken no more than a few words when Hartnett was back on his feet once more. The mention of Rupert's name had forced him into action.

Rupert, he proclaimed, had just contacted three American journalists to write his personal biography. The defence wanted access to any material that Rupert had passed to the journalists.

The three judges had no knowledge of the publishing project and felt they had no jurisdiction to make any ruling on the matter. Aware that such legal cases are won and lost on obscure legal points, Hartnett asked the court to note his submission. Before he sat down, the barrister announced that his client would possibly commence proceedings in America in an attempt to gain access to the files.

Rush watched the complex legal arguments and felt inner rage when he saw McKevitt being afforded the privilege of sitting with his legal team. The more he watched McKevitt, the angrier he felt. When the court adjourned for lunch at 1 p.m., McKevitt made his way back towards the dock, smiling at his wife and supporters. In the throes of depression and thinking about how his wife died, Rush lashed out.

'What about Omagh? You're nothing but a thug. That's all you are. A thug,' he shouted.

Afraid and embarrassed, McKevitt stared at the ground and made his way back to his cell. The court went silent as Rush returned to his seat. The judges looked startled. A detective took Rush aside and told him to stay quiet. Rush was angry and hurt. He was consumed by inner rage and didn't apologise. He felt pleased with himself.

'McKevitt thought he was some sort of special category prisoner when he was given permission to sit with his legal team. I brought him back down to size,' Rush said later. 'I didn't regret it for one moment.'

THE TRIAL FINALLY got underway when Birmingham concluded his speech. Garda witnesses were called and gave their evidence.

The first witness was Peter Maguire of Special Branch, who had been promoted to Chief Superintendent.

Maguire had just begun to deliver his testimony when Hartnett stood up yet again and made another submission. He wanted to cut to the chase. The defence, he said, intended to adjourn cross-examination of everyone in anticipation of Rupert's evidence. Hartnett was not one of those men who could leave a subject hanging and go on to another; he wanted Rupert in the witness box as quickly as possible.

This was a prelude to what would be later described as the most vigorous cross-examination ever conducted in the Special Criminal Court. The defence team was armed with realms of damming information about Rupert's nefarious professional and private life. The judges accepted the submission and adjourned the proceedings until the following Monday. Rupert would be questioned then.

THE COURT RECONVENED the following Monday at 11 a.m. Hartnett swung into action from the beginning and applied to have a number of garda witnesses removed from court. First on his list was Martin Callinan, the new chief at Crime and Security, and Diarmuid O'Sullivan of Special Branch. But he went further. He wanted any detective who had interviewed McKevitt ushered outside.

Birmingham, who listened attentively to the argument, was equally quick in his response. He stood to his feet and asked the court to remove Bernadette Sands, who was sitting in the public gallery. The judges looked at each other quizzically and retired to consider the respective submissions. When they returned, they said Callinan and O'Sullivan could stay along with the detectives who arrested and interviewed McKevitt. However, they accepted that four detectives from the NSU, should go. Bernadette Sands was permitted to stay. Hartnett had won a battle of sorts but the war was not over yet.

From the very beginning, McKevitt was aware that he was not the principle attraction in his own trial. It seemed a miracle to anyone who knew the workings of the RIRA that Rupert had gotten so close to the Quartermaster. McKevitt was generally regarded as a disciplined republican. He was security conscious. The question was how had he allowed himself to be so compromised. Everyone wanted to see the spy who had fooled the Quartermaster.

The only giveaway sign of Rupert's presence near the court that day was the sound of a garda helicopter circling overhead. But at approximately 11.54 a.m., having exchanged more stern words with Hartnett, Birmingham asked the gardaí to fetch the witness Dave Rupert. With that the court fell silent as the giant figure of Rupert appeared at the door.

And he didn't disappoint. He wore a smart grey suit, a black shirt, and silk tie. The giant American bowed his head, walked through the door, and made his way to the witness box as a crowd of spectators watched. He was a giant of a man.

Rupert himself made no eye contact with McKevitt as he sat into the witness box. He also ignored the outburst of whispers his arrival caused and focused his attention on the three judges.

McKevitt was shocked. He watched the witness with frightening attention but the two men never made eye contact. In reality, McKevitt was on the verge of a breakdown. He looked at Rupert's demeanour almost in disbelief. He sat motionless in the court not knowing what to say. Only then did he realise that he was finished.

Birmingham formally introduced the witness and began asking him questions about his evidence. Rupert answered in a concise and clear manner although he spoke in a deep American drawl. The defence watched in fascination, following his every word. Hartnett seemed content not to interrupt his evidence until Rupert began talking about Murray and O'Neill, the two republicans from Sligo. The mention of these names prompted the barrister to jump to his feet once again.

In a forceful way, he proclaimed that such evidence was hearsay, and he went further, accusing Birmingham of leading the witness. Hartnett intervened on no fewer than five occasions in relation to this point. He would not yield.

The judges, he said without fear of contradiction, should retire to consider the matter. The judges returned minutes later and rejected his submission. The spy proceeded to recount his incredible story about how he infiltrated the RIRA.

THE CROSS-EXAMINATION began the following Wednesday at 2.45 p.m. At first Hartnett was polite to Rupert.

'Do your moral teachings compel you to be honest in your dealings with others?' the barrister asked.

'Yes, they do,' answered the witness.

The question was the precursor to a robust cross-examination. In contrast to everyone's expectations, the defence had uncovered a mountain of damning information about Rupert.

Hartnett took as long as he could because this was the right time for an assault on Rupert's character. The defence knew he had engaged in sharp practices, defrauded friends and family, and conned his way through life. Rupert was exposed as a crook. The defence presented the court with just about every conceivable type of damning evidence that could be imagined. Far from being a bastion of virtue, Rupert was forced to admit he had consorted with Mafia types in Florida after fleeing bankruptcy proceedings in America, and swindled people out of money.

The litany of crimes he perpetrated seemed endless. Hartnett spoke with energy and precision in the hope of exposing Rupert for the gangster that he was but his efforts were wasted. If Rupert did not wish to answer a question, he would simply say, 'I cannot recall.'

On one day alone he repeated these words over 300 times. The public gallery would often break into laughter when Hartnett would ask him about his private life and the many women that featured in his life.

As the days passed, Rupert came under more pressure. The American religiously maintained he had never been involved in crime. He repeated his denials and challenged anyone to contradict him. In the middle of the proceedings, Hartnett produced a document, which clearly showed him to be economical with the truth.

The file was an MI5 document that referred to an officer called 'Witness C'. The document, which was heavily edited and barely legible, quoted Rupert as saying that he was involved in smuggling and other criminal activity in the past.

There was more to come. Crime and Security and MI5 had always been nervous of Rupert and Hartnett read reports of the same into the court's record.

At one stage, Hartnett produced a MI5 report headed 'An Garda Síochána Assessment of Rupert.' In this document, Jennings was quoted as stating that he had 'no confidence' in Rupert and he 'did not trust him'.

The worst was yet to come. The defence produced documents that showed Rupert received bonus payments from MI5. The defence hoped the production of these documents would grate the judge's nerves but they didn't.

Although the witness was subjected to a cross-examination, the defence did not question him in any great detail about McKevitt. The cross-examination in many ways was irrelevant. At the very end, Hartnett proclaimed aloud that Rupert had never met McKevitt at all and said his evidence was lies. This brief statement was the only challenge to Rupert's evidence concerning McKevitt and the RIRA. Rupert had spent 11 days in the witness box.

The drama, however, didn't end there.

IN THE LAST week of the trial, the defence identified a contradiction in Rupert's evidence and that provided by the NSU. The discrepancy was contained in secret files that were disclosed to the defence in the last week of the trial. In his statement to Callinan, Rupert said he had attended an IRA Army Council meeting on 17 February 2000. The NSU reports situated McKevitt at his home on the same day. The contradiction was obvious.

The error gave Hartnett an opening to attack.

His argument, in brief, was that Crime and Security had deliberately withheld the documents. When the defence saw the enormity of the contradiction, Hartnett demanded a mistrial.

'My Lords, this recently disclosed material seriously undermines Mr. Rupert's credibility as a witness. If these documents had been disclosed prior to the commencement of the trial they would have enabled the Defence to present its case differently. My Lords, somebody took a decision to withhold this information which directly attacks Mr. Rupert's credibility as a witness,' the barrister proclaimed.

Hartnett believed there was merit in his argument. He then accused the gardaí of deliberately withholding the files and asked for the trial to be ended. The three judges listened attentively before adjourning the proceedings.

THE COURT RESUMED hearing the case at 11 a.m. on 24 July and surprised many by rejecting the application. The judges based their reasons on solid and coherent grounds. The Special Criminal Court, announced Judge Johnson, comprises a panel of professional judges.

'It is our opinion that the documents in question were not deliberately withheld. However, we do believe that the documents should have been disclosed at an earlier date, but they were not. The trial will proceed.'

Hartnett was quick to respond.

'My Lords, if we had known what was in these documents we would have restructured our defence. At this time, we cannot trawl through almost 4,000 documents. My Lords, this trial should not be allowed to proceed.

'Tactical decisions were made by some person and documents were withheld. Information was withheld and to say now that the key prosecution witness can be recalled is nothing short of hypocrisy. Furthermore, I must point out the inadequate and unsatisfactory manner with which the prosecution has drip fed documents over a two-year period. This is most unsatisfactory. My Lords, at this point I request that the court adjourn as I must consult with my client.'

The court was adjourned once more. Then something happened that no one expected.

Having vanished into a legal briefing for 15 minutes with McKevitt and the defence team, McGuill returned to the court and asked Birmingham if they could talk privately.

The assembled gardaí knew something serious was about to happen.

When Hartnett returned, he stood up and addressed the court in his thundering voice.

'My Lords, I must inform the court that Mr. Michael McKevitt has discharged his entire legal team. We will now leave the court.'

And with that, Hartnett stood to his feet, and made for the door followed by the defence team. McKevitt had adopted a new strategy.

WHEN MCKEVITT WATCHED Rupert deliver his evidence, he knew his only alternative was to run his defence as if he was preparing to appeal his future conviction. From this moment onwards, every statement and comment he made was crafted with the sole intention of appealing what he presumed would be a conviction. McKevitt was now playing a long game. Everything he said had a designed purpose.

Therefore, when the judges asked if he had anything to say in the absence of legal representation, McKevitt took the opportunity to address the court.

'If I may I would like to inform the court of the reasons why I have dismissed my legal representatives and of my future intentions regarding the remainder of this trial,' he said in his flat County Louth accent.

'Firstly, I would like to thank all of my legal team for their unrelenting work over the past five weeks. I genuinely appreciate their efforts on my behalf and I sincerely thank them. Over the past two and a half years, the defence has steadfastly pursued all relevant Garda surveillance reports and all relevant FBI and MI5 documentation. This has been no easy task.

'Our difficulties were compounded by the fact that this court had no jurisdiction to compel the FBI and MI5 to disclose any relevant documentation. Furthermore, our attempts to attain disclosure of Garda surveillance reports were also continually obstructed. The court is aware that on Friday, 18 July 2003, the prosecution disclosed material that contradicted Mr. Rupert's statement, which is contained in the book of evidence.

'In his statement, Mr. Rupert alleged that I attended an IRA Army Council meeting on 17 February 2000. However, in contrast, the recently disclosed Garda surveillance report situates me at my home on this date. Why were these important surveillance reports withheld for two and a half years and disclosed twenty-two days into the trial, after Mr. Rupert had presented his testimony? This is just one small example of the difficulties the defence has been faced with.

'The prosecution cannot claim that they did not have ample requests for disclosure. Nor can they point to an oversight. Twelve months ago, my solicitor, Mr. James McGuill, wrote to the state prosecutor seeking the disclosure of all relevant Garda surveillance reports. Yet disclosure was continually denied. The defence was told that there was no relevant undisclosed material. Indeed, in October 2002, Chief Superintendent Callinan, in an affidavit presented to this court during a four-day disclosure hearing, stated that all undisclosed documents were either irrelevant or were being withheld on grounds of national security. The recent disclosure of these extremely important surveillance reports has rendered worthless the assurances of Chief Superintendent Callinan. Why were these relevant legal documents concealed for two and a half years on grounds of national security, only to be subsequently considered eligible for disclosure on Friday, 18 July 2003, twenty two days into the trial and after Mr. Rupert has presented his evidence?

'The disclosure of these documents was in no way detrimental to national security. However, prompt disclosure would have been detrimental to an effective prosecution of this case and to the advantage of the defence. Perhaps here lies the true reason for concealment?'

McKevitt read from a prepared script. The speech was well written, concise and bore the hallmarks of a legal document.

'How could Chief Superintendent Callinan claim that these recently disclosed surveillance reports were irrelevant? These surveillance reports were clearly relevant to my case. The defence prepared its case on the basis of Mr. Rupert's statements, which were contained in the book of evidence. If these surveillance reports had been promptly disclosed prior to the commencement of the trial, the defence would have reassessed its strategy, the presentation of its case and its cross-examination of Mr. Rupert.

'Somebody took a decision to withhold this information which directly attacks Mr. Rupert's credibility as a witness. I find this totally unacceptable. These developments pose a further serious question: What other material is being withheld?'

McKevitt spoke without fear of contradiction. The prosecution's failure to disclose the files was tantamount to perverting the course of justice as far as he was concerned. Of course, everyone knew he was guilty. He still could not talk about the RIRA or Rupert's allegations but he continued to protest.

'My decision to dismiss my legal team was a decision that was reluctantly forced upon me for the reasons I have just outlined. The prosecution of this case is founded upon concealment and not disclosure. It relies solely upon the word of an MI5 Agent whom Mr. Hugh Hartnett SC stated and I quote "had perjured himself during his three weeks in the witness box".

'I find myself in agreement with Detective Diarmuid O'Sullivan who, during my detention in Balbriggan Garda Station on 28 March 2001 at 11 a.m. informed me that my arrest and arraignment was "a political order from on high".

'For five weeks I have persevered with my legal team in asserting my innocence. But this task has been rendered impossible by the events, which have transpired in this very courtroom. Therefore, I will not participate any further in this political show trial and I now withdraw with my dignity intact.'

McKevitt sat down not quite sure what to do next.

'Very well Mr. McKevitt,' said Justice Johnson.

'The panel of judges will now adjourn to consider the legal implications of your decision. You are under the custody of the court. Therefore, you are not permitted to withdraw from this court.'

None of the judges were fooled by the speech. Justice Johnson moved quickly to eliminate the ambiguities and made his own pronunciation.

'Mr. McKevitt has discharged his legal team and has intelligently and understandably informed the court why he has taken this decision and why he is no longer participating in this trial. However, the court will not accede to Mr. McKevitt's request to absent himself from this trial. Would you like to respond Mr. McKevitt?'

McKevitt was more than taken aback. He was playing a long game but the judge had cut the game short.

'With respect, I sincerely hope that you fully understand my position. Once again I wish to inform the court that I have withdrawn from this political show trial and I have no further interest in it. The court has decided to hold me here. I must stress that I remain here under protest.'

The judges remained firm and said the trial would continue. And it did. More gardaí gave evidence against McKevitt. After each witness had presented his evidence, Justice Johnson made a point of specifically asking McKevitt if he wished to cross-examine the witness. He declined.

The day after the dramatic events, McKevitt refused to leave his holding cell. The judges ordered the prison officers to bring him up but he resisted. This was all an act. His decision to remain in his cell was nothing more than advance planning for an appeal hearing.

The prosecution's case ended on 28 July when Birmingham called the last Garda witness. The judges then retired to consider their verdict. This was delivered on Wednesday, 6 August 2003.

EPILOGUE

AN AIR OF excitement enveloped the Special Criminal Court when it reconvened to deliver judgement on the fate of Michael McKevitt. The public gallery was full to capacity.

Lawrence Rush was there with Victor Barker who had travelled from London to witness the calamitous event in the history of the Real IRA. Although Barker had queued from early that morning, he had failed to find a seat in the public gallery.

Wandering around the court, the only available space he managed to find was the bench left vacant by McKevitt's legal team. Unsure of the protocols, Barker sat into the solicitors' bench. When a confused garda asked if he was a solicitor, he replied yes and sat back. The bell sounded minutes later at 11 a.m. signalling the imminent appearance of the three judges.

McKevitt was nowhere to be seen. The judges asked him to appear in the dock but he refused. On that note, the judges began delivering their judgement.

Guilty to the core, McKevitt was convicted on both counts. The judges pronounced him guilty of directing the activities of an organisation styling itself Óglaigh na hÉireann and guilty of membership of the same organisation.

The judgement was 43 pages long. Justice Johnson had presided throughout the hearing and so read out the considered decision.

Rupert, he said, was a very truthful witness who had considerable knowledge of the republican movement and who referred to people by name.

The judgement was carefully crafted. In the court's opinion, Rupert was not an informant but a paid agent of the FBI. The proof was there in black and white. The contract Rupert signed with the FBI made him an agent.

The strategy adopted by the defence had been to discredit the witness, and show him to be unreliable and untruthful. The strategy devised and executed by the defence had not worked. Finally, Justice Johnson proclaimed that the court was satisfied beyond all reasonable doubt that McKevitt had indeed directed and controlled the activities of an unlawful organisation for which a suppression order was in existence. McKevitt was guilty.

On the charge of IRA membership, the wise judge said the court accepted the uncontested evidence of Chief Superintendent Michael Finnegan that the accused was a member of the IRA.

McKevitt's reaction to the decision was witnessed by no one. He had refused to leave the court's holding cell to hear the verdict and instead sent up a handwritten note, which was not read out.

IN ACCORDANCE WITH tradition, a member of the investigation team was invited to take the stand to tell the court about McKevitt. The judges take such evidence into account when deciding on an appropriate sentence. Diarmuid O'Sullivan of Special Branch was given sole responsibility for this task. He sat into the witness box and promised to tell the whole truth and nothing but the truth.

McKevitt, he said without fear of contradiction, was a former Quartermaster General of the Provisional IRA. O'Sullivan gave a brief synopsis of McKevitt's extraordinary life.

The accused, he said, had been a member of the IRA since the 1970s, and as Quartermaster General was responsible for procuring arms and explosives, including the importation of large quantities of arms from Libya. He had no previous convictions. The judges listened attentively. When O'Sullivan finished talking, the judges announced the court would adjourn and deliver an appropriate sentence the next day. The courtroom was then cleared.

The relatives of those murdered in the Omagh bombing suffered a mixture of excitement and despair at McKevitt's conviction. Outside the court, Michael Gallagher, Lawrence Rush and Victor Barker addressed crowds of journalists and television crews. Rush stated he was delighted with the conviction but said that nothing would ever bring back his wife. He had watched the trial unfold with more than a degree of scepticism. He knew Rupert had lied in court and was a crook but McKevitt was a danger to society. McKevitt had got his just desserts.

Outside the court, Barker and Gallagher addressed the crowd and publicly thanked Rupert for helping to put McKevitt behind bars. It was Barker that gave the most poignant speech.

'I take no pleasure in seeing Michael McKevitt being deprived of seeing his children. It gives me no pleasure at all. I know what it's like not to see your child but hopefully this court case will stop the violence.'

THE SENTENCING OF McKevitt was a straightforward affair and lasted no more than 20 minutes when the Special Criminal Court opened the next morning. Membership of the IRA carries a maximum sentence of seven years, while the charge of directing terrorism carries a maximum penalty of life imprisonment. The court went silent as the judges proceeded to jail McKevitt for 20 years.

The task of passing sentence was left to Justice Johnson who proclaimed that McKevitt played a leading role in the RIRA. This was a lenient sentence as far as the judges were concerned. Justice Johnson announced the court had contemplated a 25-year sentence on the directing charge. The judge referred to the evidence presented by O'Sullivan when he outlined incidents involving the RIRA and the depth of McKevitt's involvement in the paramilitary organisation.

The bombing of Omagh and the massacre of the 29 innocent victims was mentioned briefly.

The judge made a point of saying the sentence was not imposed in revenge for the Omagh bombing because the offences for which McKevitt was convicted were outside the date of the bombing.

'The court must not be seen to seek revenge for that atrocity, and would not seek to do so.'

In sentencing McKevitt, the judges took into account his age, his young family, the period of time already spent in custody and the fact that he had no previous convictions.

The Special Criminal Court believed McKevitt should be afforded the chance to rehabilitate himself. However, McKevitt never heard the kind words afforded to him. He had decided to remain in the holding cell though he did send a message to the court through a prison officer asking for permission to appeal his conviction. When McKevitt realised that he would have to make a personal appearance in court if he wanted to appeal, he realised his error and made his way hastily to the dock.

'I would like to apply for leave to appeal,' he said.

Justice Johnson looked him straight in the face and said 'refused.'

'That's fine,' said McKevitt.

IN THE DARKEST of subterfuge, Barker had arranged one final meeting with the RIRA before he left Ireland that day. When he finished addressing the assembled media outside the Special Criminal Court, he left for the village of Swords in north Dublin where he made his way to the Hawthorn Hotel.

Barker wanted something positive to come out of the trial. There had been enough bloodshed and enough misery. He fervently believed that anything was possible given that McKevitt and Campbell were now behind bars.

Waiting inside the hotel was a RIRA contact. The two men shook hands and ordered tea and sandwiches. Barker wanted to talk peace. He asked his contact if the new Army Council would agree to meet him face to face. He was told that this was out of the question for the time being.

The conversation went nowhere from the start. The two men argued about the history of the RIRA, the Good Friday Agreement and the morality of murder. Barker didn't need a fortune teller to tell him he was wasting his time. Though his republican contact sympathised with his plight and sincerely appreciated his convictions, there was nothing he could do. The RIRA had no intention of disbanding or embracing constitutional politics. Barker heeded the message but said aloud that he would never stop trying to bring about some sort of dialogue. The two men left the hotel after an hour of heated debate and arguments. The two men departed on good terms.

Barker was due to catch a flight to London but there was one question that lingered in his mind. He wanted to know if McKevitt's conviction would stop the RIRA.

His contact answered the question the only way he knew how.

'Victor, it's a storm in a tea-cup. McKevitt will be forgotten about in two weeks time. The army, be it the Provos or the Real IRA, will always be there. That's just the way it is.'

The conclusion of the trial marked the end of McKevitt, but not the end of the RIRA. The organisation continues to mount sporadic attacks in Northern Ireland and remains a serious threat to the Northern Ireland Peace Process. The RIRA Army Council still remains committed to its objectives and has refused to engage in any political dialogue.

The secret army that McKevitt established in the winter of 1997 has murdered 30 people and unborn twin girls. This is the legacy of the RIRA.

LIST OF ABBREVIATIONS

ASU	Active Service Unit
CIRA	Continuity IRA, the military wing of Republican Sinn Féin
ERU	Emergency Response Unit, an armed unit attached to Special Branch.
FBI	Federal Bureau of Investigation.
HME	Home-made explosive
GHQ	General Headquarters
IFC	Irish Freedom Committee
IRA	Provisional IRA
NBCI	National Bureau of Criminal Investigation.
NSU	National Surveillance Unit
O/C	Officer Commanding
RIRA	Real IRA
RSF	Republican Sinn Féin. Breakaway group from Provisional Sinn Féin led by Ruairí Ó Brádaigh.
TPU	Time-and-power-units. The timing mechanism used to detonate bombs.
MI5	Military Intelligence 5, otherwise known as the British Security Service
MI6	Military Intelligence 3, otherwise known as the Secret Intelligence Service.

APPENDIX

Pages 191-204: Evidence presented to the Special Criminal Court in the trial of Colm Murphy. The accused was convicted of conspiracy to cause an explosion.

Pages 208-220: Evidence presented to the Special Criminal Court in the trial of Michael McKevitt. The accused was convicted of IRA membership and directing terrorism.

Pages 221-225: Evidence presented to the Special Criminal Court in the trial of Michael McKevitt. The accused was convicted of IRA membership and directing terrorism.

Pages 227-229: Evidence presented to the Special Criminal Court in the trial of suspects arrested at Stamullen in County Meath. Séamus McGrane, Séamus McGreevey and Martin Conlon pleaded guilty to training people to use firearms.

Damien Lawless, Anthony Ryan and his brother Alan Ryan, pleaded guilty to getting training in firearms. John McDonagh pleaded guilty to the unlawful possession of an assault rifle, a pistol, a sub-machinegun and ammunition at Stamullen. He also admitted participating in training or drilling in the use of firearms.

One of the two youths arrested at the camp also pleaded guilty to a charge under the Offences Against the State Act.

Another Dublin schoolboy pleaded guilty to getting drilling in the use of firearms. He was originally charged before the Dublin Juvenile Court and was returned for trial to the Special Criminal Court on the direction of the Director of Public Prosecutions. He was the youngest person ever to appear before the Special Criminal Court.

Pages 229-232: Evidence presented to the Special Criminal Court in the trial of Michael McKevitt. The accused was convicted of IRA membership and directing terrorism.

Page 241: Evidence presented to the Special Criminal Court in the trial of Michael McKevitt. The accused was convicted of IRA membership and directing terrorism.

Page 245: Evidence presented to the Special Criminal Court in the trial of Michael McKevitt. The accused was convicted of IRA membership and directing terrorism.

Page 247-250: Evidence presented to the Special Criminal Court in the trial of Michael McKevitt. The accused was convicted of IRA membership and directing terrorism.

Pages 251-257: Evidence presented to the Special Criminal Court in the trial of Michael McKevitt. The accused was convicted of IRA membership and directing terrorism.

Pages 264-267: Evidence presented to the Special Criminal Court in the trial of Liam Campbell. The accused was convicted of IRA membership.

Pages 268-269: Evidence presented to the Special Criminal Court in the trial of Michael McKevitt. The accused was convicted of IRA membership and directing terrorism.

Pages 269-270: Evidence presented to the Special Criminal Court in the trial of Declan Carroll. The accused was convicted of IRA membership.

Page 270: Evidence presented to the Special Criminal Court in the trial of Michael McKevitt. The accused was convicted of IRA membership and directing terrorism.

Page 271: Evidence presented to the Old Bailey in London in the trial of Michael McDonald, Fintan O'Farrell and Declan Rafferty. The three pleaded guilty to conspiracy to cause an explosion.

Page 272-273: Evidence presented to the Special Criminal Court in the trial of Alan and Kenneth Patterson. Both pleaded guilty to the unlawful possession of explosive substances in Dublin and at or near McEntee Avenue in Dundalk.
   Alan Patterson also pleaded guilty to additional charges of unlawful possession of three-quarters of a kg of Semtex explosive, an air pistol and a quantity of ammunition at Marmion Court, Dublin.

Page 273: Evidence presented to the Old Bailey in London in the trial of Michael McDonald, Fintan O'Farrell and Declan Rafferty. The three pleaded guilty to conspiracy to cause an explosion.

Pages 273-277: Evidence presented to the Special Criminal Court in the trial of Michael McKevitt. The accused was convicted of IRA membership and directing terrorism.

Page 278: Taken from affidavits lodged in the Belfast High Court by solicitors acting for relatives of those murdered in the Omagh bombing.

Pages 280-284: Evidence presented to the Special Criminal Court in the trial of Michael McKevitt. The accused was convicted of IRA membership and directing terrorism.

Pages 284-286: Evidence presented to the Special Criminal Court in the trial of Dermot Gannon, Anthony and Gabriel Donohue. Gannon was convicted of IRA membership. Anthony Donohue and Gabriel Donohue pleaded guilty to the unlawful possession of a semi-automatic .22 rifle with a telescopic sight, a bolt action .22 rifle and 31 rounds of ammunition and four shotgun cartridges.

Page 286-287: Evidence presented to the Special Criminal Court in the trial of Richard Whyte and John Maloney. The two were convicted of IRA membership.

Pages 287-288: Evidence presented to the Special Criminal Court in the bail application and trials of Declan Carroll, Seán Mulligan and Robert Brennan. Carroll and Mulligan were convicted for IRA membership. Robert Brennan was found guilty of IRA membership. He was also convicted of the unlawful possession of a stun-gun at the Neptune Beach Hotel, Bettystown, County Meath. Campbell's trial has to come to court.

Page 290: Evidence presented to the Special Criminal Court in the trial of Liam Campbell. The accused was convicted of IRA membership.

Pages 291-292: Evidence presented to London's Old Baily in the trial of Robert and Aiden Hulme and Noel Maguire. The three were convicted for conspiring to cause explosions.

Pages 316-333: Evidence presented to the Special Criminal Court in the trial of Michael McKevitt. The accused was convicted of IRA membership and directing terrorism.

INDEX